D1384732

W.E.B.
DU BOIS
SPEAKS

BY PHILIP S. FONER

The Life and Writings of Frederick Douglass (4 vols.)
History of the Labor Movement in the United States (4 vols.)
A History of Cuba and Its Relations with the United States (2 vols.)
The Complete Writings of Thomas Paine (2 vols.)
Business and Slavery: The New York Merchants and the Irrepressible Conflict
The Fur and Leather Workers Union
Jack London: American Rebel
Mark Twain: Social Critic
The Jews in American History: 1654-1865
The Autobiographies of the Haymarket Martyrs
The Case of Joe Hill
The Letters of Joe Hill
The Bolshevik Revolution: Its Impact on American Radicals, Liberals, and Labor
The Black Panthers Speak
Helen Keller: Her Socialist Years
The Basic Writings of Thomas Jefferson
The Selected Writings of George Washington
The Selected Writings of Abraham Lincoln
The Selected Writings of Franklin D. Roosevelt

W.E.B.
DU BOIS
SPEAKS

Speeches and Addresses
1890-1919

Edited by Dr. Philip S. Foner

With a tribute by
Dr. Martin Luther King, Jr.

PATHFINDER
New York   London   Sydney   Toronto

First edition 1970
Sixth printing 1988

Acknowledgements:
For permission to reprint the specified material acknowledgements are
gratefully made to:
Mrs. Martin Luther King, Jr., and *Freedomways, A Quarterly Review of
the Negro Freedom Movement* for "Honoring Dr. Du Bois" by Martin
Luther King, Jr.
Henry Miller and Grove Press, Inc., for the quotation from *Plexus*.
Copyright © 1963 by Henry Miller, copyright © 1965 by Grove Press, Inc.

Pathfinder
410 West Street, New York, New York 10014
Distributors:
Africa, Europe, and the Middle East:
Pathfinder, 47 The Cut, London, SE1 8LL, England
Asia, Australia, and the Pacific:
Pathfinder, P.O. Box 153, Glebe, Sydney, NSW 2037, Australia
Canada:
Pathfinder, 410 Adelaide St. W., Suite 400, Toronto,
Ont., M5V 1S8, Canada
New Zealand:
Pilot Books, Box 8730, Auckland, New Zealand

CONTENTS

Editor's Introduction 1
Honoring Dr. Du Bois, *by Dr. Martin Luther King, Jr.* 12

1. A Pageant in Seven Decades, 1878-1938 *(1938)* 21
2. The Conservation of Races *(1897)* 73
3. Careers Open to College-Bred Negroes *(1898)* 86
4. The Study of the Negro Problems *(1898)* 102
5. Address to the Nations of the World *(July 1900)* 124
6. On Booker T. Washington *(1903)* 128
7. The Training of Negroes for Social Power
   (October 17, 1903) 130
8. Credo *(October 1904)* 142
9. The Niagara Movement *(September 1905)* 144
10. The Economic Future of the Negro *(1906)* 150
11. We Claim Our Rights *(August 1906)* 170
12. The Value of Agitation *(March 1907)* 174
13. Is Race Separation Practicable? *(May 1908)* 179
14. Politics and Industry *(May 31, 1909)* 187
15. The Evolution of the Race Problem
    (June 1, 1909) 196
16. Race Prejudice *(March 5, 1910)* 211
17. The Negro Problem *(July 1911)* 218
18. How to Celebrate the Semicentennial of the
    Emancipation Proclamation *(February 2, 1912)* 226
19. Disfranchisement *(1912)* 230
20. Socialism and the Negro Problem
    (January 1913) 239
21. The African Roots of War *(May 1915)* 244
22. The Problem of Problems *(December 27, 1917)* 258
23. The Great Migration North *(1918)* 268
24. The Future of Africa — A Platform
    (January 6, 1919) 272

Notes 276
Index 285

Your country? How come it's yours? Before the Pilgrims landed, we were here. Here we have brought our three gifts and mingled them with yours; a gift of story and song—soft, stirring melody to an ill-harmonized and unmelodious land; the gift of sweat and brawn to beat back the wilderness, conquer the soil, lay the foundations of the vast, economic empire two hundred years before your weak hands could have done it; the third a gift of the spirit. . . . Our song, our toil, our cheer. . . . Would America have been America without her Negro people?

W. E. B. Du Bois—The Souls of Black Folk

Once upon a time in my younger years and in the dawn of this century I wrote: "The problem of the twentieth century is the problem of the color line." . . . In 1925, as in 1899, I seem to see the problem of the twentieth century as the problem of the color line."

W. E. B. Du Bois, "Worlds of Color," *Foreign Affairs,* III, April 1925, p. 423.

EDITOR'S INTRODUCTION

In his *Autobiography*, published after his death, Dr. W. E. B. Du Bois wrote: "In June 1890, I received my bachelor's degree from Harvard *cum laude* in philosophy. I was one of five graduating students selected to speak at commencement. My subject was 'Jefferson Davis.' I chose it with deliberate intent of facing Harvard and the nation with a discussion of slavery as illustrated in the person of the president of the Confederate States of America. Naturally, my effort made a sensation." Bishop Potter of New York wrote in the Boston *Herald* that after hearing Du Bois's address, "I said to myself: 'Here is what an historic race can do if they have a clear field, a high purpose, and a resolute will.'"

The press published excerpts from Du Bois's speech which was titled, "Jefferson Davis as a Representative of Civilization." To Du Bois, Davis was a typical representative of "Teutonic civilization," the embodiment of "the idea of the Strong Man." The idea converted "a naturally brave and generous man" into a "Jefferson Davis — now advancing civilization by murdering Indians, now hero of a national disgrace called by courtesy, the 'Mexican War'; and finally, as the crowning absurdity, the peculiar champion of a people fighting to be free in order that another people shall not be free. Whenever this idea has for a moment escaped from the individual realm, it has found an even more secure foothold in the policy and philosophy of the state. The Strong Man and his mighty Right Arm has become the Strong Nation with its armies. Under whatever guise, however a Jefferson Davis may appear as man, as race, or as nation, his life can only logically mean this: the advance of a part of the world at the expense of the whole; the overweening sense of the 'I' and the consequent forgetting of the 'Thou.'"

Thus in what was one of his earliest public speeches, W. E. B. Du Bois already stressed themes which were to be identified with him for the remainder of his long life: hatred of and contempt for the domination of the oppressed by the oppressors; the plundering of the American continent by the white settlers, and opposition to aggressive wars and imperialism.

We are indebted to the New York *Age*, a leading black newspaper of the early eighteen-nineties edited by T. Thomas Fortune, for a report of what was probably Du Bois's next public speech. Fortune quoted the young Du Bois in order to criticize his opposition to the Lodge Federal Elections Bill which would have protected Negro political rights but was defeated in a Republican Congress. Clearly, from the excerpt of Du Bois's speech quoted in the *Age*, he was closer at this time to the position of Booker T. Washington than was Fortune, although within a few years, Du Bois was to become Washington's most famous critic and Fortune was to assume the role of Washington's defender. At any rate, here is the report of Du Bois's speech and Fortune's comment as published in the New York *Age* of June 13, 1891 under the heading, "He is Young Yet":

"Here's some funny talk recently indulged in by Mr. W. E. B. Du Bois of Harvard College, at a race meeting in Boston:

"'The whole underlying idea of the Federal Elections bill was wrong. Granted even that it would succeed in putting a few more Negroes into office, it would not benefit the colored people. The underlying idea of the measure was that law can accomplish everything; that if you have an evil in the community, all you have to do is to pass a law against it, and presto, it is gone. We must ever keep before us the fact that the South has some excuse for its present attitude. We must remember that a good many of our people south of Mason and Dixon's line are not fit for the responsibilities of republican government. When you have the right sort of black voters you will need no election laws. The battle of my people in the South must be a moral one, not a legal or physical one.'

"Mr. Du Bois is young yet. He does not know as much about some things as he thinks he does. The Federal Elections bill was based upon the underlying principle embodied in section one of article fifteen of the Federal Constitution, which declares that the right of citizens of the United States to vote shall not be denied or abridged by the United States or by any State on account of race, color or previous condition of servitude. What Mr. Du Bois has to say after the first sentence of his remark, is so much humbug based upon no provision in the Constitution and at war with all the principles predominant in our system of government. Southern newspapers may praise Mr. Du Bois' remarks, but they represent simply the opinions of a very young man who will think and talk differently a few years hence."

It was indeed an accurate prediction!

An account of a lecture delivered by Dr. Du Bois in Philadelphia early in 1902 appeared in *The Colored American*, a black weekly published in Washington D. C. in its issue of January 18, 1902:

"Before a highly cultured audience, Prof. Bernhardt [sic] Du Bois, delivered a very interesting lecture on Thursday evening at the Parish Building of the Church of the Crucifixion. His subject was 'African Slave Trade.' Prof. Du Bois has been engaged by the University Extension Centre to deliver the course of lectures on 'slavery' before the Bainbridge Street Centre. His lecture was well illustrated by African views thrown on canvas. The Philadelphia public is greatly pleased with the manner and style of the lecture and already feels great enlightment upon the subject of slavery. His next subject will be the 'Dark Continent.'"

When a young man of twenty-five years, William Edward Burghardt Du Bois told himself in his own diary, "be the truth what it may, I shall seek it on the pure assumption that it is worth seeking — and Heaven nor Hell, God nor Devil shall turn me from my purpose till I die." When Dr. Du Bois died in Accra, Ghana, at the age of ninety-five, it could truly be said of him that here was the end of a life unswervingly dedicated to truth.

What is happening in the United States on the battle-front of democracy versus racism stems back many years. But certainly one of the milestones in this long struggle was the Niagara Movement which was inaugurated at a meeting in Buffalo, New York, in July 1905, and which led to the establishment of the National Association for the Advancement of Colored People five years later. Dr. Du Bois, founder of the Movement, was present at the inaugural meeting, and when they met again the next year at Harper's Ferry, West Virginia, on ground hallowed by the martyrdom of John Brown, he delivered the historic address. Taking direct issue with the policy and program of Booker T. Washington for the Negro, under which the black American would not ask for social and political and civil equality in return for a pledge that he would be provided with industrial training and the opportunity to take a place in the rapidly expanding commercial and industrial economy of the nation, Du Bois declared:

"We will not be satisfied to take one jot or tittle less than our full manhood rights. We claim for ourselves every single right that belongs to a freeborn American, political, civil, and social; and until we get these rights we will never cease to protest and assail the ears of America."

In his books, articles, and speeches, and in the pages of *The Crisis*, monthly organ of the NAACP, which he founded in 1910 and edited for almost a quarter of a century, Du Bois continued to express this clear, unqualified demand for the complete liberation of his people from the heritage of slavery and racism. And he called for resistance. When in 1911, a mob of over 400 whites lynched a Negro in Coatesville, Pennsylvania, burning him to death in the public streets, Du Bois wrote in *The Crisis*: "Let every black American gird up his loins. We have crawled and pleaded for justice and we have been cheerfully spat upon and murdered and burned. We will not endure it forever. If we are to die, in God's name, let us perish like men and not like bales of hay."[1]

At its zenith, *The Crisis* had 100,000 readers. This meant that it went every month into one-tenth of the Negro homes of the entire nation. This vast readership breathlessly awaited the arrival of each number. The hallmark stamped on every page was Du Bois's own message— it is a thing of pride to be a Negro. Du Bois's influence was felt by untold thousands of young black Americans in all walks of life—farm workers in the South, industrial laborers in Birmingham and Detroit, writers, artists, lawyers, teachers. Here is what a distinguished Negro historian and educator, Dr. Horace Mann Bond, has to say of the influence of *The Crisis* under Du Bois's editorship:

"I was an avid reader of *The Crisis*, from my earliest literate days. We lived in rural Kentucky places and my isolation from the world was greater because I read omnivorously. Through *The Crisis* Du Bois helped shape my inner world to a degree impossible to imagine in the world of contemporary children, and the flood of various mass media to which they are exposed. I remember the pleasant faces of brown and black children pictured in the magazine; I remember the photographs of decently garbed men and women of color, never seen elsewhere in the publications that came to our home; and I remember also the horrifying cartoons depicting 'lynch law that frequently appeared in the magazine. . . .

"The cartoons were strong stuff for a child, perhaps, as were the factual accounts of the lynchings through burnings, ending with fragments of fingers and toes for sale as souvenirs for the mob; the lynchings through hangings, the lynchings through gunshot, the mass lynchings through disfranchisement and discrimination and brutalizing oppressions of all sorts. Yet I am glad that through Du Bois I had these vicarious experiences with the real and brutal world of race and color, as with the real world of black men and women clothed in beauty and dignity. . . .

"And Africa! For an American child growing up between 1910 and 1920, there was scarcely an antidote anywhere for the poisonous picture of Africa, and of Africans, painted in the school geographies, the newspapers and magazines, and by the movies. *The Crisis* magazine gave me the one antidote available. From the earliest days of *The Crisis*, Africans were revealed as intelligent human beings. I have long counted it as one of my great blessings that I read Du Bois on Africa when I was very young."

Dr. Bond touches in his last paragraph one of Du Bois's signal contributions to the struggle for democratic rights in the United States. This was his refusal to accept the conception of Negro advancement as a purely domestic affair to be resolved only by and in the United States; and his insistence upon portraying this struggle in the world context of the liberation of all subject and oppressed peoples in Africa, Asia, and the Americas from the domination of colonialism, imperialism, and monopoly capitalism. It was thus no accident that his labors to win respect and equal justice for Negro Americans by setting right the record of the Reconstruction period and of the role of black Americans in the history of the United States went hand in hand with his pioneering work in sweeping aside the prevalent falsifications regarding the African peoples and their history and bringing to light what African culture was before slavery and colonialism descended upon it. His lifelong twin aim as a scientist was to assemble in encyclopedic form the full truth of black American history and culture and African history and culture.

The young Dr. Du Bois went to Atlanta University in 1897 to pioneer in developing a systematic, rounded, 100-year program of studies of Negro life, operating on "the firm belief that race prejudice was based on widespread ignorance," and that the "long-term remedy was truth; carefully gathered scientific proof that neither color nor race determine the limits of a man's capacity or desert." He began to produce these studies, one a year for more than a decade, on selected aspects of Negro life. His plan was to repeat them, in a recurring cycle of ten studies in succeeding decades — "until gradually a foundation of carefully ascertained fact would build a basis of knowledge, broad and sound enough to be called scientific in the best sense of the term."

But Du Bois's outlook for a serene life of scholarship

was soon shattered by the racist violence directed against his people. He tells us:

"I faced situations which called — shrieked for action, even before any detailed, scientific study could possibly be prepared. . . . I saw before me a problem that could not await the last word of science, but demanded immediate action to prevent social death."

And so it was that W. E. B. Du Bois left the relative calm of academic life and plunged into the urgent practical struggles. He continued to be the highly perceptive student of society; but he had come to understand that "there could be no rift between theory and practice"; that "the social scientist could not sit apart and study *in vacuo*"; and that even "the ordered knowledge which research and tireless observations must give must be sought in the midst of action."

Herein lies one of the chief keys to the development of this most remarkable man; a profound unity of scholarship and struggle — of theoretical insight combined with practical leadership in the arena of social conflict — the one continuously reinforcing and deepening the other. On the one hand, there was the author of such definitive works of scholarship as *The Suppression of the African Slave Trade to the United States of America; The Philadelphia Negro; John Brown; Black Reconstruction; Black Folk, Then and Now; The World and Africa;* along with such literary gems as *The Souls of Black Folk, Darkwater, Dusk of Dawn,* several novels, many plays and poems, hundreds of articles, plus the founding and editing during the early nineteen-forties (following his return to Atlanta) of *Phylon — The Atlanta University Review of Race and Culture.*

On the other hand, there was the leader of hosts of spirited battles on the Negro freedom front, founder and continuing chairman of the Pan-African Congress, Envoy Extraordinary and Minister Plenipotentiary to Liberia, cochairman of the Council on African Affairs, longtime fighter for peace, including the founding of the Peace Information Center, for which the United States Government, to its shame, tried to imprison him in 1951, American Labor Party candidate for United States Senator, and uncompromising fighter for civil liberties. Finally, there was the advocate of socialism for about forty-five years, the man who looked confidently to the socialist future of all mankind — which he declared "is coming as sure as the rolling of the stars," and who, in his ninety-third year, joined the Communist Party of the United States.

"Without struggle there is no progress," wrote Frederick Douglass. "No sound effort is in vain, least of all a struggle with high ideals and personal integrity," wrote Dr. Du Bois. And again: "We refuse to allow the impression to remain that the Negro-American assents to inferiority . . . . the voice of protest of ten million Americans must never cease to assail the ears of their fellows, so long as America is unjust."

Truly a remarkable and unique figure: a magnificent poet and writer of prose, a great historian, anthropologist, and sociologist, creative editor, constructive statesman, tireless organizer in the liberation struggles of his people, a man who was throughout his life passionately devoted to freedom, peace, and human dignity. I count it as one of my greatest privileges that I had frequent opportunities both in this country and abroad to meet and discuss problems of mutual interest in the field of scholarship with this most remarkable man. It was Dr. Du Bois who encouraged me to undertake the collection and editing of the writings and speeches of Frederick Douglass, who provided insights into aspects of Douglass's long career in the struggle for the full freedom of black Americans. I felt especially rewarded by his praise of the four volumes of the *Life and Writings of Frederick Douglass* after they were published.

While Dr. Du Bois was a prolific writer, he was also a frequent figure on the lecture platform. On one occasion while early at Atlanta, he delivered twenty-three lectures and talks in a period of three weeks. The speaking trip extended from the University of Chicago in the Midwest, to Madison Avenue Presbyterian Church in New York City, to Benedict College in South Carolina. During his quarter of a century as editor of *The Crisis,* he was often touring the country in behalf of the NAACP. Few if any conferences dealing with the Negro problem both here and abroad took place without an address by Dr. Du Bois. Although he spoke to audiences of all kinds, not merely to meetings of Negroes, and on a wide variety of subjects such as the labor movement, socialism, colonialism and imperialism, peace, women's rights, his speeches always linked the subject of the hour with the special problems facing black people in the United States, Africa, and Latin America.

As a speaker, Dr. Du Bois was no impassioned orator. His speeches, regardless of the type of audience he addressed, reflected the same clear, beautiful and dignified prose which featured his prose writings, and many of his speeches were published without the slightest change as articles. Yet his speeches always had a remarkable effect on the listener, for Dr. Du Bois hit out with tremendous impact against the hypocrisies and cruelties of American society, especially in relation to its treatment of its black citizens.

Commenting on a speech Dr. Du Bois delivered in the summer of 1911 at the Universal Races Congress in London, the *Manchester Guardian* observed:

"The speaker was Dr. W. E. B. Du Bois. He spoke with astonishing mastery, lucidity and perfection of phrase. The manner was spontaneous, yet every sentence was in place. The address was so simple that an intelligent child could have followed the argument, yet it handled so closely the fundamental issue that no specialist who heard it would have refused his tribute of admiration. As a piece of exposition, as an example of oratory exactly suited to its purpose, it was by far the finest thing the Congress produced."

Henry Miller, who heard Dr. Du Bois speak to an audience made up largely of Jewish people on New York's East Side, wrote in *Plexus*:

"It was quite a time before Du Bois appeared on the platform. When he did it was with the air of a sovereign mounting his throne. The very majesty of the man silenced any would-be demonstration. There was nothing of the rabble-rouser in this leonine figure—such tactics were beneath him. His words, however, were like cold dynamite. Had he wanted to, he could have set off an explosion that would rock the world. But it was obvious that he had no intention of rocking the world—not yet, at any rate. As I listened to his speech I pictured him addressing a body of scientists in much the same way. I could imagine him unleashing the most devastating truths, but in such a manner that one would be left stunned rather than moved to action. . . .

"Du Bois was no rabble-rouser. No, but to a man like myself it was all too obvious that what his words implied were—'Assume the spirit of liberty and you will be free!'"

In introducing Dr. Du Bois to the audience of the Chicago Forum in March 1929, Fred Atkins Moore, Forum Director, correctly described him as "unquestionably one of the ablest speakers for his race not only in America but in the whole wide world." Dr. Du Bois occupied this position until his death in 1963.

Except for the first speech in this collection, all of Dr. Du Bois's addresses are arranged chronologically. The opening speech, delivered in 1938, has been placed first because the information in this autobiographical address will be helpful in enabling the reader to understand many of the issues in the selections that follow.

Until recently, this outstanding and prolific black scholar was treated with scorn by the academic establishment and confined to oblivion by most white scholars in the fields of history, economics, and sociology. But today Dr. W. E. B. Du Bois is widely considered to deserve the title of Father of Black Scholarship as well as the Father of Pan-Africanism. His books are selling at a greater rate than at any time during his long lifetime. And while the government of the United States, once again to its shame, denied a visa to Mrs. Shirley Graham Du Bois, his widow, the Black Academy of Arts and Letters, founded in April 1969, announced its intention to enroll W. E. B. Du Bois as one of three persons in its Hall of Fame, and has asked the government to grant Mrs. Du Bois a visa so that she could accept the citation honoring her husband.

A number of anthologies of selections from the writings of W. E. B. Du Bois have appeared in recent years. But the present volumes are the first comprehensive collection of the speeches of this great black American. In nearly all cases the speeches in this collection are published in their entirety. Wherever omissions occur they have been properly indicated. In each case the selection is preceded by an introductory note to place it in its historical framework, and, wherever it was deemed necessary, explanatory notes have been furnished to provide information on personalities and events referred to by Dr. Du Bois. With each selection is given the source. In a number of cases, the speeches were delivered without any special covering title. I have taken the liberty of furnishing a title where none appeared.

I wish to express my deep appreciation to the staffs of the Lincoln University Library, the Schomburg Collection of the New York Public Library, the New York Public Library, the Library of Columbia University, the Library of Congress, the Library of Howard University, the Library of Fisk University, the Library of Atlanta University, and the Library of Talladega College for assistance in the use of their collections of Dr. Du Bois.

I wish also to thank Mrs. Martin Luther King, Jr. and *Freedomways* for permission to reprint the late Dr. King's tribute to Dr. Du Bois. I wish to express my gratitude to Mrs. Shirley Graham Du Bois for her cooperation in the project.

Philip S. Foner
Lincoln University, Pennsylvania

HONORING DR. DU BOIS

by Dr. Martin Luther King, Jr.

*On the hundredth birthday of Dr. W. E. B. Du Bois,
February 23, 1968,* Freedomways Magazine *sponsored
an International Cultural Evening at Carnegie Hall in
New York City. The meeting launched an "International
Year" (1968) honoring Dr. Du Bois's life and works.
The Centennial Address that evening was delivered by
Nobel Laureate Dr. Martin Luther King. This was the
last major address of Dr. King before his assassination.*

Tonight we assemble here to pay tribute to one of the
most remarkable men of our time.

Dr. Du Bois was not only an intellectual giant exploring
the frontiers of knowledge, he was in the first place a
teacher. He would have wanted his life to teach us something about our tasks of emancipation.

One idea he insistently taught was that black people
have been kept in oppression and deprivation by a poisonous fog of lies that depicted them as inferior, born
deficient and deservedly doomed to servitude to the grave.
So assiduously has this poison been injected into the mind
of America that its disease has infected not only whites
but many Negroes. So long as the lie was believed, the
brutality and criminality of conduct toward the Negro
was easy for the conscience to bear. The twisted logic ran
—if the black man was inferior he was not oppressed—
his place in society was appropriate to his meager talent
and intellect.

Dr. Du Bois recognized that the keystone in the arch of oppression was the myth of inferiority and he dedicated his brilliant talents to demolish it.

There could scarcely be a more suitable person for such a monumental task. First of all he was himself unsurpassed as an intellect and he was a Negro. But beyond this he was passionately proud to be black and finally he had not only genius and pride but he had the indomitable fighting spirit of the valiant.

To pursue his mission, Dr. Du Bois gave up the substantial privileges a highly educated Negro enjoyed living in the North. Though he held degrees from Harvard and the University of Berlin, though he had more academic credentials than most Americans, black or white, he moved South where a majority of Negroes then lived. He deliberately chose to share their daily abuse and humiliation. He could have offered himself to the white rulers and exacted substantial tribute for selling his genius. There were few like him, Negro or white. He could have amassed riches and honors and lived in material splendor and applause from the powerful and important men of his time. Instead, he lived part of his creative life in the South — most of it in modest means and some of it in poverty and he died in exile, praised sparingly and in many circles ignored.

But he was an exile only to the land of his birth. He died at home in Africa among his cherished ancestors and he was ignored by a pathetically ignorant America but not by history.

History cannot ignore W. E. B. Du Bois. Because history has to reflect truth and Dr. Du Bois was a tireless explorer and a gifted discoverer of social truths. His singular greatness lay in his quest for truth about his own people. There were very few scholars who concerned themselves with honest study of the black man and he sought to fill this immense void. The degree to which he succeeded discloses the great dimensions of the man.

Yet he had more than a void to fill. He had to deal with the army of white propagandists — the myth-makers of Negro history. Dr. Du Bois took them all on in battle. It would be impossible to sketch the whole range of his intellectual contributions. Back in the nineteenth century he laid out a program of a hundred years of study of problems affecting American Negroes and worked tirelessly to implement it.

Long before sociology was a science he was pioneering in the field of social study of Negro life and completed works on health, education, employment, urban conditions and religion. This was at a time when scientific inquiry of Negro life was so unbelievably neglected that only a single university in the entire nation had such a program and it was funded with $5,000 for a year's work.

Against such odds Dr. Du Bois produced two enduring classics before the twentieth century. His *Suppression of the African Slave Trade* written in 1896 is Volume I in the Harvard Classics. His study *The Philadelphia Negro*, completed in 1899, is still used today. Illustrating the painstaking quality of his scientific method, to do this work Dr. Du Bois personally visited and interviewed 5,000 people.

He soon realized that studies would never adequately be pursued nor changes realized without the mass involvement of Negroes. The scholar then became an organizer and with others founded the NAACP. At the same time he became aware that the expansion of imperialism was a threat to the emergence of Africa.

He recognized the importance of the bonds between American Negroes and the land of their ancestors and he extended his activities to African affairs. After World War I he called Pan-African Congresses in 1919, 1921 and 1923, alarming imperialists in all countries and disconcerting Negro moderates in America who were afraid of this restless, militant, black genius.

Returning to the United States from abroad he found his pioneering agitation for Negro studies was bearing fruit and a beginning was made to broaden Negro higher education. He threw himself into the task of raising the intellectual level of this work. Much later in 1940 he participated in the establishment of the first Negro scholarly publication, *Phylon.* At the same time he stimulated Negro colleges to collaborate through annual conferences to increase their effectiveness and elevate the quality of their academic studies.

But these activities, enough to be the lifework for ten men, were far from the sum of his achievements. In the six years between 1935 and 1941 he produced the monumental seven-hundred page volume on *Black Reconstruction in America*, and at the same time writing many articles and essays. *Black Reconstruction* was six years in writing but was thirty-three years in preparation. On its publication, one critic said: "It crowns the long, unselfish and brilliant career of Dr. Du Bois. It is comparable in clarity, originality and importance to the Beards' *Rise of American Civilization*." The *New York Times* said, "It is beyond question the most painstaking and thorough study ever made of the Negroes' part in Reconstruction," and the New York *Herald Tribune* proclaimed it "a solid history of the period, an economic treatise, a philosophical discussion, a poem, a work of art all rolled into one."

To understand why his study of the Reconstruction was a monumental achievement it is necessary to see it in context. White historians had for a century crudely distorted the Negro's role in the Reconstruction years. It was a conscious and deliberate manipulation of history and the stakes were high. The Reconstruction was a period in which black men had a small measure of freedom of action. If, as white historians tell it, Negroes wallowed in corruption, opportunism, displayed spectacular stupidity, were wanton, evil and ignorant, their case was made. They would have proved that freedom was dangerous in the hands of inferior beings. One generation after another of Americans were assiduously taught these falsehoods and the collective mind of America became poisoned with racism and stunted with myths.

Dr. Du Bois confronted this powerful structure of historical distortion and dismantled it. He virtually, before anyone else and more than anyone else, demolished the lies about Negroes in their most important and creative period of history. The truths he revealed are not yet the property of all Americans but they have been recorded and arm us for our contemporary battles.

In *Black Reconstruction* Dr. Du Bois dealt with the

almost universally accepted concept that civilization virtually collapsed in the South during Reconstruction because Negroes had a measure of political power. Dr.
Du Bois marshaled irrefutable evidence that, far from
collapsing, the southern economy was recovering in these
years. Within five years the cotton crop had been restored
and in the succeeding five years had exceeded prewar
levels. At the same time other economic activity had ascended so rapidly the rebirth of the South was almost completed.

Beyond this he restored to light the most luminous
achievement of the Reconstruction — it brought free public
education into existence not only for the benefit of the
Negro but it opened school doors to the poor whites. He
documented the substantial body of legislation that was
socially so useful it was retained into the twentieth century
even though the Negroes who helped to write it were
brutally disenfranchised and driven from political life.
He revealed that far from being the tragic era white historians described, it was the only period in which democracy existed in the South. This stunning fact was the
reason the history books had to lie because to tell the
truth would have acknowledged the Negroes' capacity
to govern and fitness to build a finer nation in a creative
relationship with poor whites.

With the completion of his book *Black Reconstruction*,
despite its towering contributions, despite his advanced
age, Dr. Du Bois was still not ready to accept a deserved
rest in peaceful retirement. His dedication to freedom drove
him on as relentlessly in his seventies as it did in his
twenties. He had already encompassed three careers. Beginning as a pioneer sociologist he had become an activist to further mass organization. The activist had then
transformed himself into a historian. By the middle of the
twentieth century when imperialism and war arose once
more to imperil humanity he became a peace leader. He
served as chairman of the Peace Information Center
and like the Rev. William Sloane Coffin and Dr. Benjamin
Spock of today he found himself indicted by the government and harried by reactionaries. Undaunted by obstacles and repression, with his characteristic fortitude

he fought on. Finally in 1961 with Ghana's independence established, an opportunity opened to begin the writing of an African Encyclopedia and in his ninety-third year he emigrated to Ghana to begin new intellectual labors. In 1963 death finally came to this most remarkable man.

It is axiomatic that he will be remembered for his scholarly contributions and organizational attainments. These monuments are imperishable. But there were human qualities less immediately visible that are no less imperishable.

Dr. Du Bois was a man possessed of priceless dedication to his people. The vast accumulation of achievement and public recognition were not for him pathways to personal affluence and a diffusion of identity. Whatever else he was, with his multitude of careers and professional titles, he was first and always a black man. He used his richness of talent as a trust for his people. He saw that Negroes were robbed of so many things decisive to their existence that the theft of their history seemed only a small part of their losses. But Dr. Du Bois knew that to lose one's history is to lose one's self-understanding and with it the roots for pride. This drove him to become a historian of Negro life and the combination of his unique zeal and intellect rescued for all of us a heritage whose loss would have profoundly impoverished us.

Dr. Du Bois *the man* needs to be remembered today when despair is all too prevalent. In the years he lived and fought there was far more justification for frustration and hopelessness and yet his faith in his people never wavered. His love and faith in Negroes permeate every sentence of his writings and every act of his life. Without these deeply rooted emotions his work would have been arid and abstract. With them his deeds were a passionate storm that swept the filth of falsehood from the pages of established history.

He symbolized in his being his pride in the black man. He did not apologize for being black and because of it, handicapped. Instead he attacked the oppressor for the crime of stunting black men. He confronted the establishment as a model of militant manhood and integrity. He defied them and though they heaped venom and scorn on him his powerful voice was never stilled.

And yet, with all his pride and spirit he did not make a mystique out of blackness. He was proud of his people, not because their color endowed them with some vague greatness but because their concrete achievements in struggle had advanced humanity and he saw and loved progressive humanity in all its hues, black, white, yellow, red and brown.

Above all he did not content himself with hurling invectives for emotional release and then to retire into smug passive satisfaction. History had taught him it is not enough for people to be angry — the supreme task is to organize and unite people so that their anger becomes a transforming force. It was never possible to know where the scholar Du Bois ended and the organizer Du Bois began. The two qualities in him were a single unified force.

This life style of Dr. Du Bois is the most important quality this generation of Negroes needs to emulate. The educated Negro who is not really part of us, and the angry militant who fails to organize us have nothing in common with Dr. Du Bois. He exemplified black power in achievement and he organized black power in action. It was no abstract slogan to him.

We cannot talk of Dr. Du Bois without recognizing that he was a radical all of his life. Some people would like to ignore the fact that he was a Communist in his later years. It is worth noting that Abraham Lincoln warmly welcomed the support of Karl Marx during the Civil War and corresponded with him freely. In contemporary life the English-speaking world has no difficulty with the fact that Sean O'Casey was a literary giant of the twentieth century and a Communist or that Pablo Neruda is generally considered the greatest living poet though he also served in the Chilean Senate as a Communist. It is time to cease muting the fact that Dr. Du Bois was a genius and chose to be a Communist. Our irrational obsessive anticommunism has led us into too many quagmires to be retained as if it were a mode of scientific thinking.

In closing it would be well to remind white America of its debt to Dr. Du Bois. When they corrupted Negro history they distorted American history because Negroes are too big a part of the building of this nation to be written out of it without destroying scientific history. White America, drenched with lies about Negroes, has lived too long in a fog of ignorance. Dr. Du Bois gave them a gift of truth for which they should eternally be indebted to him.

Negroes have heavy tasks today. We were partially liberated and then re-enslaved. We have to fight again on old battlefields but our confidence is greater, our vision is clearer, and our ultimate victory surer because of the contributions a militant, passionate black giant left behind him.

Dr. Du Bois has left us but he has not died. The spirit of freedom is not buried in the grave of the valiant. He will be with us when we go to Washington in April to demand our right to life, liberty and the pursuit of happiness.

We have to go to Washington because they have declared an armistice in the war on poverty while squandering billions to expand a senseless, cruel, unjust war in Vietnam. We will go there, we will demand to be heard, and we will stay until the administration responds. If this means forcible repression of our movement, we will confront it, for we have done this before. If this means scorn or ridicule, we will embrace it for that is what America's poor now receive. If it means jail we accept it willingly, for the millions of poor already are imprisoned by exploitation and discrimination.

Dr. Du Bois would be in the front ranks of the peace movement today. He would readily see the parallel between American support of the corrupt and despised Thieu-Ky regime and northern support to the southern slave-masters in 1876. The CIA scarcely exaggerates, indeed it is surprisingly honest, when it calculates for Congress that the war in Vietnam can persist for a hundred years. People deprived of their freedom do not give up — Negroes have been fighting more than a hundred years and even if the date of full emancipation is uncertain, what is explicitly certain is that the struggle for it will endure.

In conclusion let me say that Dr. Du Bois's greatest virtue was his committed empathy with all the oppressed

and his divine dissatisfaction with all forms of injustice.
Today we are still challenged to be dissatisfied. Let us
be dissatisfied until every man can have food and material
necessities for his body, culture and education for his
mind, freedom and human dignity for his spirit. Let us
be dissatisfied until rat-infested, vermin-filled slums will
be a thing of a dark past and every family will have a
decent sanitary house in which to live. Let us be dissatisfied until the empty stomachs of Mississippi are filled and
the idle industries of Appalachia are revitalized. Let us
be dissatisfied until brotherhood is no longer a meaning-
less word at the end of a prayer but the first order of
business on every legislative agenda. Let us be dissatisfied
until our brother of the Third World — Asia, Africa, and
Latin America — will no longer be the victim of imperialist
exploitation, but will be lifted from the long night of poverty, illiteracy and disease. Let us be dissatisfied until
this pending cosmic elegy will be transformed into a creative psalm of peace and "justice will roll down like waters
from a mighty stream."

Freedomways, Second Quarter, Spring 1968, pp. 104-111.

1

A PAGEANT IN SEVEN DECADES
1878-1938

Three autobiographies of W. E. B. Du Bois have been published: Darkwater: Voices from within the Veil, *published in 1921;* Dusk of Dawn: An Essay toward an Autobiography of a Race Concept, *issued in 1940, and* The Autobiography of W. E. B. Du Bois, *published in 1968, five years after Du Bois's death. In 1961 Folkways Records issued "W. E. B. Du Bois – A Recorded Autobiography."*

In 1938 Du Bois celebrated his seventieth birthday. He was then Professor of Sociology at Atlanta University, and to mark the occasion he was asked to address the University Convocation and review his life. The address was later published as a pamphlet by Atlanta University. It is not mentioned in most of the existing bibliographies of writings and speeches of W. E. B. Du Bois. It is reproduced here in its entirety.

I have been asked to review my life and I have chosen to essay this from the aspect of a historical pageant of humankind in which I have been a more or less active spectator, and whose end and meaning I have sought to see. It is not easy to do this; deeds, facts and fancies flow so ceaselessly and, with occasional whirlpools, so smoothly on, that one grasps and arranges them and views them with difficulty. Temptation to topical treatment is barred by the alchemy of time which not simply prolongs life but successively changes all perspective and interpretation. I find. it better then to group my years in

decades from childhood to today; seeking in each term
of ten years the more or less elusive unity that may lie
therein and checking somewhat my present memory by
such documents as may partially re-create the past.

*The First Decade — Childhood, 1868-1878 — birth-10
years.* — The year of my birth was the year that the freedmen of the South were enfranchised and for the first time
as a mass took part in government. Conventions with
black delegates voted new constitutions all over the South;
and two groups of laborers — freed slaves and poor whites
— dominated the former slave states. It was an extraordinary experiment in democracy. Thaddeus Stevens, the
clearest-headed leader of this attempt at industrial democracy, made his last speech impeaching Andrew Johnson
on February 16[1] and on February 23 I was born.

I had a pleasant childhood. I can remember no poverty
although my family was certainly poor. I represented
the third generation from three small-landholding brothers
on my mother's side and the fourth generation from a
West Indian planter on my father's. The outstanding thing
in my earliest memory was the school. In a letter which
I began to my grandmother in 1877, after conventional
thanks for some present, I plunged right into the real
subject, "My schoolhouse stands a little way from Main
Street." I remember it vividly; down a lane with a great
chokecherry tree on the right; on the left the wooden primary and grammar school and farther on the right, the
brick grammar and high school. I attended these schools
regularly from five or six years of age until I was sixteen with hardly a day's absence.

The town and its surroundings were a boy's paradise:
there were mountains to climb and rivers to wade and
swim; lakes to freeze and hills for coasting. There were
orchards and caves and wide green fields; and all of it
was the free property apparently of the children of the
town. My family were pleasant and miscellaneous: the
father was dead before I can remember; the mother brown
and quietly persistent; the aunts and one uncle a bit cen-
sorious but not difficult to get on with; and then an endless vista of approving cousins.

The town was shut in by its mountains and provincialism — cut off both from Boston and New York state. My first glimpse of the outer and wider world was through Johnnie Morgan's news shop which occupied the front end of the post office. There newspapers and books were on display and I remember very early seeing pictures of "U. S." Grant and of Tweed who was beginning his extraordinary career in New York state;[2] and later of Hayes and the smooth and rather cruel face of Tilden. Of the great things happening in the United States at that time, we were touched only by the Panic of 1873. When my uncle came home from the little town east of us where he was the leading barber, he brought me, I remember, a silver dollar which was an extraordinary thing; up to that time I had seen nothing but paper money. I do not remember hearing anything said about the Fifteenth Amendment which became law in 1870; but there were a few new colored people, "contrabands," who came to town. One family particularly I liked, they were so jolly and darkly handsome.

Charles Sumner died and the Freedmen's Bank closed when I was but six years old, and when I was eight there came the revolution of 1876. But I hardly knew of it. And, too, of the world overseas: the Franco-Prussian War; the ups and downs of Disraeli and Gladstone; the opening of the Suez Canal— of these things my little village said nothing nor did they mention the fact that the Medji Emperors of Japan ascended to new and ever growing power in the year I was born.

The Second Decade— Youth, 1878-1888 — 10-20 years. — The United States in the decades 1870-1890 was an extraordinary country. Grant, Hayes, Garfield, Arthur and Grover Cleveland were presidents. James G. Blaine was an aspirant who barely missed the highest office, and the country was reckless and prosperous, squandering its seemingly endless resources, tying east and west with railways, exploiting iron and coal and oil and making fortunes for a new and ruthless caste of businessmen who were cashing in on the cost of Civil War. The results of this I could easily see in my town. I grew up in the midst of definite ideas as to wealth and poverty, work and charity. Wealth was the result of work and saving, and the rich rightly inherited the earth. The poor, on the whole, were to be blamed. They were lazy or unfortunate and, if unfortunate, their fortunes could easily be mended by thrift and sacrifice.

There were some differences of wealth in Great Barrington; there were mills and millowners; there were German and Irish factory hands. Singularly enough I knew the millowners and their children much better than I knew the workers, but I was no flunky for the rich. My people always had a certain independence. They were by occupation small farmers, servants, laborers, barbers and waiters. They earned their way. I early came to understand that to be "on the town," the recipient of public charity, was the depth not only of misfortune but of a certain guilt. I presume some of my folk sank to that but not to my knowledge. We earned our way.

I have a postcard dating from 1883 in which "Miss Smith," September 19, writes, "We would like to have you come certainly next Saturday as you did last week to do some splitting for us." This was a matter of splitting up kindling for two maiden ladies and was one of my ways of beginning financial independence. I remember well my first regular work: as a high-school lad I went early of mornings and filled one or two of the so-called baseburning stoves with coal in a little millinery shop. I received twenty-five cents a week which represented the beginning of affluence. From then on, all through my high-school course, I worked after school and on Saturdays, mowing lawns, doing errands, and for a few months through the goodwill of Johnnie Morgan, I rose to be local correspondent of the *Springfield Republican.* For some time, too, I sent weekly letters to the New York *Age,*[3] and before the A & P stores dealt in groceries and simply were selling tea, I was one of their local agents.

Thus in all sorts of little ways I managed to earn some money and never asked nor thought of gifts save in one case: my school principal suggested, quite as a matter of fact, that I ought to take the college preparatory course in high school, which involved Latin and Greek. This meant a considerable expenditure for books, but the wife of one of the millowners, or rather I ought to describe her as the mother of one of my playmates, offered to furnish all the necessary high-school books, which became my one charity.

The other class of rich folk with whom I came in contact were summer boarders who made yearly incursions from New York. I think I was most impressed by their clothes. Outside of that there was little reason so far as I could see to envy them. The children were not very strong and rather too well-dressed to have a good time playing. There were few slum areas in my town and almost no crime. The one indulgence was liquor and there my mother quietly took a firm stand. I was never to enter a saloon. I never did. Alcohol gave perhaps the one reaction that this pleasant but rather drab little town had against the monotony of life, and rich and poor got drunk more or less regularly. I have seen a millowner staggering; and my own very dignified uncle used to come home now and then walking very straight.

In one respect my training in this town has had rather momentous results. It was not good form in New England or in Great Barrington to express yourself volubly, to give way to emotion—people held themselves in. They were sparing even of their greetings. There was only on the street a curt "Good Morning" to those whom you knew and no greeting at all for others. The result was that because of this and probably from growing racial consciousness I was early thrown in upon myself. I found it difficult and even unnecessary to approach other people and by that same token my own inner life grew perhaps the richer. Later the habit of repression often returned to plague me, for so early a habit could not easily be unlearned.

I entered high school at the age of twelve and was graduated at the age of sixteen in 1884. I had during that time my first chance to travel and to get little glimpses of the world. I was sent, for instance, by my mother across the state to see my grandmother and grandfather in New Bedford. I wrote back about this in 1883, "The house is white with green blinds. The yard is full of flow-

ers. Grandma is about my color and taller than I thought.
I like her very much. Grandpa is short and rather thick
set. I like him better than I thought I would. He says
very little but speaks civilly when I say something to him.
Grandma says by and by he will talk more."

When I was graduated from the high school we all had
speeches and mine was on Wendell Phillips. He had died
in February and I spoke in June, fired by new and unusual knowledge of his sort of man. Then there came
in my life the first great change. My mother died and it
was decided that I was too young to go to college. I sus-
pect that money matters had something to do with it.
At any rate instead of being able to go to Harvard in
the fall of 1884, as I had fondly hoped, I was given a
job and promised that the next fall I should begin my
college work.

The job brought me in curious touch with the world.
There was a great uncle of mine, Tom Burghardt, whose
tombstone I had seen often in the village graveyard. My
family used to say in undertones that the money of Tom
Burghardt helped to build the Pacific Railway and that
it came in this wise: Nearly all his life Tom Burghardt
was a servant in the Kellogg family, only the Kelloggs
forgot to pay him but did give him a handsome burial.
Then Mark Hopkins married into the family and used
presumably my uncles's unpaid wages, with other assets,
to make millions in railways. His widow came back to
Great Barrington and planned a mansion out of the beautiful blue granite which formed our hills. A host of workmen, masons, stonecutters, and carpenters were assembled
and in the summer of 1884 I was made timekeeper for the
contractors, receiving the fabulous wage of a dollar each
day.

It was a most interesting experience and had bits of
romance. There was the English architect who appeared
on the scene and the colored steward who committed
suicide when the architect married the widow; then came
the death of the widow and the passing of the Hopkins
millions into foreign hands. In the meantime the fabrica-
tion and growth of this marvelous palace proceeded, beautiful beyond anything that Great Barrington had seen;

and always I could sit and watch it grow and handle delegated powers in dismissing workmen and rewarding them.

Finally in the fall of 1885 there came a proposal which made all my cousins and aunts raise their eyebrows. I was to have a scholarship to go South to Fisk University. The South had an unholy name in my village and the family was not at all sure that I ought to go. Only one black Burghardt had ever gone South and he a Union soldier, but I never hesitated. I started out and went into Tennessee at the age of seventeen to become a sophomore at Fisk University. It was to me an extraordinary experience. I was thrilled to be for the first time among so many people of my own color or rather of such various and such extraordinary colors, which I had not seen before, but who seemed close bound to me by new and exciting ties. I had never seen such beautiful girls in my life or men who gave themselves such merited airs.

The three years here were years of growth, strength and expanding ambition. I learned new things about the world. I came in contact for the first time with a sort of violence that I had never realized in New England. I remember going down and looking wide-eyed at the door of a public building filled with buckshot where the white editor of the leading daily paper had been publicly murdered the day before. I was astonished to find many of my fellow students carrying firearms and to hear their stories of adventure. I suddenly determined that I was going out to teach during the summer vacations. It was not necessary. My scholarship would have supported me but it was adventure. I walked into east Tennessee ten or more miles a day until at last in a little valley I found a place where they had had a Negro public school only once since the Civil War and there for two successive summer terms I taught at $28 and $30 a month; paid immediately in promises and in cash three or four months later.

I began my writing and public speaking at Fisk. I wrote an article of which the *Century Magazine* said, "We shall be glad to print 'The New Negro' if we may take our time and we are afraid we shall have to take a great deal." It did, for it hasn't been printed yet. For three years

I was on the editorial staff of the *Fisk Herald,* as editor-in-chief the last year, contributing essays and one novel. I became a considerable orator and for a long time the older students of Fisk took deep joy in remembering the debate where in the very midst of impassioned periods I forgot my lines.

The persistence, however, which I had learned in New England stood me now in good stead. The interlude at Fisk did not turn me from it. When I heard that Harvard was offering scholarships in various parts of the country I immediately wrote and to the astonishment of teachers and fellow students, not to mention myself, received Price Greenleaf aid of $300. I was graduated from Fisk in 1888 and took as my subject Bismarck. It showed my already growing interest in the wider world. I knew of the great jubilee of Queen Victoria, of the aftermath of the Franco-Prussian War and the triumph of the Mahdi in Khartoum. I had followed the fortunes of Gladstone and Salisbury and was filled with enthusiasm at the rise of the new German Empire under Bismarck. So I talked of Bismarck and then turned back to the North.

Third Decade— Education, 1888-1898— 20-30 years. — This decade covered the years of my education at Harvard and at Berlin and the beginning of my teaching career. The members of the Fisk Glee Club went to Lake Minnetonka, a resort in Minnesota, for the summer of 1888, with the idea of working in the dining room and giving concerts. I was to act as their business manager. During college I had developed as the executive and planner, the natural secretary of affairs rather than the ornamental president and chairman. The only difficulty about the Minnesota excursion was that I had never worked in a hotel in my life; I did not know how to wait on table and therefore became one of the busboys. It was so unusual a pageant to watch the dining room that I made no tips and for a long time had difficulty in getting enough to eat, not realizing that servants in great hotels are not systematically fed. But after the season I went on ahead and succeeded in making a respectable number of concerts for the students who followed me down all the way to Chicago;

while I went on to Harvard to enter the junior class in the fall of 1888.

The Harvard of 1888 was an extraordinary aggregation of great men. Not often if ever since that day have so many distinguished teachers been together in one place and at one time. There was William James, the psychologist; Palmer in ethics; Royce and Santayana in philosophy; Shaler in geology; and Hart in history. The president was the cold, precise but exceedingly efficient Charles William Eliot and there were a dozen lesser lights. By extraordinary good fortune I was thrown into contact with most of these men. I was repeatedly a guest in the house of William James; of all teachers, he was my closest friend. I was a member of the philosophical club; I talked often with Royce and Shaler; I sat alone in an upper room and read Kant's *Critique* with Santayana; I became one of Hart's favorite pupils and was afterwards guided by him through my graduate course and started on my work in Germany.

It was an extraordinary opportunity for a young man and I think I realized it. I evolved habits of work rather different from those of most of the other students. I burned no midnight oil. I did my studying in the daytime and had my day planned out almost to the minute. I spent a great deal of time in the library and did my assignments with persistent thoroughness and with a rather interesting prevision of the kind of work I wanted to do later. I have before me a theme which I wrote October 3, 1890, for Barrett Wendell, the great pundit of Harvard English. I said: "Spurred by my circumstances I have always been given to systematically planning my future, not indeed without many mistakes and frequent alterations, but always with what I now conceive to have been a strangely early and deep appreciation of the fact that to live is a serious thing. I determined while in high school to go to college — partly because other men went, partly because I foresaw that such discipline would best fit me for life. I believe foolishly perhaps but sincerely that I have something to say to the world, and I have taken English 12 in order to say it well." Barrett Wendell rather liked that last sentence; he read it to the class.

I tried to take culture out into the colored community of Boston; I visited, joined clubs, lectured, and once actually gave the *Birds of Aristophanes* in a colored church on Thanksgiving night. The matter of meeting my college expenses presented some difficulties. I had scholarships for $300 for both college years but that was not enough. One year after careful calculation I found that I needed $50 more and noted with interest that this was exactly the stipend of the Boylston prizes in oratory. I had to have one of the prizes in order to make ends meet for the year and I got it. Then with a colored classmate, Clement Morgan, who was also a Boylston prize man, I made a tour of the summer resorts of New England. We gave readings in hotels, parlors and churches and did in this way much toward making our expenses. In my senior year the death of my last near relative, my grandfather, left me a fortune of $400.

In 1890, I took my bachelor's degree from Harvard and was one of the six commencement speakers, taking as my subject Jefferson Davis.[4] On the platform of Sanders Theatre were President Eliot, the Governor of Massachusetts and the Bishop of New York. I am glad that the New York *Nation* could say July 3, 1890, that I handled the theme "with absolute good taste, great moderation, and almost contemptuous fairness."

I was graduated just at the beginning of the term of President Harrison when the trusts were dominating industry and the McKinley tariff making that domination easier.[5] The understanding between the industrial North and the new South was being perfected, and in 1890 a series of disfranchising laws was passed by the southern states destined in the next six years to make voting by southern Negroes practically impossible. Already I had received more education than most young white men, having been continuously in school from the age of six to the age of twenty-two. But I did not yet feel prepared. I knew that to cope with the new and extraordinary situation then building in the United States I needed to go further and that as a matter of fact I had just well begun my training and my knowledge of social conditions.

On the other hand, I was quite penniless, with no resources in wealth or friends. I applied for a fellowship in the graduate school. If I had not gotten it, I should have had to go to work; but I was appointed Henry Bromfield Rogers fellow for a year, and later the appointment was renewed so that from 1890 to 1892 I was a fellow in Harvard University, studying in history and what would have been social science if Harvard had then recognized such a field.

I worked on my thesis, "The Suppression of the Slave Trade," taking my master's degree in 1891 and hoping to get my doctor's degree in another two years. Then came one of those tricks of fortune which seem partly due to chance, but in this case undoubtedly due to a good deal of stubborn persistence. In 1882 the Slater Fund for the education of Negroes had been established, and the board in 1892 was headed by ex-President Rutherford B. Hayes. President Hayes at Johns Hopkins University talked frankly in 1890 about the plans of the Fund. He said among other things that they had wanted to find some young colored men to whom they could give a chance for graduate training, but they had only been able to find "orators."

The statement was brought to my attention at a card party one evening, and it not only made me good and mad but also set me thinking. I wrote President Hayes. I received a pleasant reply saying that they did not have any present plans for such scholarships. That really aroused me. I proceeded to get letters from every person I knew in the Harvard Yard and places outside and literally deluged the unfortunate chairman of the Slater Fund. He wrote again and said that he was sorry but the plan had been given up; that they might otherwise have given me some attention.

It has been my experience that most of my small successes have been due to steps that I have taken after all hope seemed lost. I sat down and proceeded to write Mr. Hayes a letter that could be described as nothing less than impudent. I intimated plainly that somebody was lying. I reiterated my plans and added many written references. President Hayes was undoubtedly disturbed and almost apologized to me, reiterating his good faith and

promising to take up the matter the next year with the
board. Whereupon promptly the next year I proceeded to
write the board: "At the close of the last academic year at
Harvard, I received the degree of master of arts, and was
reappointed to my fellowship for the year 1891-92. I
have spent most of the year in the preparation of my
doctor's thesis on the suppression of the slave trade in
America. I prepared a preliminary paper on this subject
and read it before the American Historical Association
at its annual meeting at Washington during the Christmas
holidays. The paper will shortly be published in their
proceedings and a preliminary report of it may be seen
in the *Independent* of January 7, 1892, pages 10-11;
also in *Congregationalist* of about the same date. The
first draft of the larger thesis was completed March 28
and it will be formally finished May 1, and, I hope, eventually published; besides this I have worked on a number
of general studies. Properly to finish my education, a careful training in a European university for at least a year
is, in my mind and the minds of my professors, absolutely
indispensable. I therefore desire, respectfully to lay these
suggestions before you: First, that the board grant me
aid to study at least a year abroad under the direction
of the graduate department of Harvard or other reputable
auspices. Second, if this be not practicable, that the board
loan a sufficient sum for this purpose."

The Trustees of the Slater Fund granted my request and
gave me $750, half gift and half loan, to study in Europe.
I shall never forget my interview with ex-President Hayes
in the old Astor House in New York, nor the extravagant
shirt I immediately bought in celebration. In the summer
I sailed for Europe, saw Holland and the Rhine, and
lived in a fine German family in Eisenach with a group
of gay young folk who made me realize that white folk
were human.

In the fall I went up to Berlin and registered in the University. In groups of one hundred we were ushered into
a room. "It was a large room, with high ceiling, and a
row of four windows on one side in the deep recesses of
which stood busts of Berlin's famous professors. The
center of the room was occupied by chairs, in which the

students seated themselves; at the upper end was a long table about which perhaps a dozen officials were grouped. Near the left end was the present year's *rector magnificus,* the widely famous Rudolf Virchow, doctor of medicine, laws and philosophy, city councillor and member of the Reichstag. He is a meek and calm looking little man, white-haired and white-bearded, with a kindly face and a pleasant voice. At smaller tables arranged before the windows were the deans of the various faculties. . . . Recognizing with some difficulty my Germanicized name I presented myself with trepidation at the bar. The stiff secretary (it's quite the thing to be stiff in new Germany) with my help more clearly deciphered my name, ascertained under which faculty I wished to study, firmly declined to examine any of my sheepskins, and passed me over to the rector; Rector Virchow smiled benignantly, made some remark as to my faculty, and after filling out the blanks with some remarkably poor writing, presented me with a large 24 by 18 inch sheet of paper: this stated that a certain Gulielmus had in the general goodness of his heart endowed the present Mr. Virchow with various powers; among these was that of making me (who was described with some infelicity of phrase as a 'most ornamented young man') a legalized and licensed student of the University of Berlin."

I had again at Berlin as at Harvard unusual opportunity. Although a foreigner I was admitted my first semester to two semesters under Schmoller and Wagner, both of them the most distinguished men in their lines, and I received eventually from both of them pleasant testimony of my work. My work was in economics, history and sociology. I sat under the voice of the fire-eating Von Treitschke and heard him assert the general inferiority of mulattoes and mixed races; I wrote on American agriculture for Schmoller and discussed social conditions in Europe with teachers and students. But more especially I traveled; living cheaply I saved good sums for the numerous vacations. I went to the Hansa cities; I made the celebrated Hartzreise up to the Brocken in the spring.

My Christmas vacation I spent in making a trip through south Germany along with a German-American and an

Englishman. We visited Weimar, Frankfort, Heidelberg and Mannheim. During Christmas and New Year's we stopped in a little German dorf in the Rheinfalz, where I had an excellent opportunity of studying the peasant life closely and comparing it with country life in the South. We visited perhaps twenty different families, talked, ate and drank with them; listened to their gossip and history, attended their assemblies, etc. We then went to Strassborg, Stuttgart, Ulm, Muenchen, Nuernburg, Prague and Dresden. In those places we stayed from one to five days, following our Baedeker closely, and paying much attention to the Muenchner and Dresden art galleries. The trip cost about $80. Later I went down to Italy, to Genoa, Rome and Naples and over to Venice and Vienna and Budapest and finally up to Krakau, where the father of a fellow student was the head of the Polish library and where I learned of the race problems of the Poles, and then came by Breslau back to Berlin.

I have a curious document of a birthday which came in Berlin in 1893. "Today I am a quarter of a century old. It seems so strange—my boyhood and youth are but memories now and I am a full-grown man. I wonder what the next quarter of a century will bring me—if it will be as rich in work and happiness as the past—as awfully full of fulfilled plans. . . . These twenty-five years of mine have been rich in personal history. I remember school days, the brook by Sumner's house, the attic rooms where we lived, the little stove that used to fall down and the window I proudly called a bay window. I remember little sorrows of life when I found no companions to play with and busied myself in making great plans for a toy with which I could play alone. I remember the gate where I looked into the great town—wonderful world to me then."

I returned to the United States by way of Paris, where I stayed as long as possible and then having reduced myself almost to the last cent, took passage to the United States in the steerage, quite penniless. It was by no means a pleasant trip, but perhaps it was a good introduction to the new life, because now at last at twenty-six years of age and after twenty years of study I was coming home to look for a job and to begin work. I need not dwell on the difficulties of landing that job. It was a disturbed world in which I landed; 1892 saw the high tide of lynching in the United States, 235 untried Negroes being slaughtered in that one year. Cleveland had entered his second term in 1893, and the Chicago Exposition had taken place. The Dreyfus case had opened in France with his conviction and imprisonment and he was destined for twelve years to suffer martyrdom. The war between China and Japan broke out the year of my return, and Nicholas II was ruling in Russia.

I wrote everywhere offering my services and at last received three offers. On August 17, 1894, the chair of Latin and Greek at Wilberforce University, Ohio, with a salary of $800 was offered, which I immediately accepted with gratitude. A little later there came an offer of a position at Lincoln Institute in Missouri at $1,050, but I stuck to my first promise; and finally August 25 I received this telegram from Tuskegee, "Can give you mathematics if terms suit. Will you accept? Booker T. Washington." It would be interesting to speculate just what would have happened if I had accepted the last offer instead of the first.

Wilberforce was a small denominational college married to a state normal school. The church was too poor to run the college, the state did not want the normal school, and there were consequently enormous difficulties in both church and state politics. Into this institution I landed with the cane and gloves of my German student days; with my rather inflated ideas of what a university ought to be and with a terrible plainness of speech that was continually getting me into difficulty; when, for instance, very suddenly and without warning the student leader of a prayer meeting announced that Professor Du Bois would lead us in prayer, I simply answered, "No, he won't," and as a result nearly lost my job. It took a great deal of explaining to the board of bishops why a professor in Wilberforce should not be able any time to lead in extemporaneous prayer. I was really saved by the fact that I was so willing to do endless work when the work seemed to me worth doing. My program for a

day at Wilberforce looks almost as long as a week's
program today. I taught Latin, Greek, German, and English and wanted to add sociology to it but the college
demurred. I had charge of the most unpleasant of the
duties of discipline and did outside work in study and
investigation; I met many new friends: first of all, my
wife; then my good friend Charles Young, not long graduated from West Point; Charles Burroughs was a student
in my classes; Paul Laurence Dunbar came over from
Dayton to read to us. I had known his work but was
astonished to find that he was a Negro.[6]

We younger teachers had a hard team fight at Wilberforce and soon saw that we were licked. It was impossible for me especially to stay, for I had talked too plainly
and acted too independently. When, therefore, a temporary
appointment came from the University of Pennsylvania,
it was a message from heaven. I was offered work for one
year as "assistant instructor" for $600. I accepted forth-
with and in addition to that showed my faith in life by
getting married. My wife was one of the Wilberforce students and lived in Iowa, where the marriage took place
in the fateful year 1896. In that year the great battle of
Adua occurred, when Abyssinia overthrew Italy and when
England, suddenly seeing two black nations in ascendan-
cy, threw her army back into the Sudan and recaptured
Khartoum. The next year when my son was born, there
burst in the United States the free-silver controversy of
Bryan and McKinley and it was that year that President
Bumstead of Atlanta University asked me to come to Atlanta and take charge of the work in sociology and of the
new conferences on the Negro problem which the university
was inaugurating.

*Fourth Decade— Research and Propaganda— 1898-1908
— 30-40 years* — This fourth decade was the real beginning
of my lifework. My education was finished and I had
traveled in the world. The two years at Wilberforce being
a sort of uneasy prelude, I began with my advent into
the University of Pennsylvania a planned career which had
an unusual measure of success and yet was in the end
pushed partly aside by forces which, if not beyond my

control, were certainly of tremendous weight. My vision was in the beginning clear. The Negro problem called for systematic investigation and intelligence. The world was thinking wrong about races because it did not know. The ultimate evil was ignorance and its child, stupidity. The cure for it was knowledge based on study. The opportunity opened at the University of Pennsylvania was exactly what I wanted. I had tried to teach social science at Wilberforce outside my overloaded program but they did not want it. At the University of Pennsylvania I ignored the pitiful stipend. It made no difference to me that I was put down as an "assistant instructor" and even at that my name never actually got into the catalogue; it goes without saying that I did no instructing and rather to my dismay I found as much jealousy and politics in this great white institution as in the smaller black one.

But here at least I had a clear-cut job. The city of Philadelphia at that time had a social theory, and the theory was that this great, rich and famous municipality, founded by godly Quakers, was going to the dogs because of the crime and venality of its Negro citizens. These Negroes lived largely centered in a slum at the lower end of the seventh ward. Philadelphia wanted to prove all this by figures and I was the man they picked to do it. Of this thought and plan I neither knew or cared. I was simply asked to study, know and tell. I saw here a chance to study a historic group of black folk and to show exactly what their place was in the community. I did the work despite extraordinary difficulties both within and without the group. The Negroes resented being studied at all and especially by a colored stranger; the whites endured the study as a gesture toward an answer which they already knew.

I made a study of the Philadelphia Negro so thorough that it has withstood the criticism for forty years. It was as complete a scientific answer as could have been given under the limitations of time and money; it showed the Negro group as a symptom and not a cause; as a striving, palpitating human group and not an inert, sick body of crime; it traced, analyzed, charted and counted. It left few untouched queries. At the end of that study I an-

nounced with a certain pride my general plan of studying
the Negro problem and published papers on the matter
in the *Annals of the American Academy* in 1898.[7]

With this program clearly in mind I came to Atlanta
University. There was at the last moment a curious little
hitch based on that old matter of extemporaneous public
prayer. Dr. Bumstead and I compromised on the Episcopal prayer book and afterwards I added certain prayers
of my own. I am not sure that they reached heaven but
they certainly reached my audience.

Without thought or consultation, I rather preemptorily
changed the plans of the first two Atlanta Conferences.
They had been conceived as conferences on city problems
contrasting with the increasingly popular conferences on
rural problems held at Tuskegee. But I was not thinking
of mere conferences. I was thinking of a comprehensive
plan for studying a human group and if I could have
carried it out as completely as I conceived it, the American Negro would have contributed to the development
of social science in this country an unforgettable body
of work. Social scientists were at that time thinking in
terms of theory and of vast and tenuous laws; while I
had for study a concrete group of living beings set off
by themselves and capable of almost laboratory experiment. I laid down a program of a hundred years, in
which taking annually aspect after aspect of the group
life of Negroes for a decade, we could repeat and broad-
en and concentrate our attention, sharpen our tools of
investigation and improve our methods, so that we would
accumulate an increasing living body of scientifically ascertained fact to make the so-called Negro problems, and
through them the problem of all social living, clearer
and surer and more definite.

Something of this was accomplished. For thirteen years
we poured forth a series of studies limited, incomplete,
only partially conclusive, and yet so much better done
than any other attempt at such work anywhere else in
the world that they gained attention in America, Europe,
Asia and Africa.[8] Nevertheless, at the very time when
they were beginning to achieve widening success, there

cut across this plan of science a red ray of emotion which could not be ignored.

I remember when it first, as it were, pulled me off my feet.

A poor Negro in central Georgia, Sam Hose, had killed his landlord in a wage dispute. He could not be found for days; then at last a new cry was raised that he had raped the landlord's wife. It was obviously and clearly a trumped-up charge to arouse the worst passions of the countryside, and the mob roared. I wrote out a careful and reasoned statement concerning the evident facts and started down to *The Constitution,* carrying in my pocket a letter of introduction which I had to Joel Chandler Harris.[9] I did not get there. On the way the news met me: Sam Hose had been lynched and they said that his knuckles were on exhibition at a grocery store on Mitchell Street. I turned back to the university. I suddenly saw that complete scientific detachment in the midst of such a South was impossible.

Nevertheless, I tried to keep my mounting indignation within bounds. I went on with my studies, but together with other black Georgians: W. J. White, John Hope, H. R. Butler and others, I sent out memorials and petitions and protests. One in 1899, which I wrote, said, "Race antagonism and hatred have gone too far in this state; let us stop here; let us insist that they go no further; let us countenance no measure or movement calculated to increase that deep and terrible sense of wrong under which so many today labor. May the twentieth century of the Prince of Peace dawn upon an era of generous sympathy and forbearance between these two great races in Georgia, and not upon a season of added injustice and antipathy." Another, a year or so later, said, "'From each according to his ability—to each according to his needs' is the ideal of modern society, and in the light of this dictum, there is not a boy in Georgia today so poor or so black as not to deserve from the state free common-school training." And a third which came out of a great Macon mass meeting: "Popular government in the United States is not a failure, but it is having in these days a severe and critical trial. Its success in the future depends upon the ability of great classes of men to rise above prejudice and do strict justice to their fellowmen. And today strict justice in Georgia demands free common-school training for every single child of the state."

With all this I stuck to my scientific work. I helped prepare in 1900 a sociological exposition of the American Negro for the Paris Exposition, which gained a grand prize for the exhibit and a gold medal for myself. I attended at that time a first Pan-African Conference in London with Bishop Walters, where I met the Colensos and Samuel Coleridge-Taylor. I was elected a member of the American Association for the Advancement of Science in 1900 and made a fellow in 1904.

I not only published the conference reports yearly but wrote magazine articles in the *World's Work,* and in the *Atlantic Monthly,* where I was a fellow contributor with Woodrow Wilson on a symposium. I testified before Congressional Commissions in Washington and appeared on the lecture platform with Walter Page, afterwards war ambassador to England. I had wide correspondence with men of prominence in America and Europe: Lyman Abbott of the *Outlook;* E. D. Morel, the English expert on Africa; Max Weber of Heidelberg; Professor Wilcox of Cornell; Bliss Perry of the *Atlantic Monthly;* Horace Traubel, the great protagonist for Walt Whitman; Charles Eliot Norton and Talcott Williams. I began to be regarded by some as having definite information on the Negro to which they might listen with profit.

At the same time there was cause for increasing apprehension. First of all, and for me most astonishing, we could not get money for our work in the Atlanta Conferences and our studies of the Negro problem. My theory had been that just as soon as the world saw the value of our studies, the raising of funds would be the easiest thing in the world. I received for the whole thirteen years that I was then at Atlanta University an annual salary of only $1,200. The whole cost of the conference and studies never exceeded $5,000 a year and usually it was considerably less. The work was done at first in a spare bedroom of my apartment and finally in the attic of Stone

Hall, where adequate but rather inaccessible rooms were provided. I had no skilled assistants and yet my dream was still splendid. If in a properly equipped institution I could have gathered four or five well-equipped young students, some tabulating machines and a small corps of traveling investigators, we could at a cost of $10,000 to $25,000 a year have absolutely reconstituted the basis of fact and argument concerning the American Negro. But we could not get $5,000 even; and then to make the situation worse there came the controversy with Booker T. Washington, which turned from me and from Atlanta University the sympathy of many men who had money to give.

It was no controversy of my seeking; quite the contrary. I was, in my imagination, a scientist and neither a leader nor an agitator; I had nothing but the greatest admiration for Mr. Washington and Tuskegee and I had applied in 1894 at both Tuskegee and Hampton for work; if the telegram from Tuskegee had reached me before the Wilberforce bid, I should doubtless have gone there. Certainly I knew no less about mathematics than I did about Latin and Greek. But no sooner was my work at Atlanta University under way than pressure began to be placed upon me to leave there and go to Tuskegee. There again I was not adverse in principle to Tuskegee, except that I had started a job and wanted to continue it; surely if my work was worth support, it was worth support at Atlanta University as much if not more than elsewhere.

I remember that a letter came from Wallace Buttrick late in 1902 asking that I attend a private conference in New York with Felix Adler and William H. Baldwin, Jr., George Foster Peabody and Robert Ogden. The object of the conference was ostensibly the condition of the Negro in New York City. I went to the conference and did not like it. Most of the more distinguished persons were not present. The conference itself amounted to little, but I was whisked over to William H. Baldwin's Long Island home and there what seemed to me to be the real object of my coming was disclosed. Mr. Baldwin was at that time a prime mover of the Tuskegee board of trustees, and slated to be president of the Pennsylvania Railway;

he was the rising industrial leader of America. Both he
and his wife insisted that my place was at Tuskegee; that
Tuskegee needed the kind of development that I had been
trained to give. I could not help being impressed and I
promised to think the matter over. Later I had two personal interviews with Mr. Washington. He encouraged
me to talk but he said very little himself. I could get no
clear understanding of just what I was going to do at
Tuskegee if I went. I was given to understand that the
salary and accommodations would be satisfactory. Later
in the year I went to Bar Harbor for a series of speeches
in behalf of Atlanta University and while there met Jacob
Schiff, the Schieffelins and Merriam of Webster's dictionary.
I had dinner with the Schieffelins and their mother, the
daughter of John Jay: and again was urged to go to
Tuskegee.

But by that time my mind was made up. I was growing
increasingly uncomfortable under Mr. Washington's various
statements of his program, his depreciation of the value of
the vote, his evident dislike of Negro colleges, and his
general attitude, which seemed to place the onus of blame
for the race problems upon the Negro himself rather
than upon the whites. I attended several conferences at
Hampton and found myself consenting by silence to a
systematic attack on Negro colleges.

I determined on a decisive step. I had been asked some-
time before by A. C. McClurg and Company of Chicago
if I did not have material for a book, and I suggested
a social study which should be perhaps a summing up
of the work of the Atlanta Conferences or at any rate
a broad scientific treatise which required some time. They
asked, however, if I did not have some essays that they
might put together and issue immediately, and they in-
stanced the articles in the *Atlantic Monthly* and other
places. I demurred because essays usually fell so flat.
Nevertheless, I got together a series of my fugitive pieces
and added a frank evaluation of Booker T. Washington
and sent them on. *The Souls of Black Folk* was published
in 1903, and in 1938 it is still selling.

This settled definitely any further question of my going
to Tuskegee, but it also aroused apprehension. Various

friends of the Negro desired to keep Negro thought from splitting into a pro-Washington and an anti-Washington camp. After all, Mr. Washington had accomplished much, and a new basis of understanding on the Negro seemed to most white people in sight. Every effort must be made to preserve unity of effort. I was asked in 1903 to join Mr. Washington and his friends in a conference to be held in New York to talk of a common program. I assented and as I wrote to Kelly Miller:

"I think this will be a chance for a heart-to-heart talk with Mr. Washington. I propose to stand on the following platform:

1. Full political rights on the same terms as other Americans.
2. Higher education of selected Negro youth.
3. Industrial education for the masses.
4. Common-school training for every Negro child.
5. A stoppage to the campaign of self-depreciation.
6. A careful study of the real condition of the Negro.
7. A national Negro periodical.
8. A thorough and efficient federation of Negro societies and activities.
9. The raising of a defense fund.
10. A judicious fight in the courts for civil rights.

Finally, the general watchword must be, not to put further dependence on the help of the whites but to organize for self-help, encouraging 'manliness without defiance, conciliation without servility.'"

The matter dragged on with some argument as to who should be invited. The general invitation to the conference went out in October 1903, when Mr. Washington sent out the following circular letter: "You will perhaps recall that about the middle of last February I addressed you a letter concerning a private conference to be attended by about fifteen or eighteen of our most prominent men, representing various sections of the country and various race interests, for the purpose of considering quietly all the weighty matters that now confront us as a race. The meeting was not called at the time hoped for in my last correspondence for the reason that there was delay and some disappointment in providing funds for the expenses of the meeting.

That feature has now been provided for in a way that will not make those who attend the conference feel obligated to any individual or organization and leave them free for open and frank discussion.

"I very much hope that you can now see your way to attend such a conference in New York City to be held, if possible, on the sixth, seventh, and eighth of January, 1904."

The conference took place in Carnegie Hall, New York. There was some plain speaking but it was overborne by almost fulsome praise of Mr. Washington from the lips of various invited guests like Andrew Carnegie and Lyman Abbott. It ended in the appointment of a committee of three, of which I was one, who were to select a sort of racial steering committee called the Committee of Twelve. Nothing really came of this. The two other members of the committee organized it in my absence, placed the full power in the hands of Mr. Washington, who was to carry on the work with funds the source of which I did not know. I resigned forthwith and was pretty roundly condemned for my lack of "cooperation," but I was indignant at what seemed to me an effort to buy agreement and smother dissent under a dictatorship.

Things now began to move swiftly. In Boston a new colored weekly newspaper, the Boston *Guardian*, was organized by two young radicals: Monroe Trotter and George Forbes. [10] They were bitter in their attacks upon Mr. Washington, and I got myself in hot water by publishing a statement in the *Guardian* concerning the venality of certain Negro papers whom I charged had sold out and were viciously attacking every Negro who did not agree with Mr. Washington. It was a charge which I could not support by concrete facts, but it was true in the sense that there had been organized at Tuskegee a literary bureau to emphasize Mr. Washington's ideas in the Negro press and to stop the widespread criticism against him. The methods used are common today: distribution of advertising; sending out of special correspondence and distributing other favors; but it seemed to me then that this kind of propaganda was monstrous and dishonest and I resented it. On the other hand, the public expression of this resentment caused many people to think that I was wild and unfair in my statements and, beyond that, it undoubtedly made it increasingly difficult for Dr. Bumstead to raise funds for Atlanta University. In the fall of 1904 the printing of our conference report was postponed by the trustees until special funds could be secured. I did not at the time see the handwriting on the wall. I did not realize how strong the forces were back of Tuskegee and how they might interfere with my plan of scientific study of the Negro.

My first thought was in order to state our case and honest criticism we needed a journal. I had already helped an A. U. graduate to establish a printing press in Memphis. Out of this might arise a vehicle for both opinion and fact which would help me carry on my scientific work and at the same time be a forum less radical than the *Guardian* and more rational than the rank and file of Negro papers then so largely arrayed with Tuskegee. I wrote to Jacob Schiff reminding him of having met him in Bar Harbor in 1903. "I want to lay before you a plan which I have and ask you if it is of sufficient interest to you for you to be willing to hear more of it and possibly to assist in its realization. The Negro race in America is today in a critical condition. Only united concerted effort will save us from being crushed. This union must come as a matter of education and long continued effort. To this end there is needed a high class journal to circulate among the intelligent Negroes, tell them of the deeds of themselves and their neighbors, interpret the news of the world to them and inspire them toward definite ideals. Now we have many small weekly papers and one or two monthlies and none of them fill the great need I have outlined. I want to establish therefore for the nine million American Negroes and eventually for the whole Negro world a monthly journal."

Mr. Schiff wrote back courteously, saying: "Your plans to establish a high-class journal to circulate among the intelligent Negroes is in itself interesting and on its face has my sympathy. But before I could decide whether I can become of advantage in carrying your plans into effect, I would wish to advise with men whose opinion in such a matter I consider of much value."

Nothing came of this because, as I might have known, most of Mr. Schiff's friends were strong and sincere advocates of Tuskegee. Then came a new and surprising turn to the whole situation which, in the end, quite changed my life. In the early summer of 1905, Mr. Washington went to Boston and arranged to speak in a colored church to colored people, a thing which he did not often do in the North. Trotter and Forbes, editors of the *Guardian*, determined to heckle him and make him answer certain questions with regard to his attitude toward voting and education. William H. Lewis, a lawyer whom I had introduced to Mr. Washington, had charge of the meeting; the result was a disturbance, magnified by the newspapers into a riot, which resulted in the arrest of Mr. Trotter, and eventually he served a term in jail.

Later, I explained to Mr. George Foster Peabody, in answer to a query, my own connection with and attitude toward this occurrence. "I did not arrive in Boston until after the Zion Church disturbance. Before seeing the account in the morning papers, I had no inkling or suspicion in any way of the matter. I did not know Mr. Washington was in Boston or intending to go there, as I had just left him at Tuskegee. I had had no correspondence with Mr. Trotter for six months, save in regard to a boarding place. When I arrived in Boston and heard of the meeting, I told Mr. Trotter and Mr. Forbes in plain terms my decided disapproval of the unfortunate occurrence and my conviction that it would do harm."

When, however, Mr. Trotter was jailed, my indignation overflowed. Trotter was headstrong but sincere. He must not be made a martyr. I sent out from Atlanta in June 1905, "a call to a few selected persons for organized determination and aggressive action on the part of men who believe in Negro freedom and growth." I proposed a conference during that summer to "oppose firmly present methods of strangling honest criticism, to organize intelligent and honest Negroes, and to support organs of news and public opinion." Fifty-nine men from seventeen different states signed a call for a meeting near Buffalo, New York, during the week of July 9, 1905. I went to Buffalo and hired a little hotel on the Canada side of the river at Fort Erie and waited for the men to attend the meeting called for July 11, 12, 13 and 14. If sufficient men had not come to pay for the hotel, I should certainly have been in bankruptcy and perhaps in jail; but as a matter of fact, twenty-nine men, representing fourteen states, came. The Niagara Movement was organized January 31, 1906, and was incorporated in the District of Columbia with the following principles:

1. Freedom of speech and criticism.
2. Unfettered and unsubsidized press.
3. Manhood suffrage.
4. The abolition of all caste distinctions based simply on race and color.
5. The recognition of the principles of human brotherhood as a practical present creed.
6. The recognition of the highest and best human training as the monopoly of no class or race.
7. A belief in the dignity of labor.
8. United effort to realize these ideals under wise and courageous leadership.

The Niagara Movement created furor and the most disconcerting criticism. I was accused of acting from motives of envy of a great leader and of being ashamed of the fact that I was a member of the Negro race. The leading weekly of the land, the New York *Outlook,* pilloried me with scathing articles and the Negro weeklies, with few exceptions, went mad. But the movement went forward. The next year, 1906, instead of meeting in secret, we met publicly at Harper's Ferry, the scene of John Brown's raid, and had, in significance if not numbers, one of the greatest meetings that American Negroes have ever held. We made pilgrimage at dawn barefooted to the scene of Brown's martyrdom and we talked some of the plainest English that had been given voice by black men in America.

Now the fat was in the fire and my career as a scientist was beginning to be swallowed up in my role as propagandist. This was not at all to my liking. I was no natural

leader of men. I could not slap people on the back and
make friends of strangers. I could not easily break down
an inherited reserve and a cold, biting, critical streak.
Nevertheless, having put my hand to the plow I could
not turn back. The Niagara Movement met with less
momentum in Boston in 1907 and in Oberlin in 1908
and then practically became merged into a new and en-
veloping movement which started with a conference in 1909
and was incorporated as the National Association for the
Advancement of Colored People in 1911.

While now I was being swept on in this current to a new
and different mode of expression, I continued to cling to
my scientific work. In 1906, I outlined that work to Andrew Carnegie hoping to interest him in the Atlanta Conferences and reminding him that I had been presented to
him and Carl Schurz some years before. I said: "I en-
close herewith a report on Negro Crime, which is the ninth
annual report published by the Conference. The object
of this Conference is the systematic and exhaustive study
of the American Negro, in order that in the future philanthropists and others who seek to solve this serious set of
problems may have before them a carefully gathered body
of scientifically arranged facts to guide them.

"The studies mentioned above have been widely used;
they are in all the large libraries of the world including
the British Museum, the Library of Congress, Harvard
University, etc. They have been commended by periodicals
like the *Outlook*, the *Nation*, the London *Times*, the *Spectator*, and the *Manchester Guardian;* they have been favor-
ably spoken of by men like G. Stanley Hall, Walter F.
Willcox, Talcott Williams, and most of the teachers of
economics and sociology in American colleges." There was
no response, but still I pushed on.

I approached the United States Commissioner of Labor
in 1906 with a proposal for a study of Lowndes County,
Alabama. I was going to take a single county of a former
slave state with a large majority of Negroes and make
a social and economic study from the earliest times where
documents were available, down to the present, supple-
mented by studies of official records and a house-to-house
individual canvass. I plied Commissioner Neill with plans

and specifications until at last he authorized the study. Helped by Monroe Work now at Tuskegee Institute and R. R. Wright now a bishop of the A. M. E. Church and a dozen or more local employees I settled at the Calhoun School and began the study. It was carried on with all sorts of difficulties including the greeting of my agents with shotguns in certain parts of the county; but it was eventually finished. The difficult schedules were tabulated and I think myself that it was the most complete study of the sort that has ever been made. It included maps of the chronological division of the land; studies of the distribution of labor; investigations of the relation of landlord and tenant; a review of the political organization and of the family life and distribution of the population. I went to Washington and I spent some weeks there revising and perfecting it. It was accepted by the government and $2,000 paid for it, most of which went back to Atlanta University in repayment of funds which it had kindly furnished me to carry on the work.

But the study was not published. I finally approached the bureau and tried to find out when it would be published — and was told that the bureau had decided not to publish the manuscript since it "touched on political matters." I was astonished and disappointed, but after a year I went back to them again and asked if they would allow me to have the manuscript published since they were not going to use it. They told me it had been destroyed.

And to complete this strange picture, while I was down in Lowndes County finishing this study, there came the news of the Atlanta riot. I took the next train for Atlanta and my family. On the way I wrote the "Litany of Atlanta."[11]

Meantime I had started in Memphis, with the help of two graduates of Atlanta University, the little printing shop that I have mentioned, and from this was published a weekly paper called *The Moon,* beginning in 1906. *The Moon* was in some sort precursor of *The Crisis.* It was published for a year in Memphis, and then the printing office given up; and in 1907, in conjunction with two friends in Washington, there was issued a miniature monthly called the *Horizon.* The *Horizon* was published from 1907 to 1910, and in the fall of 1910, *The Crisis* was born.

So my work in Atlanta and my dream of the settlement of the Negro problem by science faded. I began to be acutely conscious of the difficulty which my attitudes and beliefs were making for Atlanta University. For a while I thought of withdrawing in 1906, when I was offered the position of assistant superintendent of schools of Washington, D. C. But even there, fear of my "radicalism" took the matter up even to President Theodore Roosevelt, and the offer, while never withdrawn, was not pressed. Finally, after the conference of 1909 in New York, the new organization of the National Association for the Advancement of Colored People was formed, and I was asked to come as Director of Publications and Research.

The Fifth Decade— Editor— 1908-1918— 40-50 years.— The span of my life from 1908 to 1918 is chiefly the story of *The Crisis* magazine under my editorship, but it had also an astonishing variety of subsidiary interests and activities.

Beginning a little before this period I continued my visits to Europe. I went in 1900 and again by the grace of an English friend in 1907; I took part in the great Races Congress in 1911 and went again in December 1918, just after the Armistice. This close touch with Europe and European developments had much to do with my understanding of social problems and trends of the world. I followed the development of English imperialism and the forces in England, France, Italy and Germany which resulted in the Balkan War, the World War and eventually the Russian Revolution. In the United States I studied the political development from the free-silver controversy led by Bryan, through the administrations of Theodore Roosevelt and Taft, and especially the Bull Moose campaign and the election of Wilson.

I kept on writing and publishing not with as much concentration of effort as I ought to have, but with some effectiveness. In 1907 appeared *The Negro in the South—* from lectures, two by myself and two by Mr. Washington. In 1909 I published *John Brown*, one of the best written of my books, but one which aroused unfortunate jealousy. In 1915 I published my volume on *The Negro*. To this must be added part of a bulletin in the twelfth census and several magazine articles; and, of course, eight years of *The Crisis*.

I was active in the organization of the new National Association for the Advancement of Colored People but carefully avoided the temptation of becoming its executive head. I still clung to my idea of investigation in lines which would temper and guide my exposition of a racial philosophy; and for that reason I determined from the beginning to make my work with the Association not that of executive secretary but editor of an official organ to be established. There was opposition to this from the first. First of all, organs of this sort were known to be usually costly and the organization had no money. Secondly, organs were of doubtful efficiency. My good friend, Albert E. Pillsbury, attorney general of Massachusetts, wrote and said feelingly: "If you have not decided upon a periodical, for heaven's sake don't. They are as numerous as flies"— and he meant to conclude about as useful. I came to New York to occupy a bare office; associated with a treasurer who said frankly, "I don't know who is going to pay your salary. I have no money," and with a generally critical, if not hostile, public which expected the National Association for the Advancement of Colored People to launch upon a bitter attack upon Booker T. Washington and Tuskegee.

My first job was to get *The Crisis* going, and arriving in August I finally got the first copy off the press in November 1910. It came at the psychological moment and its success was phenomenal. From the one thousand which I ventured to publish first it went up a thousand a month until by 1918 (due, of course, to special circumstances) we published and sold over a hundred thousand copies.

With this organ of propaganda and defense we were able to organize one of the most effective assaults of liberalism upon reaction that the modern world has seen. We secured extraordinary helpers; great lawyers like Moorfield Storey and Louis Marshall; earnest liberals like Villard, Milholland, John Haynes Holmes, Mary Ovington, Jane Addams, the Spingarns, Charles Edward Russell and William English Walling. We gained a series of court victories before the highest courts of the land which perhaps never have been equalled, beginning with the overthrow of the vicious Grandfather Clauses in 1915 and the breaking of the backbone of segregation in 1917. Above all we could, through *The Crisis* and our officers, our secretaries and friends, place consistently and continuously before the country a clear-cut statement of the legitimate aims of the American Negro and the facts concerning his condition. We organized his political power and made it felt and we started a campaign against lynching and mob law which was the most effective ever organized and at long last seemed to bring the end of the evil in sight.

With these efforts came other activities. I lectured widely in nearly every state in the Union. I furnished information to people everywhere on all sorts of subjects closely and remotely connected with race problems, and carried on from time to time studies and investigations. I was held more responsible for the success of the National Association for the Advancement of Colored People than I cared to confess to myself; than most other people wanted to admit. I had to spread myself over a whole field of activities when I should have done great deal better work if I could have confined myself to writing and study.

The development of *The Crisis* where most of my writing was done was interesting and difficult. It was impaired first and last by lack of trained business management. For the most part I was my own business manager which meant the loss of much time in learning and details. Then there was the delicate matter of policy; of how far I should express my own ideas and reactions in *The Crisis* or the studied judgment of the organization. From first to last I thought strongly, and as I still think rightly, to make the opinion expressed in *The Crisis* a personal opinion; because as I argued, no organization can express definite and clear-cut opinions; so far as this organization comes to conclusions it states them in its annual resolutions but *The Crisis* states openly the opinion of its editor so long as that opinion is in general agreement with that of the organization.

This of course was a dangerous and delicate matter bound eventually to break down in case there was any considerable divergence of opinion between the organization and editor. It was perhaps rather unusual that for two decades the two lines of thinking ran so largely together. If on the other hand *The Crisis* had not been in a sense a personal organ and the expression of myself, it could not possibly have attained its popularity and effectiveness. It would have been the dry kind of organ that so many societies support for purposes of reference and not for reading. It took, on the part of the organization, a great deal of patience and faith to allow me the latitude that they did for so many years; and on the other hand I was enabled to lay down for the National Association for the Advancement of Colored People, a clear, strong and distinct body of doctrine that could not have been built up by majority vote. It was probably inevitable that in the end a distinct and clear-cut difference of opinion on majority policies should lead to the dissolution of this interesting partnership.

One of the first difficulties that the National Association met was the case of its attitude toward Mr. Washington. I carefully tried to avoid any exaggeration of differences of thought; but to discuss the Negro question in 1910 was to discuss Booker T. Washington and almost before we were conscious of the inevitable trends we were challenged from Europe. Mr. Washington was in Europe in 1910 and made some speeches in England in his usual conciliatory lines. John Milholland who had been so dominant in the organization of the National Association immediately wrote me and said that American Negroes must combat the idea that they were satisfied with conditions. I, therefore, wrote an appeal to England and Europe.

"If Mr. Booker T. Washington, or any other person, is giving the impression abroad that the Negro problem in America is in process of satisfactory solution, he is giving an impression which is not true. We say this without personal bitterness toward Mr. Washington. He is a distinguished American and has a perfect right to his opinions. But we are compelled to point out that Mr. Washington's large financial responsibilities have made him dependent on the rich charitable public and that, for this reason, he has for years been compelled to tell, not the whole truth, but that part of it which certain powerful interests in America wish to appear as the whole truth. In flat contradiction, however, to the pleasant pictures thus pointed out, let us not forget that the consensus of opinion among eminent European scholars who know the race problem in America, from de Tocqueville down to von Halle, de Laveleys, Archer and Johnston, is that it forms the gravest of American problems. We black men who live and suffer under present conditions, and who have no reason, and refuse to accept reasons, for silence, can substantiate this unanimous testimony."

In furtherance of this statement and in anticipation of the meeting of the Races Congress, Mr. Milholland arranged that I should go early to the conference and make some addresses. The plan simmered down to a proposed address before the Lyceum Club, the leading women's group of London, and there it ran against the opposition of an American woman who wrote: "I think there is serious objection to entertaining Dr. Du Bois at the Lyceum." The result was a rather acrimonious controversy, in which I tried gently to withdraw but was unable to and finally, led by Her Highness the Ranee of Sarawak and Dr. Etta Sayre, a luncheon was held at the Lyceum Club with a bishop and two countesses and several knights and ladies and with Maurice Hewlett and Sir Harry Johnston.

The Races Congress would have marked an epoch in the racial history of the world if it had not been for the World War. As it was, it was a great and inspiring occasion, bringing together representatives of numerous ethnic and cultural groups and bringing new and frank conceptions of scientific bases of racial and social relations of people. I had a chance twice to address the Congress and to write one of the two poems which greeted the assembly.

Returning to the United States, I was plunged into the Bull Moose campaign. I thought I saw a splendid chance for a third-party movement on a broad platform of votes for Negroes and industrial democracy. Sitting in the office of *The Crisis,* I wrote out a proposed plank for the Progressives to adopt at their Chicago meeting: "The Progressive Party recognizes that distinctions of race or class in political life have no place in a democracy. Especially does the party realize that a group of ten million people who have in a generation changed from a slave to a free labor system, reestablished family life, accumulated a billion dollars of real property, including twenty million acres of land, and reduced their illiteracy from 80 to 30 percent, deserve and must have justice, opportunity and a voice in their own government. The party, therefore, demands for the American of Negro descent the repeal of unfair discriminatory laws and the right to vote on the same terms on which other citizens vote."

This was taken to Chicago by Joel E. Spingarn and advocated by two other directors of the Association, Dr. Henry Moskowitz and Jane Addams. They worked in vain for its adoption. Theodore Roosevelt would have none of it. He told Mr. Spingarn frankly that he should be "careful of that man Du Bois" who was in Roosevelt's opinion a dangerous person. The Bull Moose convention not only refused to adopt a plank anything like this but refused to seat most of the colored delegates, elected a southern "lily white" to run on the ticket with Mr. Roosevelt and finally succeeded in making Woodrow Wilson president of the United States.

Immediately Bishop Walters and myself conceived the idea that Mr. Wilson might be approachable. I proposed to throw the weight of *The Crisis* against Roosevelt and Taft and for Wilson, and Bishop Walters went to see him. He secured from Woodrow Wilson a categorical expression over his signature "of his earnest wish to see justice done the colored people in every matter; and not mere grudging justice, but justice executed with liberality and cordial good feeling. I want to assure them that should I become president of the United States they may count upon me for absolute fair dealing, for everything by which I could assist in advancing the interest of their race in the United States." In this effort to divide the Negro vote which was successful to an unusual degree, we were cruelly disappointed when the Democratic Congress met. There was the greatest flood of discriminatory bills both in Congress and among the states that has probably ever been introduced

since the Civil War. Only united and determined effort
defeated bills against intermarriage and for other discriminations in eight states, and while most of the proposed legislation in Congress was kept from the statute
books, the administration carried out a segregation by
color in the various departments which we had to fight
for years and vestiges of which even remain today.

In other respects our lines were cast in difficult places.
The socialists began to consider the color question and to
discriminate against the membership of colored people in
the South, lest whites should not be attracted. Mr. Villard
tried to get the president to appoint a National Race
Commission to be privately financed to the extent of
$50,000 but nothing could be done; and suddenly war and
revolution struck the world: the Chinese Revolution in
1912, the Balkan War in 1913 and finally in 1914 the
World War. In that very year the National Council of
Social Agencies met in Memphis without daring to discuss
the color question but Spingarn and I went down and
held open meetings advertising "for all who dared hear the
truth." We had an interesting time. This success and the
death of Booker T. Washington in 1915 led to the first
Amenia conference and united the American Negro in one
program of advance.

Finally the World War touched America; with it and in
anticipation of it came a sudden increasing of lynching
including the horrible burning at Dyersburg; there came
renewed efforts at segregation; the refusal to let Negroes
volunteer; the whole extraordinary difficulties of the draft
and the question of Negro officers. The Association itself
hesitated. It did not want openly to advocate segregation
but Spingarn, chairman of the board, and of *The Crisis,*
went ahead and the students of Howard and other schools
backed our efforts. We finally succeeded in arranging for
an officers' camp at Des Moines where seven hundred
officers were eventually given commissions. At the same
time there was the increased migration of Negroes to the
North, the riots at East St. Louis and the rebellion of Negro soldiers at Houston, the shelving of Colonel Young
and the alleged German plots.

The Sixth Decade — Editor and Traveler — 1918-1928 — 50-60 years. — I review the sixth decade of my life with some misgivings and difficulties of judgment. It was in many respects a culmination and yet again it represented, as it seems to me now, a vast dissipation of energy which might to better purpose have been concentrated in fewer lines. I am not altogether sure of this. There were so many things to do; so many paths that presented themselves as duties which must be followed that I was perhaps more or less helpless in the grasp of forces mightier than my will. Because, after all, the decade following the war was a time of tremendous crisis and changes and no single life could escape the paradox and confusion to which all life, and especially life in culture lands, was subjected.

My career had at this time a certain sense of drama. I had never before seen Theodore Roosevelt but in November 1918, I presided at a meeting in Carnegie Hall where he made his last public speech, appearing together with Irwin Cobb and a representative of the French High Commission. I remember my introduction: "I have the honor to present Theodore Roosevelt." Then on my fiftieth birthday there was a public celebration and many kindly messages. *The Crisis* had reached a monthly circulation of 68,000 and during the year I had a little dinner with Glendowen Evans, Margaret DeLand and William James. John Hope wrote: "How glad I am that your fiftieth birthday is going to be such a happy one because you can look back on so much good work done. But not the good work alone. What you may look back upon with greatest comfort is good intention."

And Albert Bushnell Hart wrote a word which one quotes with a certain diffidence: "Out of his fifty years of life I have followed a good thirty — and have counted him always among the ablest and keenest of our teacher-scholars, an American who viewed his country broadly."

Finally I prize most highly the tribute of President Bumstead: "First of all, let me express the keen satisfaction I take in having been the one chiefly responsible, perhaps, for bringing Doctor Du Bois to Atlanta University. I cannot but smile when I think of the objections and misgivings of some of our trustees and other friends when he

came. We wanted a professor of sociology with special
reference to investigating conditions concerning the Negro;
and I said that Doctor Du Bois was the one man, white or
black, far and away best fitted for the position. But how
about his religion — he's studied in Germany — perhaps if
you scratch him, you'll find an agnostic. Now it is true
that Atlanta University has always had a pronounced religious, though undenominational, life   . . so I must needs
have some assurance on this point. But, as Doctor Du
Bois will remember, they were not very easy to get. He
seemed to be one of those persons who, when asked about
their religion, reply that they 'have none to speak of.'
But though reluctant to speak of his religion or to say
what he would do at Atlanta, I observed that at the time
of my interview with him he was living with his newly
wedded bride in the center of the Negro slums in Philadelphia, doing the beneficent work to which Provost Harrison
had called him, and I thought there were some indications
of genuine religion in that fact.

"So, in spite of objections and misgivings, Doctor Du
Bois came to Atlanta University, and we held him there
for thirteen years notwithstanding several offers to go elsewhere and get double the salary that we could afford to
pay him. His work became a memorable part of the history of the institution."

The most important work of the decade as I now look
back upon it was my travel. Before 1918 I had made
three trips to Europe; but now between 1918 and 1928
I made four trips of extraordinary meaning: to France
directly after the close of the war and during the Congress
of Versailles; to England, Belgium, France and Geneva in
the earliest days of the League of Nations; to Spain, Portugal and Africa in 1923 and 1924; and to Germany,
Russia, and Constantinople in 1927. I could scarcely have
encompassed a more vital part of the modern world picture
than in those stirring journeys. They gave me a depth of
knowledge and a breadth of view which was of incalculable value for realizing and judging modern conditions,
and above all the problem of race in America.

But this was only part of my work: in the United States
I was still fighting the battle of liberalism against race

prejudice; trying to adjust war and postwar problems to the questions of racial justice; trying to show from the injustices of wartime what the new vision must encompass; fighting mobs and lynchings; encouraging Negro migration; helping women's suffrage; encouraging the new rush of young blacks to college; watching and explaining the political situation and traveling and lecturing thousands of miles and in hundreds of centers. In addition to this I was encouraging the writing of others and trying to help develop Negro art and literature. Besides editing *The Crisis* continuously, I published *Darkwater* in 1920; *The Gift of Black Folk* in 1924; the article on Georgia "In These United States" in 1924; and the concluding chapter in *The New Negro* in 1925, besides a number of magazine articles. Most of the young writers who began what was called the renaissance of Negro literature in the twenties began their first publication in *The Crisis* magazine.

Above all in these days I made two efforts toward which I look back with infinite satisfaction: the two-year attempt in the *Brownie's Book* to furnish a little magazine for Negro children in which my efforts were ably seconded by Augustus Dill and Jessie Fauset; and most especially my single-handed production of the pageant "The Star of Ethiopia." The pageant was an attempt to put into dramatic form for the benefit of large masses of people, a history of the Negro race. It was first attempted in the New York celebration of Emancipation in 1913; it was repeated with magnificent and breath-taking success in Washington with 1,200 participants; it was given again in Philadelphia in 1916; and in Los Angeles in 1924.

Finally in New York I attempted a little theatre movement which went far enough to secure for our little group second prize in an international competition. In 1918 I was asked rather suddenly by the NAACP to go to Europe right after the Armistice, to investigate the treatment of Negro soldiers and keep the record straight; and then at the behest of a group of American Negroes I considered that the interests of Africa ought to be represented during the peace efforts following the war. With infinite difficulty and through the cooperation of Blaise Diagne, the French deputy from Senegal, I succeed in gathering in February

1919, at the Grand Hotel in Paris a Pan-African Congress of fifty-seven delegates including sixteen American Negroes, twenty West Indians, and twelve Africans. France, Belgium, and Portugal were represented by officials.

This was to my mind but a beginning and in 1921 I returned and held a Second Pan-African Congress in London, Brussels and Paris from August 28 to September 6. There were 113 accredited delegates from twenty-six different groups including thirty-five from the United States, thirty-nine from Africa and the rest from the West Indies and Europe. Among the speakers were Sir Sidney now Lord Olivier, Florence Kelly, Bishop Hurst, Paul Otlet, often called the father of the League of Nations, Senator La Fontaine of Belgium, Dr. Vitellian, former physician of Menelik of Abyssinia, General Sorelas, Blaise Diagne, Norman Leys, and others. The attention which the congress evoked all over Europe was astonishing. It was discussed in the London *Times, Observer* and *Daily Graphic;* in the Paris *Petit Parisian, Matin* and *Temps;* in the *Manchester Guardian* and in practically all the daily papers of Belgium. It led to heated debate in Brussels touching the rights of these delegates to discuss the relation of colonies and it emphasized in the minds of all of us the consequent importance of such discussions.

Two of us visited the League of Nations and the International Labor Office with petitions and suggestions. In 1923 a third Pan-African Congress, less broadly representative than the second, but nevertheless of some importance was held in London, Paris and Lisbon; and thence I went to Africa and for the first time saw the homeland of the black race.

It was the time when the U. S. had disappointed Liberia by not granting her a promised loan and a gesture of goodwill was in order. At the suggestion of William H. Lewis I was therefore designated by cable as special minister plenipotentiary and envoy extraordinary to represent President Coolidge at the inauguration of President King. In the presence of the diplomatic and consular representatives of England, France, Germany, Spain, Belgium, Holland and Panama I had the honor to tell the president of Liberia: "Your Excellency: . . . I am sure that in this

special mark of the President's favor, he has had in mind
the wishes and hopes of Negro Americans. He knows
how proud they are of the hundred years of independence
which you have maintained by force of arms and by
brawn and brain upon the edge of this mighty continent;
he knows that in the great battle against color caste in
America, the ability of Negroes to rule in Africa has been
and ever will be a great and encouraging reinforcement."

At the London meeting of the third Pan-African Congress, Harold Laski, H. G. Wells, and Sir Sidney Olivier
spoke, and Ramsay MacDonald promised to speak to us
but was hindered by the sudden opening of the campaign
which eventually made him prime minister of England.
Among other efforts, at this time we held conferences with
members of the Labour Party of England at which Mrs.
Sidney Webb, Mr. Clynes and others were present. We
emphasized the importance of labor solidarity between
white and black labor in England, America and elsewhere.
In Portugal our meeting was attended by cabinet ministers and deputies and though small was of great interest.

To return again to the fight in the United States, there
arose early in this decade the case of Marcus Garvey. I
heard of him first when I was in Jamaica in 1915 when
he sent a letter "presenting his compliments" and giving
me "a hearty welcome to Jamaica, on the part of the
United Improvement and Conservation Association." Later
he came to the United States. In his case, as in the case
of others, I have repeatedly been accused of enmity and
jealousy, which have been so far from my thought that
the accusations have been a rather bitter experience. In
1920 when his movement was beginning to grow in America I said in *The Crisis* that he was "an extraordinary
leader of men" and declared that he had "with singular
success capitalized and made vocal the great and long
suffering grievances and spirit of protest among the West
Indian peasantry." On the other hand, I noted his difficulties of temperament and training, inability to get on
with his fellow workers, and denied categorically that I
had ever interfered in any way with his work.

Later when he began to collect money for his steamship
I characterized him as a sincere and hard-working idealist

but called his methods bombastic, wasteful, illogical and almost illegal and begged his friends not to allow him foolishly to overwhelm with bankruptcy and disaster one of the most interesting spiritual movements of the modern world. But he went ahead, wasted his money, got in trouble with the authorities and was deported. As I said at the time: "When Garvey was sent to Atlanta, no word or action of ours accomplished the result. His release and deportation was a matter of law which no deed or wish of ours influenced in the slightest degree. We have today, no enmity against Marcus Garvey. He has a great and worthy dream. We wish him well. He is free; he has a following; he still has a chance to carry on his work in his own home and among his own people and to accomplish some of his ideas. Let him do it. We will be the first to applaud any success that he may have."

I felt for a moment during the war that I could be without reservation a patriotic American. The government was making sincere efforts to meet our demands. It had commissioned over seven hundred Negro officers; I had had a personal interview with Newton Baker, secretary of war, and he had made categorical promises; Wilson had spoken out against lynching; and I had myself been offered a captaincy in the Intelligence Service, afterwards to be sure rather incontinently withdrawn as the higher command realized just who I was. Nevertheless, I tried to stand by the country and wrote the widely discussed editorial "Close Ranks" in which I said to the Negroes: forget your grievances for the moment and stand by your country. [12]

I am not sure that I was right but certainly my intentions were. I did not believe in war, but I thought that in a fight with America against militarism and for democracy we could be fighting for the emancipation of the Negro race. With the Armistice came disillusion. I saw the mud and dirt of the trenches; I heard from the mouths of soldiers the kind of treatment that black men got in the American army; I was convinced and said that American white officers fought more valiantly against Negroes within our ranks than they did against the Germans. I still believe this was largely true. I collected some astonishing documents of systematic slander and attack upon Negroes and demands upon the French for insulting attitudes toward them, and when I published these documents in America the government started to interfere by refusing *The Crisis* mailing facilities; then realizing that this was an admission of guilt, they quickly withdrew their prohibition.

I was especially upset by the mobs and lynchings during this time: by that extraordinary upheaval wherein for several hours black men fighting against a mob practically held the city of Washington in their hands; then the riot and murder in Chicago. We fought back through the National Association for the Advancement of Colored People, the columns of *The Crisis*, through lectures and articles with every force at hand. Mary Talbert started the Anti-Lynching Crusaders and with her help and that of the secretary, James Weldon Johnson, we raised a defense fund of $70,000 and put the Dyer Lynch Bill through the House of Representatives and onto the floor of the Senate.[13]   It was not until years after that I knew what killed that anti-lynching bill. It was a bargain between the South and the West by which lynching was permitted on condition that the Japanese were excluded.

Court cases kept pressing upon us: there were the Elaine riots and the Arkansas cases, there was the Sweet case in Detroit,[14] and equally significant to my mind but to few other Negroes the Sacco-Vanzetti case in Massachusetts.[15] We continued winning court victories and yet somehow, despite them, we did not seem to be getting far. We added to the Grandfather Case of 1915 and the Segregation Case of 1917, the victories in the Arkansas cases, the white primary case and another segregation case in the high courts, in addition to the eventual freeing of Dr. Sweet and his family. Still injustice prevailed. In the case of the Mississippi flood the Red Cross allowed the Negroes to be treated as slaves and peons, and in Okolona the Episcopal church refused to prosecute a white murderer on its own school grounds. Above all there came disquieting situations among Negro students: a strike at Hampton, disturbed conditions at Wilberforce, turmoil at Howard, and an uprising at Fisk.

It was thus a decade of infinite effort and discouraging turmoil. I suppose it had to be. I suppose that with the best will, it would have been impossible for me to concentrate on a few great lines of creative effort. I had to be a part of the revolution through which the world was going and to feel in my own soul the scars of its battle. Two things made a sort of finale to the decade: the fourth Pan-African Congress held in New York in 1927 with Dantes Bellegarde, George Sylvain and other speakers; and news of the Congress of British West Africa which began its meetings in 1920 and forced the British government to the greatest step toward democratic method ever taken in black colonies. And finally, to my surprise and quite against my best judgment, there was given for me upon my return from Africa at the Cafe Savarin in New York, a dinner. Among the speakers were Heywood Broun, Walter Hampden and Mrs. Bethune, and tributes were sent by Witter Bynner, Zona Gale and Eugene O'Neill. It was a very beautiful and touching tribute.

Seventh Decade— The Teacher and Writer— 1928-1938— 60-70 years. — Gradually in the last ten years of my life it has dawned upon me with increasing clarity just what the essential change in the world has been since the era of war and depression and how the tactics of those who live for the widest development of men must change accordingly. It is not a matter of change in ideals but of decisive change in the methods by which ideals are to be approximated.

As I now look back, I see in the crusade waged by the National Association for the Advancement of Colored People from 1910 to 1930 one of the finest efforts of liberalism to achieve human emancipation; and much was accomplished. But the essential difficulty with liberalism of the twentieth century was not to realize the fundamental change brought about by the worldwide organization of work and trade and commerce. Karl Marx had emphasized in the nineteenth century the overwhelming influence of the economic activities of men upon their thought and actions; but it was not until the twentieth century that it became clearer and clearer to those who observed and thought, that modern business enterprise organized for private profit was throttling democratic government, choking art and literature and making work and industry a paradox by systematically increasing the number of unemployed and dislocating industry itself by periodic depressions.

During the decade, 1918-1928, the world tried to "recover" from the disaster of the World War. We strove to "restore prosperity," to "get back to normalcy" and to return to the same sort of world as the one that had just committed suicide. After ten years of confused effort, it became increasingly clear that the disaster was far greater and deeper than most men dreamed, and that not recovery but fundamental change in the very bases of government and civilization faced us. With the worldwide depression, even the dullest began to conceive the size of the disaster that had overwhelmed mankind.

Moreover the words of the prophets who for nearly a century had been warning mankind now began to sound clear: freedom, that fine dream of the eighteenth century, had been during the nineteenth persistently interpreted as license for business enterprise, until it had not only reforged shackles for the human spirit, but actually reestablished human slavery, first by transporting labor and then by making worldwide the domination of capital. Armed rivalry for monopolizing wealth and services had led to commercial imperialism, world war and universal poverty. We were now faced with enormously difficult tasks of reconstructing the economic foundations of civilization and building thereon a new heaven and a new earth for the free and creative spirit of man.

The first answer was the practically universal abandonment of democratic control in government and social development for oligarchy. This proved unexpectedly easy because already before the war democracy was so widely a form of words and pious belief and not a practical reality. We held to the forms of voting and popular election, but did not believe nor practice the substance. Throughout European culture, government had passed into the hands of industry, and industry was not controlled by democratic methods. When now the realities of

the situation were posed to men, two radical solutions
were suddenly resorted to: Russian communism and
fascism. They both did away with democracy, and substituted oligarchic control of government and industry of
thought and action. [16] Communism aimed at eventual democracy and even elimination of the state, but sought this
by a dogmatic program, laid down ninety years ago by a
great thinker, but largely invalidated by nearly a century
of extraordinary social change. Fascism sought to take
complete control of the state, ostensibly for the good of all
the people, but practically for the good of the dominant
classes. Both dictatorships were forced to consolidate their
power by assassination and mass propaganda of every
sort.

All this in the years since the war I had been observing
in every part of the world, and I had been trying desperately and unremittingly, to spy out in the Universal
Gloom a path for the American Negro. One thing I knew
and knew well: we could not afford to sit and wait; we
must actively and intelligently press forward toward goals
consistent with the new ways of a world about to be born.
The problem of a minority group in a world torn by old
and new national and racial division was of enormous
difficulty: it was idle for us simply to repeat the old slo-
gans of democracy in an oligarchic world; no matter how
strongly we, with all forward-looking thinkers, might en-
visage a birth of democracy, we knew or should know,
that at present, our problem was economic rather than
political reform; this economic reconstruction was now in
progress — amid turmoil and contradiction, beclouded by
a thousand irrelevances and bedeviled by every art of
selfishness, but nevertheless clearly in progress. My problem was — How can American Negroes join this movement and intelligently reenforce it, for their own good
and the good of all men?

In the organization whose leadership I then shared, I
saw few allies impressed as I was to an ever increasing
degree, as to the immediate necessity of a reorientation
of objectives in order to make our original and unshak-
able ideals realizable. It was a problem not of change of
goal but of method. I looked about for allies and looked

where man ever looks in such crisis — to youth. I thought that just as a quarter century earlier, the NAACP was recruited from clear-eyed and courageous young folk, so today, a reorganization of our aims could be led by a similar group.

For this reason the Second Amenia Conference was called, seventeen years after the first. The first Amenia conference in 1916 met at a strategic time. It brought together on the beautiful farm of Joel Spingarn, where once John Burroughs had studied and dreamed, men and women representing all elements of leadership in the Negro race, together with white friends of prominence and influence. It was an unusually successful effort, and there on the old farm and around the dark still lake, while there was war in Europe and unrest in the United States, a hundred or more Negroes came together and a half dozen whites with messages from three presidents of the United States and other distinguished persons and we agreed upon a liberal program which included a plea for education, a warning against factionalism, a need for interracial understanding and a forward movement. Our essential agreement on a program of advance was gratifying and epochmaking. But as I now see, we did not then sufficently appreciate the spadework which had gone before and which for ten years had been preparing the minds of Americans, black and white, for a new deal in race relations and renewed effort toward racial equality.

In 1933, the situation was different. We met at the beginning rather than at the end of a period of preparatory discussion. We were still mentally whirling in a sea of inconclusive world discussion. We could not really reach agreement as a group, because so many of us as individuals had not made up our minds on the essentials of coming social change. The attendance was sifted — perhaps too much so; outside of four of the Elder Statesmen, the median age was thirty — persons just out of college, their lifework begun but not settled. They were teachers, social workers, professional men, and two artisans. The discussion was indeterminate and the resolutions contradictory; it was agreed that "the primary problem is economic" but the conclusion was that this problem could not be

approached from the point of view of race, but only from
that of a united group of laborers cutting across racial
lines. This was of course the intrusion of communistic
dogma — ideally right, and practically unworkable. If the
workers of the world would unite in unselfish cooperation
to uplift the laboring mass, the millenium would be in
sight. But we cannot expect of the age-long underprivi-
leged worker, that which the educated and advanced have
not envisaged; namely, the ignoring of race prejudice at
just the era when it is being artificially stimulated by
every human device.

Our program then must begin at home. Whatever just
objection there be to racial efforts in a day when biologic
races have been proved a myth, the reality of cultural
groups like the American Negro, whether called "races"
or what not, not only must be admitted but used as units
of social uplift. I began then, despite the fact that the most
courageous of the Negro youth seemed rushing down
steep places into the sea of communistic dogma, without
stopping to ask how far this dogma applied to our situation — I began advocating a program of economic organization within the Negro group, designed to prepare
us for effective citizenship in the new industrial democracy
which the world is slowly but surely approaching.

No sooner had I come to this conclusion than I knew
that I was out of touch with my organization and that the
question of leaving it was only a matter of time. This
was no easy decision; to give up *The Crisis* was like
giving up a child; to leave the National Association was
leaving the friends of a quarter of a century. But on the
other hand staying meant silence and a repudiation of
what I was thinking and planning. My cutting away, therefore, from this work did not conform to any of the ordinary patterns. A good many of my friends and most
onlookers are still puzzled. They tried to classify this
break of ties as a question of dismissal, of quarrel, of
incompatability of age and youth, or other classifications
of the sort. It was none of these. I could have stayed with
the National Association to the end of my working days
or at least as long as it continued to exist. There was
no greater friction within its organization than is inevi-

table to every human machine; but there was a clear difference of point of view. The Association in the matter of segregation emphasized a part of its program more than it emphasized before. We had recognized and used segregation in the matter of schools and colleges, in matter of religion, in the matter of the officers' camp; but we had fought its further spread.

At this point I came advocating a new segregation in economic lines; in precisely the lines of business and industry whither the National Association for the Advancement of Colored People was not prepared to go. It was not an absolute difference of principle, but it was a grave difference of further procedure, and therefore I gave up my connection with the Association, saying: "In thirty-five years of public service my contribution to the settlement of the Negro problem has been mainly candid criticism based on a careful effort to know the facts. I have not always been right, but I have been sincere, and I am unwilling at this late day to be limited in the expression of my honest opinions in the way in which the Board proposes. . . . I am, therefore, resigning from my position as Director of Publications and Research, Editor of *The Crisis*, member of the Board of Directors of the National Association for the Advancement of Colored People, and member of the Spingarn Medal Committee—this resignation to take effect immediately." The Association was good enough to express in return appreciation of the work I had done while associated with it.

In the meantime I had already been turning to work which was in a sense a renewal of my early work and research from 1908 to 1918. Already as early as 1909 I had planned an *Encyclopedia of the Negro*, had secured on my board of advisers Flinders Petrie, Sir Harry Johnston, Giuseppe Sergi, Dr. J. Deniker, William James, and Franz Boas; and on my proposed board of editors I had practically all the leading Negroes of the United States who were inclined toward research, but my change to New York and the work of starting *The Crisis* and then the World War put this quite out of my mind. The project was reviewed by the Phelps-Stokes Fund and today, backed by anthropologists all over the world, we are seeking a quarter of a million dollars to realize this dream.[17]

On the other hand my interest in Reconstruction which had begun in 1910 was renewed. In that year I had read a paper on "Reconstruction and its Benefits" before the American Historical Association. At the suggestion of the president, Albert Bushnell Hart, and others like Dunning of Columbia this paper was published. Finally in 1932 I asked the Rosenwald Fund to give me funds by which I could finish it. They did and the book *Black Reconstruction in America* was published in 1935.

By that time I was teaching at Atlanta University. There again I was carrying out the thread of a long dream. As early as 1905 I had been one of a group interested in uniting the various colored colleges into one university. Later, in 1909, President Hope and I worked out an interchange of lectures. He wrote me February 16, 1910: "I hope and believe this is the beginning of new and larger things in an educational way among our Colored institutions"; and later, April 21, 1910, he added: "I feel a downright enthusiasm over the beginning that our two schools made this year and hope that, now that we have made a start and have some slight idea of what can be accomplished, the two schools may next year do larger things."

John Hope and I had long been intimate and sympathetic friends and in the earlier part of this same year he had written me quite frankly a letter which I can now without betraying confidence quote:

"My impression is that *friendship* — not acquaintanceship or perfunctory intercourse but real friendship — is based not so much on agreement in opinion and policies and methods but upon downright confidence, upon simple faith, no matter what the view or appearances. You and I for nearly ten years have been friends. . . . You may remember that in the early and bitterly misunderstood efforts of the Niagara Movement, I was the only college president that ventured to attend the Harper's Ferry meeting to take part in its deliberations. You may remember, too, that while some may have answered the call to that seemingly radical meeting in New York last May, I was the only president, colored or white, of our colleges that took part in the deliberations of that meeting. I cite this to show that I have dared to live up to my views even when they threw me in the midst of the most radical. Furthermore, every man on our faculty does the same and will as long as I am head of the institution. . . . I write to ask you whether you have me in your heart— not on your calling list or your mailing list but in your heart—on your list of friends."

Before I had resigned from the National Association for the Advancement of Colored People, Hope had offered me a position in Atlanta whenever I might wish to come, and, when the actual consolidation of these schools took place, he repeated the offer. So that finally when the break came I returned to the renewed Atlanta University to carry out my independent lines of thought and express them in such writing and teaching as I might wish. In 1936, I seemed confirmed in the wisdom of my way by the panorama of the world which swept before me in London and Paris, Berlin and Vienna, Moscow and Mukden, Peiping and Shanghai, Kyoto and Tokyo, and heavenly Hawaii.

Finally I suppose upon a seventieth birthday one is presumed to have accumulated enough wisdom on the art of living to leave a wise word. There is not much that I feel moved to say; that little is this: I am especially glad of the divine gift of laughter; it has made the world human and loving, despite all its pain and wrong. I am glad that the partial Puritanism of my upbringing has never made me afraid of life. I have lived completely, testing every normal appetite, feasting on sunset, sea and hill. I have seen the face of beauty from the Grand Canyon to Capri, from the Alps to Lake Baikal, from the African bush to the Venus of Milo. I am proud of a straight-forward clearness of reason, in part a gift of the gods, but also to no little degree due to scientific training and inner discipline. By means of this I have met life face to face, I have loved a fight and above all I have done the work which I wanted to do and not merely that which men wished to pay me for. This is, I ween, the essential difference between Heaven and Hell.

Finally I have realized that the main fact of life is age and death. This makes it the more incomprehensible for me to see persons quite panic-stricken at the approach of their thirtieth birthday and prepared for dissolution at forty. Few of my friends have celebrated their fiftieth birthdays, and near none their sixtieth. Of course one sees some reasons: the disappointment at meager accomplishment which all to some extent must share, the haunting shadow of possible physical decline, the fear of death. I have been fortunate in having health and wise in keeping it. I have never shared what seems to me the essentially childish desire to live forever. Life has its pain and evil — its bitter disappointments; but in healthful length of days there is triumphal fullness of experience and infinite joy in seeing the most interesting of continued stories unfold. Not eternity but time is for the living:

> Mein Vermaechtniss, mein Vermaechtniss,
> Wie herrlich weit und breit!
> Die Zeit ist mein Vermaechtniss —
> Mein Acker ist die Ziet! [18]

A Pageant in Seven Decades 1868-1938 by William Edward Burghardt Du Bois, Professor of Sociology, Atlanta University. An address delivered on the occasion of his seventieth birthday at the University Convocation of Atlanta. Pamphlet. (Copy in Columbia University Library.)

2

THE CONSERVATION OF RACES

In March 1897 The American Negro Academy was founded. The leader and first president of the organization was Reverend Alexander Crummell, and Dr. Du Bois was one of four professors prominent in its activities and in 1899 he headed the Academy. Its chief objects were "the promotion of literature, science and art . . . the fostering of higher education, the publication of scholarly work and the defense of the Negro against vicious assault." The Academy published Occasional Papers *made up of addresses by leading black scholars. The following paper was delivered by Dr. Du Bois in 1897 and was published in the second of the Academy's* Occasional Papers.

The American Negro has always felt an intense personal interest in discussions as to the origins and destinies of races: primarily because back of most discussions of race with which he is familiar, have lurked certain assumptions as to his natural abilities, as to his political, intellectual and moral status, which he felt were wrong. He has, consequently, been led to deprecate and minimize race distinctions, to believe intensely that out of one blood God created all nations, and to speak of human brotherhood as though it were the possibility of an already dawning tomorrow.

Nevertheless, in our calmer moments we must acknowledge that human beings are divided into races; that in this country the two most extreme types of the world's races have met, and the resulting problem as to the future relations of these types is not only of intense and living interest to us, but forms an epoch in the history of mankind.

It is necessary, therefore, in planning our movements, in guiding our future development, that at times we rise above the pressing, but smaller questions of separate schools and cars, wage-discrimination and lynch law, to survey the whole question of race in human philosophy and to lay, on a basis of broad knowledge and careful insight, those large lines of policy and higher ideals which may form our guiding lines and boundaries in the practical difficulties of everyday. For it is certain that all human striving must recognize the hard limits of natural law, and that any striving, no matter how intense and earnest, which is against the constitution of the world, is vain. The question, then, which we must seriously consider is this: what is the real meaning of race; what has, in the past, been the law of race development, and what lessons has the past history of race development to teach the rising Negro people?

When we thus come to inquire into the essential difference of races we find it hard to come at once to any definite conclusion. Many criteria of race differences have in the past been proposed, as color, hair, cranial measurements and language. And manifestly, in each of these respects, human beings differ widely. They vary in color, for instance, from the marble-like pallor of the Scandinavian to the rich, dark brown of the Zulu, passing by the creamy Slav, the yellow Chinese, the light brown Sicilian and the brown Egyptian. Men vary, too, in the texture of hair from the obstinately straight hair of the Chinese to the obstinately tufted and frizzled hair of the Bushman. In measurement of heads, again, men vary; from the broad-headed Tartar to the medium-headed European and the narrow-headed Hottentot; or, again in language, from the highly-inflected Roman tongue to the monosyllabic Chinese. All these physical characteristics are patent enough, and if they agreed with each other it would be very easy to classify mankind. Unfortunately for scientists, however, these criteria of race are most exasperatingly intermingled. Color does not agree with texture of hair, for many of the dark races have straight hair; nor does color agree with the breadth of the head, for the yellow Tartar has a broader head than the German; nor, again, has the science of language as yet succeeded in clearing up the relative authority of these various and contradictory criteria.

The final word of science, so far, is that we have at least two, perhaps three, great families of human beings — the whites and Negroes, possibly the yellow race. That other races have arisen from the intermingling of the blood of these two. This broad division of the world's races which men like Huxley and Raetzel have introduced as more nearly true than the old five-race scheme of Blumenbach, is nothing more than an acknowledgment that, so far as purely physical characteristics are concerned, the differences between men do not explain all the differences of their history. It declares, as Darwin himself said, that great as is the physical unlikeness of the various races of men, their likenesses are greater, and upon this rests the whole scientific doctrine of human brotherhood.

Although the wonderful developments of human history teach that the grosser physical differences of color, hair and bone go but a short way toward explaining the different roles which groups of men have played in human progress, yet there are differences — subtle, delicate and elusive, though they may be — which have silently but definitely separated men into groups. While these subtle forces have generally followed the natural cleavage of common blood, descent and physical peculiarities, they have at other times swept across and ignored these. At all times, however, they have divided human beings into races, which, while they perhaps transcend scientific definition, nevertheless, are clearly defined to the eye of the historian and sociologist.

If this be true, then the history of the world is the history, not of individuals, but of groups, not of nations, but of races, and he who ignores or seeks to override the race idea in human history ignores and overrides the central thought of all history. What, then, is a race? It is a vast family of human beings, generally of common blood and language, always of common history, traditions and impulses, who are both voluntarily and involuntarily

striving together for the accomplishment of certain more
or less vividly conceived ideals of life.

Turning to real history, there can be no doubt, first,
as to the widespread, nay, universal, prevalence of the
race idea, the race spirit, the race ideal, and as to its
efficiency as the vastest and most ingenious invention
for human progress. We, who have been reared and trained
under the individualistic philosophy of the Declaration
of Independence and the laisser-faire philosophy of Adam
Smith, are loath to see and loath to acknowledge this
patent fact of human history. We see the Pharaohs, Cae-
sars, Toussaints and Napoleons of history and forget
the vast races of which they were but epitomized expressions. We are apt to think in our American impatience,
that while it may have been true in the past that closed
race groups made history, that here in conglomerate America *nous avons changé tout cela*—we have changed all
that, and have no need of this ancient instrument of progress. This assumption of which the Negro people are
especially fond cannot be established by a careful consideration of history.

We find upon the world's stage today eight distinctly
differentiated races, in the sense in which history tells us
the word must be used. They are the Slavs of Eastern
Europe, the Teutons of middle Europe, the English of
Great Britain and America, the Romance nations of Southern and Western Europe, the Negroes of Africa and America, the Semitic people of Western Asia and Northern
Africa, the Hindoos of Central Asia and the Mongolians
of Eastern Asia. There are, of course, other minor race
groups, as the American Indians, the Esquimaux and
the South Sea Islanders; these larger races, too, are far
from homogeneous; the Slav includes the Czech, the Mag-
yar, the Pole and the Russian; the Teuton includes the
German, the Scandinavian and the Dutch; the English
include the Scotch, the Irish and the conglomerate American. Under Romance nations the widely-differing Frenchman, Italian, Sicilian and Spaniard are comprehended.
The term Negro is, perhaps, the most indefinite of all,
combining the Mulattoes and Zamboes of America and
the Egyptians, Bantus and Bushmen of Africa. Among

the Hindoos are traces of widely differing nations, while
the great Chinese, Tartar, Corean and Japanese families
fall under the one designation — Mongolian.

The question now is: What is the real distinction between
these nations? Is it the physical differences of blood, color
and cranial measurements? Certainly we must all acknowledge that physical differences play a great part, and that,
with wide exceptions and qualifications, these eight great
races of today follow the cleavage of physical race distinctions; the English and Teuton represent the white variety
of mankind; the Mongolian, the yellow; the Negroes, the
black. Between these are many crosses and mixtures,
where Mongolian and Teuton have blended into the Slav,
and other mixtures have produced the Romance nations
and the Semites. But while race differences have followed
mainly physical race lines, yet no mere physical distinctions would really define or explain the deeper differences
— the cohesiveness and continuity of these groups. The
deeper differences are spiritual, psychical, differences —
undoubtedly based on the physical, but infinitely transcend-
ing them. The forces that bind together the Teuton nations are, then, first, their race identity and common blood;
secondly, and more important, a common history, common laws and religion, similar habits of thought and a
conscious striving together for certain ideals of life. The
whole process which has brought about these race differ-
entiations has been a growth, and the great characteristic
of this growth has been the differentiation of spiritual
and mental differences between great races of mankind
and the integration of physical differences.

The age of nomadic tribes of closely related individuals
represents the maximum of physical differences. They
were practically vast families, and there were as many
groups as families. As the families came together to form
cities the physical differences lessened, purity of blood was
replaced by the requirement of domicile, and all who
lived within the city bounds became gradually to be regarded as members of the group; i.e., there was a slight
and slow breaking down of physical barriers. This, however, was accompanied by an increase of the spiritual
and social differences between cities. This city became

husbandmen; this, merchants; another, warriors; and so on. The *ideals of life* for which the different cities struggled were different.

When at last cities began to coalesce into nations there was another breaking down of barriers which separated groups of men. The larger and broader differences of color, hair and physical proportions were not by any means ignored, but myriads of minor differences disappeared, and the sociological and historical races of men began to approximate the present division of races as indicated by physical researches. At the same time the spiritual and physical differences of race groups which constituted the nations became deep and decisive. The English nation stood for constitutional liberty and commercial freedom; the German nation for science and philosophy; the Romance nations stood for literature and art, and the other race groups are striving, each in its own way, to develop for civilization its particular message, its particular ideal, which shall help to guide the world nearer and nearer that perfection of human life for which we all long, that "one far off Divine event."

This has been the function of race differences up to the present time. What shall be its function in the future? Manifestly some of the great races of today—particularly the Negro race—have not as yet given to civilization the full spiritual message which they are capable of giving. I will not say that the Negro race has as yet given no message to the world, for it is still a mooted question among scientists as to just how far Egyptian civilization was Negro in its origin; if it was not wholly Negro, it was certainly very closely allied. Be that as it may, however, the fact still remains that the full, complete Negro message of the whole Negro race has not as yet been given to the world: that the messages and ideal of the yellow race have not been completed, and that the striving of the mighty Slavs has but begun.

The question is, then: how shall this message be delivered; how shall these various ideals be realized? The answer is plain: by the development of these race groups, not as individuals, but as races. For the development of Japanese genius, Japanese literature and art, Japanese spirit, only Japanese, bound and welded together, Japanese inspired by one vast ideal, can work out in its fullness the wonderful message which Japan has for the nations of the earth. For the development of Negro genius, of Negro literature and art, of Negro spirit, only Negroes bound and welded together, Negroes inspired by one vast ideal, can work out in its fullness the great message we have for humanity. We cannot reverse history; we are subject to the same natural laws as other races, and if the Negro is ever to be a factor in the world's history — if among the gaily-colored banners that deck the broad ramparts of civilization is to hang one uncompromising black, then it must be placed there by black hands, fashioned by black heads and hallowed by the travail of two hundred million black hearts beating in one glad song of jubilee.

For this reason, the advance guard of the Negro people — the eight million people of Negro blood in the United States of America — must soon come to realize that if they are to take their just place in the van of Pan-Negroism, then their destiny is *not* absorption by the white Americans. That if in America it is to be proven for the first time in the modern world that not only are Negroes capable of evolving individual men like Toussaint the Saviour,[1] but are a nation stored with wonderful possibilities of culture, then their destiny is not a servile imitation of Anglo-Saxon culture, but a stalwart originality which shall unswervingly follow Negro ideals.

It may, however, be objected here that the situation of our race in America renders this attitude impossible; that our sole hope of salvation lies in our being able to lose our race identity in the commingled blood of the nation; and that any other course would merely increase the friction of races which we call race prejudice, and against which we have so long and so earnestly fought.

Here, then, is the dilemma, and it is a puzzling one, I admit. No Negro who has given earnest thought to the situation of his people in America has failed, at some time in life, to find himself at these crossroads; has failed to ask himself at some time: what, after all, am I? Am I an American or am I a Negro? Can I be both? Or is it my duty to cease to be a Negro as soon as possible and be an American? If I strive as a Negro, am I not perpetuating the very cleft that threatens and separates black and white America? Is not my only possible practical aim the subduction of all that is Negro in me to the American? Does my black blood place upon me any more obligation to assert my nationality than German, or Irish or Italian blood would?

It is such incessant self-questioning and the hesitation that arises from it, that is making the present period a time of vacillation and contradiction for the American Negro; combined race action is stifled, race responsibility is shirked, race enterprises languish, and the best blood, the best talent, the best energy of the Negro people cannot be marshaled to do the bidding of the race. They stand back to make room for every rascal and demagogue who chooses to cloak his selfish devilry under the veil of race pride.

Is this right? Is it rational? Is it good policy? Have we in America a distinct mission as a race—a distinct sphere of action and an opportunity for race development, or is self-obliteration the highest end to which Negro blood dare aspire?

If we carefully consider what race prejudice really is, we find it, historically, to be nothing but the friction between different groups of people; it is the difference in aim, in feeling, in ideals of two different races; if, now, this difference exists touching territory, laws, language, or even religion, it is manifest that these people cannot live in the same territory without fatal collision; but if, on the other hand, there is substantial agreement in laws, language and religion; if there is a satisfactory adjustment of economic life, then there is no reason why, in the same country and on the same street, two or three great national ideals might not thrive and develop, that men of different races might not strive together for their race ideals as well, perhaps even better, than in isolation.

Here, it seems to me, is the reading of the riddle that puzzles so many of us. We are Americans, not only by birth and by citizenship, but by our political ideals, our language, our religion. Farther. than that, our Americanism does not go. At that point, we are Negroes, members of a vast historic race that from the very dawn of creation has slept, but half awakening in the dark forests of its African fatherland. We are the first fruits of this new nation, the harbinger of that black tomorrow which is yet destined to soften the whiteness of the Teutonic today. We are that people whose subtle sense of song has given America its only American music, its only American fairy tales, its only touch of pathos and humor amid its mad money-getting plutocracy. As such, it is our duty to conserve our physical powers, our intellectual endowments, our spiritual ideals; as a race we must strive by race organization, by race solidarity, by race unity to the realization of that broader humanity which freely recognizes differences in men, but sternly deprecates inequality in their opportunities of development.

For the accomplishment of these ends we need race organizations: Negro colleges, Negro newspapers, Negro business organizations, a Negro school of literature and art, and an intellectual clearing house, for all these products of the Negro mind, which we may call a Negro Academy. Not only is all this necessary for positive advance, it is absolutely imperative for negative defense. Let us not deceive ourselves at our situation in this country. Weighted with a heritage of moral iniquity from our past history, hard pressed in the economic world by foreign immigrants and native prejudice, hated here, despised there and pitied everywhere; our one haven of refuge is ourselves, and but one means of advance, our own belief in our great destiny, our own implicit trust in our ability and worth.

There is no power under God's high heaven that can stop the advance of eight thousand thousand honest, earnest, inspired and united people. But — and here is the rub — they *must* be honest, fearlessly criticizing their own faults, zealously correcting them; they must be *earnest.* No people that laughs at itself, and ridicules itself, and wishes to God it was anything but itself ever wrote its name in history; it *must* be inspired with the Divine faith of our black mothers, that out of the blood and dust of battle will march a victorious host, a mighty nation, a peculiar people, to speak to the nations of earth a Divine truth that shall make them free. And such a people must be united; not merely united for the organized theft of political spoils, not united to disgrace religion with whoremongers and ward-heelers; not united merely to protest and pass resolutions, but united to stop the ravages of consumption among the Negro people, united to keep black boys from loafing, gambling and crime; united to guard the purity of black women and to reduce that vast army of black prostitutes that is today marching to hell; and united in serious organizations, to determine by careful conference and thoughtful interchange of opinion the broad lines of policy and action for the American Negro.

This is the reason for being which the American Negro Academy has. It aims at once to be the epitome and expression of the intellect of the black-blooded people of America, the exponent of the race ideals of one of the world's great races. As such, the Academy must, if successful, be:

　　a. Representative in character.
　　b. Impartial in conduct.
　　c. Firm in leadership.

It must be representative in character; not in that it represents all interests or all factions, but in that it seeks to comprise something of the *best* thought, the most unselfish striving and the highest ideals. There are scattered in forgotten nooks and corners throughout the land, Negroes of some considerable training, of high minds, and high motives, who are unknown to their fellows, who exert far too little influence. These the Negro Academy should strive to bring into touch with each other and to give them a common mouthpiece.

The Academy should be impartial in conduct; while it aims to exalt the people it should aim to do so by truth — not by lies, by honesty — not by flattery. It should continually impress the fact upon the Negro people that they must not expect to have things done for them — they *must do for themselves*; that they have on their hands a vast work of self-reformation to do, and that a little less complaint and whining, and a little more dogged work and manly striving would do us more credit and benefit than a thousand Force or Civil Rights bills.

Finally, the American Negro Academy must point out a practical path of advance to the Negro people; there lie before every Negro today hundreds of questions of policy and right which must be settled and which each one settles now, not in accordance with any rule, but by impulse or individual preference; for instance: what should be the attitude of Negroes toward the educational qualification for voters? What should be our attitude toward separate schools? How should we meet discriminations on railways and in hotels? Such questions need not so much specific answers for each part as a general expression of policy, and nobody should be better fitted to announce such a policy than a representative honest Negro Academy.

All this, however, must come in time after careful organization and long conference. The immediate work before us should be practical and have direct bearing upon the situation of the Negro. The historical work of collecting the laws of the United States and of the various states of the Union with regard to the Negro is a work of such magnitude and importance that no body but one like this could think of undertaking it. If we could accomplish that one task we would justify our existence.

In the field of sociology an appalling work lies before us. First, we must unflinchingly and bravely face the truth, not with apologies, but with solemn earnestness. The Negro Academy ought to sound a note of warning that would echo in every black cabin in the land: *unless we conquer our present vices they will conquer us;* we are diseased, we are developing criminal tendencies, and an alarmingly large percentage of our men and women are sexually impure. The Negro Academy should stand and proclaim this over the housetops, crying with Garrison: *I will not equivocate, I will not retreat a single inch, and I will be heard.* [2] The Academy should seek to gather about it the talented, unselfish men, the pure and noble-minded women, to fight an army of devils that disgraces our manhood and our womanhood. There does not stand today upon God's earth a race more capable in muscle, in intel-

lect, in morals, than the American Negro, if he will bend
his energies in the right direction; if he will

> Burst his birth's invidious bar
> And grasp the skirts of happy chance,
> And breast the blows of circumstance,
>   And grapple with his evil star.

In science and morals, I have indicated two fields of
work for the Academy. Finally, in practical policy, I wish
to suggest the following *Academy Creed:*

1. We believe that the Negro people, as a race, have a
contribution to make to civilization and humanity, which
no other race can make.

2. We believe it the duty of the Americans of Negro descent, as a body, to maintain their race identity until this
mission of the Negro people is accomplished, and the ideal
of human brotherhood has become a practical possibility.

3. We believe that, unless modern civilization is a failure,
it is entirely feasible and practicable for two races in such
essential political, economic and religious harmony as the
white and colored people of America, to develop side by
side in peace and mutual happiness, the peculiar contribution which each has to make to the culture of their common country.

4. As a means to this end we advocate, not such social
equality between these races as would disregard human
likes and dislikes, but such a social equilibrium as would,
throughout all the complicated relations of life, give due
and just consideration to culture, ability, and moral worth,
whether they be found under white or black skins.

5. We believe that the first and greatest step toward the
settlement of the present friction between the races — commonly called the Negro problem — lies in the correction of
the immorality, crime and laziness among the Negroes
themselves, which still remains as a heritage from slavery.
We believe that only earnest and long continued efforts on
our own part can cure these social ills.

6. We believe that the second great step toward a better
adjustment of the relations between the races should be a
more impartial selection of ability in the economic and
intellectual world, and a greater respect for personal lib-

erty and worth, regardless of race. We believe that only earnest efforts on the part of the white people of this country will bring much needed reform in these matters.

7. On the basis of the foregoing declaration, and firmly believing in our high destiny, we, as American Negroes, are resolved to strive in every honorable way for the realization of the best and highest aims, for the development of strong manhood and pure womanhood, and for the rearing of a race ideal in America and Africa, to the glory of God and the uplifting of the Negro people.

American Negro Academy Occasional Papers, No. 2, 1897.

3

CAREERS OPEN TO
COLLEGE-BRED NEGROES

*Ten years after he had graduated from Fisk University,
Dr. Du Bois, class of 1888, delivered the commencement
address at Fisk. To the black students drawn from all
parts of the South, Du Bois outlined various careers open
to them after graduation. He urged the students to use
their newly-acquired knowledge in the service of their
people. In concluding he gave them three watchwords, the
first of which went: ". . . you are Negroes, members of
that dark, historic race that from the world's dawn has
slept to hear the trumpet summons sound through our
ears. Cherish unwavering faith in the blood of your fathers, and make sure this last triumph of humanity." In
this address one can discern the emergence of Du Bois's
concept of the "talented tenth" of the Negro people who
would utilize their knowledge to improve the status of the
black masses.*

To the young ears that hearken behind college walls at
the confused murmur of the world beyond, there comes
at times a strangely discordant note to mar the music of
their lives. Men tell them that college is a play world—
the mirage of real life; the place where men climb or seek
to climb heights whence they must sooner or later sink
into the dust of real life. Scarcely a commencement season
passes but what, amid congratulation and rejoicing, amid
high resolve and lofty sentiment, stalks this pale, half-
mocking ghost, crying to the newborn bachelor in arts:
You have played — now comes work.

And, therefore, students of the class of '98, I have thought to take this oft-repeated idea and talk with you in this last hour of your college days about the relation which, in your lives, a liberal education bears to bread-winning.

And first, young men and women, I heartily join in congratulating you to whom has been vouchsafed the vision splendid — you who stand where once I stood,

> When meadow, grove, and stream,
>   The earth, and every common sight,
> To me did seem
>   Apparelled in celestial light,
> The glory and the freshness of a dream.

And yet not a dream, but a mighty reality — a glimpse of the higher life, the broader possibilities of humanity, which is granted to the man who, amid the rush and roar of living, pauses four short years to learn what living means.

The vision of the rich meaning of life, which comes to you as students, as men of culture, comes dimly or not at all to the plodding masses of men, and even to men of high estate it comes too often blurred and distorted by selfishness and greed. But you have seen it in the freshness and sunshine of youth: here you have talked with Aristotle and Shakespeare, have learned of Euclid, have heard the solemn drama of a world, and thought the thoughts of seers and heroes of the world that was. Out of such lore, out of such light and shade, has the vision of the world appeared before you: you have not all comprehended it; you have, many of you but glanced at its brilliant hues, and have missed the speaking splendor of the background.

I remember how once I stood near the ancient cathedral at Berne, looking at the Alps; I heard the rushing waters below and knew their music; I saw the rolling fields beyond and thought them pretty; then I saw the hills and the towering masses of dark mountains; they were beautiful, and yet I saw them with a tinge of disappointment, but even as I turned away, I glanced toward the sky, and then my heart leaped — for there above the meadows and the waters, above the hills and the mountains, blazed in the evening sunshine, the mighty, snow-clad peaks of the high Alps, glistening and glorious with the hues of the rainbow, in spotless purity and awful majesty. And so many a man to whom opportunity has unveiled some revelation of the broader, truer world, has turned away from it, half seen and half known.

But some have seen the vision, have comprehended all the meaning of a liberal education; and now, as you turn away half-regretfully, half gladly, what relation has this day of transfiguration to the hard, cold paths of the world beyond these walls? Is it to be but a memory and a longing, or if more than this, how much more?

I presume that few of you have fully realized that with tomorrow morning you begin to earn your own bread and butter; that today is the commencement of a new life on which you are to find self-support by daily toil. And I am glad if you have not given this matter too much thought or worry, for, surely, if you have done well your college work you have had other things to think of, problems of life and humanity far broader than your own single destiny; not that you have neglected dreams and plans of parts that you might play in life, but that you have scarce thought out its dry details. And, therefore, to most of you the nearness of real life dawned this morning with a certain suddenness; with something of that dark dismay with which the human creator faces his own creature — with some thought, too, half of rebellion and an aimless asking: why must I turn from so pleasant a life to one hard and matter of fact? Why must I leave the pleasures of study and dear companionship and high inspiration to "bear the whips and scorns of time, the oppressor's wrong, the proud man's contumely?"

Today the paradox of life rises over you as never before, and you wonder why you, of all men, should not have been born rich and privileged, not to see the vision of the world and all the glory that shall be, fade into some distant future, leaving long paths of dirt and rocks between. All these questions you have asked, I have asked, and all men have asked, who, whether on the college ros-

trum or with the pick and shovel, have, on a commencement morning, turned from study to deeds, from ideals to
realization, from thought to life.

All this I cannot answer plainly, and yet the shadow
of answer falls on us all; for why should the sun rise if
there be neither noon nor evening, and what is a life that
is all beginning? And have not these, your college days,
been all the happier for the promise and prophecy of a
life to come?

Three universal laws underlie the necessity of earning
a living: the law of work, the law of sacrifice, the law of
service. The law of work declares that to live one must
toil continuously, zealously; the apple may hang ripe upon
the tree, but to eat we must pick it; grain will sprout and
grow, but not till we plant it; houses will shelter us and
clothes cover us only as we build and weave. Sometimes,
to be sure, it may seem that enjoyment came without work
and sacrifice — but it is not so. Someone toils, someone
delves, and though we may shift our burden on the bowed
shoulders of others — yet that is the necessity of the sick,
or the shame of the lazy, or the crime of the coward.

Blind toil alone, however, will not satisfy the wants of
aught but the lowest and simplest culture; the greater satisfaction comes from the sacrifice of today's enjoyment that
tomorrow's may be greater; of this year's consumption to
increase next year's production; of the indulgence of youth
to the vigor of old age, of the pleasure of one life to the
richer heritage of humanity; this is the law of sacrifice,
and we see it everywhere: in the fruit we save to ripen,
in the fields that lie fallow, in the years given to training
and education, and in the self-sacrifice of a Socrates, a
Darwin, or a David Livingstone.

Even this does not complete the laws of life as we find
it in the twilight of the nineteenth century. We must not
only work and sacrifice for ourselves and others, but also
render each other mutual service. The physician must heal
not himself, but all men; the tailor must mend the whole
village; the farmer must plant for all. Thus in the civilized
world each serves all, and all serve each, and the binding
force is faith and skill, and the skill is bounded only by

human possibility and genius, and the faith is faithful even to the untrue.

Such are the laws of that life, young people, which you enter today. And upon these laws have been built through the ages, in sweat of brow and sorrow of soul, all that fair world whose darkly glorious vision has made its study sweet to you, and its knowledge precious.

While these be the laws of universal life, their application differs in each age, and an equipment in life suitable to one century may be fatally unsuited to another. Therefore, you must not make the mistake of misunderstanding the age in which you live; and I especially warn you here, because as American Negroes, in the strange environment and unusual conditions of life which surround you, it will be peculiarly easy for you to fail to catch the spirit of the times; to distort the proportions of life, to seek to do what others have done better, and to seek quickly to undo what cannot legally be undone. I have often feared that the failure of many a promising young Negro was due largely to this natural ignorance.

Young Negroes are born in a social system of caste that belongs to the middle ages; they inherit the moral looseness of a sixteenth century; they learn to lisp the religious controversies of the seventeenth century; they are stirred by discussions of the rights of man that belong to the eighteenth century, and it is not wonderful if they hardly realize that they live upon the threshold of the twentieth century. You, men of Fisk, must not misunderstand your age; you must know that the world does not feel the injustice of caste as it once did, but rather sees in it some antidote for a vulgar democracy; you must remember that there are central elementary moral precepts which the world utterly refuses to excuse or palliate; you must realize that the controversies of Methodists and Baptists chiefly interest antiquarians and not active Christians of today; that we insist today on men's duties rather than their rights, and that the spirit of the century in which you will work is service not indulgence.

And surely no century more richly deserves understanding than the nineteenth. It has not the romantic interest of the fifteenth, when the world rose in a dream and wandered in the sunshine of its new discovered self, and poetry and art and tales from over seas; it has not the rugged might of that sixteenth century, when the dark monk faced the emperor of all the world, daring to be honest rather than orthodox, and crying, "Here I stand. God help me! I cannot waver."

But whatever the nineteenth century may lack in romantic or striking interest, it repays and more than repays in human opportunity, in the broadness of its conception of humanity, in the wonderful organization of effort to serve humanity. Never before have work and sacrifice and service meant so much, never before were there so many workers, such widespread sacrifice, such world-service. In the business of governing men, never before did so many take part. The issue is not altogether successful, and yet its measure of success far exceeds the wildest dreams of the world of long ago.

Never before have so many hands and heads joined to make the earth yield her increase, to make glad the waste places of the earth, to ply the loom, and whirl the spindle, and transform the useless and the worthless. On our breakfast table lies each morning the toil of Europe, Asia, and Africa, and the isles of the sea; we sow and spin for unseen millions, and countless myriads weave and plant for us; we have made the earth smaller and life broader by annihilating distance, magnifying the human voice and the stars, binding nation to nation, until today, for the first time in history, there is one standard of human culture as well in New York as in London, in Cape Town as in Paris, in Bombay as in Berlin.

Is not this, then, a century worth living in — a day worth serving? And though toil, hard, heavy toil, be the price of life, shall we not, young men and women, gladly work and sacrifice and serve "That one, far off, divine event,/ Toward which the whole creation moves"?

And we serve first for the sake of serving — to develop our own powers, gain the mastery of this human machine, and come to the broadest, deepest self-realization. And then we serve for real end of service, to make life no narrow,

selfish thing, but to let it sweep as sweeps the morning—
broad and full and free for all men and all time, that you
and I and all may earn a living and earn, too, much
more than that—a life worth living.

This, fellow workers, is the veil of toil that hangs before
the vision glorious. And yet, when on commencement
morning, we leave behind the vivid hues of this, our inspiration, believe me, it is not easy to guard the sacred image,
to keep alive the holy fire that lights and lightens life; to
hold amid the toil and turmoil of living those old ideals
fixed and tranquil before the soul. How often do we see
young collegians enter life with high resolve and lofty purpose and then watch them shrink and shrink and shrink
to sordid, selfish, shrewd plodders, full of distrust and
sneers. Woe to the man, who, with the revelation of the
world once before him, as it stands before you now, has
let it fade and whiten into common day—life is death.

But you who, firm and inspired, turn toward the work
of living, undismayed, knowing the world that was, loving
that world that is, and believing in the world that is to
be, just what can you do—what careers may you follow
to realize the ideals and hopes of this day?

You cannot surely be knights and kings and magicians,
but you can choose careers fully as wonderful and much
more useful. You look about you in the world and see
servants, they whose function it is to help the helpless,
the weak and the busy—to cook, that Washington may
command armies; to sweep, that Edison may have time
to think. You see the laborer, that wizard who places his
weak shoulders against the physical world and overturns
mountains and pushes away forests, and guides the rivers,
and garners the harvests. You see the manufacturer guiding the laborer with brains and with capital: he is the
alchemist in whose alembic dirt turns to houses, grass to
coats, and stones to food. The merchant you see standing
beside him, the prophet who enables us to laugh at famine,
and want, and waste, by bringing together buyer and
seller, maker and user, reader and writer. There is the

teacher, the giver of immortal life, the one who makes
the child to start where his fathers left off, that the world
may think on with one mind. Yonder stands the physician
with the long sought elixir of life, the lawyer clothed in
justice, the minister who seeks to add to justice righteousness, and to life ideals higher than life. Your restless eye
may easily overlook the corner where sits the scientist
seeking the truth that shall make us free, or the other,
where the artist dies that there may live a poem or painting or a thought.

All these ways of earning a living you may see in the
world, and many more. But it does not follow that you
may idly or thoughtlessly choose one as you pick a flower
on a summer's day. To choose a life calling is a serious
thing: first, you must consider not so much what you want
to do as what wants to be done; secondly, you cannot
wander at will over all the world of work that wants workers, but duty and privilege and special advantage calls to
the work that lies nearest your hands. The German works
for Germany, the Englishman serves England, and it is
the duty of the Negro to serve his blood and lineage, and
so working, each for each, and all for each, we realize
the goal of each for all.

The concrete question, then, that faces you of the class
of '98, is: what part can I best take in the striving of the
eight million men and women who are bound to me by
a common sorrow and a common hope, that through the
striving of the Negro people this land of our fathers may
live and thrive?

The most useful and universal work, and the type of all
other work, is that of the servant and common laborer.
The ordinary, unskilled part of this work I pass over —
it is useful, it is honorable, but you have been trained for
skilled work, and it is throwing away the money of this
institution if its college graduates are to become Pullman
porters. Even the higher branches of house-service, as
cooking and nursing, and the great field of skilled labor,
are rather for different training, and you will rightly leave

them to the skilled graduates of our great industrial
schools, with the sincere hope that so useful and promising
avenues will soon be filled by able and honest artisans.

The first field that opens itself to you is the calling of
the farmer. I do not mean the farmhand or the milkmaid,
nor even the agricultural scientist. I mean the man who,
by rational methods and business sense, with a knowledge
of the world market, the methods of transportation, and
the possibilities of the soil, will make this land of the South
to bloom and blossom like Belgium and Holland, France
and Germany; who will transform the slipshod, wasteful,
happy-go-lucky farming of the South into the scientific
business methods of New England and the West. There
is little more reason for leaving farming to people without
brains or culture than there would be in thus abandoning
the other great fields of industry.

Especially, however, do the Negro people need the country gentleman — the man of air and health and home and
morals; and today we have an unparalleled chance to
supply such an aristocracy. Throughout Tennessee and
Georgia and Virginia, where the young people are hurry-
ing to the industries of the cities, stand the fine old abandoned farms and decaying mansions of a gentry that has
passed. You are the ones to buy these farms at a nominal
price, start a new agriculture, and a balance for the sickly
crowding of cities and to furnish the food and material
which these cities increasingly demand, and thus help to
solve some of the most intricate of our social problems.

The next great field open to you is that of the merchant,
where again there is among Negroes no discouraging
competition, and a broad field for development.

Those Negroes who urge the blight of color prejudice
as a barrier to their entering mercantile pursuits, quite
forget that they have before them an undeveloped market
of eight million souls, and that these millions spend every
year $150,000,000 to $300,000,000, and that a part of
this expenditure, at least, could be made through Negro
merchants, if well-trained, educated, active men would only
enter this field and cultivate it. Of course, the training of

slavery was most unfortunate for business qualities. There linger among the freedmen's sons habits of laziness, of being perpetually five minutes behind time, of inattention to detail, which are fatal to modern business methods. All this can and must be unlearned, and the college man who, making himself familiar with the best business methods of a business age, starts in to open this field will not only earn and deserve a living for himself, but will make it easier for thousands to follow his example.

And this brings me to a thought that I want especially to impress upon college men: the time has come when the American Negro is being expected to take care of himself, and not much longer to depend on alms and charity; he must become self-supporting — a source of strength and power instead of a menace and a burden to the nation; the hindrance that today prevents him from fulfilling this expectation with reasonable quickness is his anomalous economic condition — his lack of remunerative employment. And you, young men and women, are the ones to supply this lack. We have workers enough, brawny and willing; we have some skill, and the industrial schools are furnishing more; moreover, a people that have today more than $26,000,000 invested in church property alone, and who spend at least $10,000,000 each year in those churches, have capital enough to collect in savings banks and put into industrial enterprises. But what we do lack, and what schools like this must begin to supply in increasing numbers is the captain of industry, the man who can marshal and guide workers in industrial enterprises, who can foresee the demand and supply it — note the special aptitude of laborers and turn it to advantage — so guide with eye and brain the work of these black millions, that, instead of adding to the poverty of the nation and subtracting from its wealth, we may add to the wealth of the land and make Negro poverty no longer a byword.

Here is a field for development such as few ages offer — a body of willing workers such as few nations furnish. And this field calls not for mere money-makers, or those who would ape the silly display and ostentation of certain

classes of Americans; nor does it call for men narrowed
and shrunk by the soul-destroying commercialism of the
hour, that philosophy which imagines men made for industry and not industry for men; but rather here is a chance
to set a nation working, to make their work more effective,
to build and fortify Negro homes, to educate Negro children, to establish institutions of protection, reform, and
rescue, and to make the Negro people able to help others
even as others have helped us.

Let us turn now to the professional class and ask about
the openings there for college-bred men. As to the demand
in one department there can be no doubt. If ever a nation
needed the gospel of health presented to them, it is the Negro race, with its alarming death rate, its careless habits, its
widows and orphans, and its sick and maimed. For the
well-trained physician, as distinguished from the quack
and the man who is too hurried to learn, there is large
and important work. The remuneration which a poor
people can pay will not be large, but the chance for usefulness and far-reaching influence on the future of our race
and country can scarcely be overestimated. Especially is
the calling open to young women, who ought to find here
congenial, useful employment, and employment, perhaps,
next in nobility to that of the noblest and best — mother-
hood.

When we come to the profession of law we have a narrower and less obvious field, one in which there is plenty
of room for success, but against the peculiar difficulties
of which young people need warning and advice. These
difficulties arise from the fact that, first, the Negro himself
furnishes little important or lucrative law business, and
secondly, even among the whites, the profession is over-
crowded and only men of ability or some wealth and much
influence can expect much success. Thus, many changes
must come before the handicap of color prejudice will allow
Negroes to start in this profession with an even chance.
Yet, here as elsewhere, blood will tell.

For thirty years the chief function of the Negro college
has been that of furnishing teachers for the Negro schools,

and the extraordinary success and value of this work has not yet been adequately recognized.´ Nevertheless, it is evident that this work has already passed through many phases and is about to pass through others. Fisk University at first furnished common-school teachers, then teachers of schools that teach common-school teachers; finally, teachers of men who teach the teachers; with each of these steps comes, to be sure, a demand for better quality, but also for a smaller quantity. The field for teaching, therefore, open to the class of '98 is smaller than that open to former classes and more exacting in its demands.

What is true now is apt to be emphasized in the future; specially trained teachers of high attainments will ever find some demand for their services. On the other hand, most college graduates will slowly turn to other work. Hereafter, when Negro education is more firmly founded, the better-trained college men will be more in demand. This, then, is a field still open — of broad usefulness and demanding the very best in character, and the better in training and knowledge, only the competition is sharp and is destined to be sharper.

I now turn to the Christian ministry with something of diffidence. The development of the Negro church has been so extraordinary, and of such deep sociological interest that its future course is a matter of great concern. As it is now, churches organized among Negroes are, for the most part, curiously composite institutions, which combine the work of churches, theaters, newspapers, homes, schools, and lodges. As a social and business institution the church has had marvelous success and has done much for the Negro people. As a religious institution, also, it has played some part, but it is needless to say that its many other activities have not increased the efficiency of its function as a teacher of morals and inspirer to the high ideals of Christianity.

An institution so popular that there is now in the United States one organization for every sixty Negro families, has, naturally, already attracted to its leadership a vast army of men. Moreover, the severest charge that can be brought against the Christian education of the Negro in the South during the last thirty years is the reckless way in which sap-headed young fellows, without ability, and in some cases without character, have been urged and pushed into the ministry. It is time now to halt. It is time to say to young men like you: qualifications that would be of no service elsewhere are not needed in the church; a general desire to be good, joined to a glib tongue, is not the sort of combination that is going to make the Negro people stop stealing and committing adultery. And, instead of aimless, wholesale invitations to enter this calling of life, we need to put our hands kindly on the shoulders of some young candidates, and tell them firmly that they are not fitted to be heads of the church of Christ.

What we need is not more but fewer ministers, but in that lesser number we certainly need earnest, broad, and cultured men; men who do a good deal more than they say; men of broad plans and far-seeing thought; men who will extend the charitable and rescue work of the churches, encourage home-getting, guard the children of the flock, not on Sundays, but on weekdays, make the people use savings banks, and, in fine, men who will really be active agents of social and moral reform in their communities. There, and there only, is the soil which will transform the mysticism of Negro religion into the righteousness of Christianity.

There is then an opening for college men in this field, but it is a field to be entered with more care than others, not with less; to be chosen by men of more stable character than others, not of less; and it is the one field where the man who doubts his fitness had best give the world the benefit of the doubt. But to those consecrated men who can and will place themselves today at the head of Negro religious life and guide this wavering people to a Christianity pure and holy and true — to those men in the day of reckoning shall surely come the benediction of a useful life, and the "Well done!" of the Master.

Finally, I come to the field of the scientist and the artist — of the men who seek to know and create. And here little can be said of openings or of hindrances — for the way of such men is the dim and unfenced moor that wends its path beyond the world into the unknown: the man who enters here must expect long journeys, poor and unknown and often discouraged. To do in science and literature today anything worth the doing, anything that is really good and lasting, is hard to anyone, impossible to many. And here the young Negro so often forgets that "art is long and time is fleeting." The first applause of his good-natured race too often turns his head; lets him rest on his oars, and instead of pursuing more doggedly the faint chance of doing some little masterpiece, he lingers upon his notoreity and puts his picture and biography in the papers.

For the man who will work and dig and starve there is a chance to do here incalculable good for the Negro race; for the woman in whose soul the divine music of our fathers has touched some answering chord of genius, there is a chance to do more than follow the masters; to all of you in whom the tragedy of life, or its fitful comedy, has created a tale worth the telling, there is a chance to gain listeners who will know no color line. Everywhere there is work to be done; in physical and social science, in literature, painting and architecture, in music and sculpture, in every place where genius and toil will unite and strive.

Let me now briefly review these fields of work:

A broad field of scientific, businesslike farming.

The uncultivated but promising field of the Negro merchant, with a constituency of eight millions.

The pressing demands for captains of industry to employ the labor, to direct the work, and develop the capacity of Negro workmen by industrial enterprise.

The large field for well-trained physicians.

Some small demand for lawyers.

A considerable field for specially-trained teachers.

The pressing necessity for fewer ministers of better type and more thorough devotion.

An ever open field for talent and application in literature, science, and art.

Such are some of the paths that open before you, class

of '98, and along these you go toward the goal you have set for yourselves. Which path you will take you must choose, and the choice is difficult. Nevertheless, it cannot be long put off—for no choice is a choice. And when you have chosen, stand by it, for the man who is ever wavering and choosing again is wasting God's time. Choose, then, remembering that failure is the lot of many men, and that no success will be so marvelous but what it beckons to greater goals beyond.

And with the lifework chosen, remember that it can become, as you will it, drudgery or heroism, prosaic or romantic, brutal or divine. Who of the world today cares whether Washington was a farmer or a merchant? Who thinks of Lincoln as a country lawyer, or reads of St. Peter, the fisherman, prays to Jesus Christ, the carpenter? If you make the object of your life-calling food and drink, food and drink it will yield you grudgingly; but if above and beyond mere existence you seek to play well your part because it is worth playing—to do your duty because the world thirsts for your service, to perform clean, honest, thorough work, not for cheap applause, but because the work needs to be done—then is all your toil and drudgery transfigured into divine service and joins the mighty lives that have swept beyond time into the everlasting world. In this sense is it, young men and women, that the vision of life you have gained here is truer and holier and more real than the narrow, sordid views of life which you meet on the streets and in the homes of smaller souls. Cling to those ideals, cherish them, and in travail and sorrow, if need be, make them more true.

It is now ten years since I stood amid these walls on my commencement morning, ten years full of toil and happiness and sorrow, and the full delight of hard work. And as I look back on that youthful gleam, and see the vision splendid, the trailing clouds of glory that lighted then the wide way of life, I am ever glad that I stepped into the world guided of strong faith in its promises, and inspired by no sordid aims. And from that world I come back to welcome you, my brothers and my sisters. I cannot promise you happiness always, but I can promise you divine discontent with the imperfect. I cannot promise you success — 'tis not in mortals to command success.

But as you step into life I can give you three watchwords: first, you are Negroes, members of that dark, historic race that from the world's dawn has slept to hear the trumpet summons sound through our ears. Cherish unwavering faith in the blood of your fathers, and make sure this last triumph of humanity. Remember next, that you are gentlemen and ladies, trained in the liberal arts and subjects in that vast kingdom of culture that has lighted the world from its infancy and guided it through bigotry and falsehood and sin. As such, let us see in you an unfaltering honesty wedded to that finer courtesy and breeding which is the heritage of the well-trained and the well-born. And, finally, remember that you are the sons of Fisk University, that venerable mother who rose out of the blood and dust of battle to work the triumphs of the Prince of Peace. The mighty blessing of all her sons and daughters encompass you, and the sad sacrifice of every pure soul, living and dead, that has made her what she is, bend its dark wings about you and make you brave and good! And then through the weary striving and disappointment of life, fear not for the end, even though you fail:

> Truth forever on the scaffold,
>   Wrong forever on the throne.
> Yet that scaffold sways the future,
>   And behind the dim unknown
> Standeth God within the shadow,
>   Keeping watch above his own.

Two Addresses delivered by Alumni of Fisk University, pamphlet, Nashville, 1898, pp. 1-14.

4

THE STUDY OF
THE NEGRO PROBLEMS

In 1897 Dr. Du Bois went to Atlanta University as Professor of Economics and History. "I was going," he wrote later, "to study the facts, any and all facts, concerning the American Negro and his plight, and by measurement and comparison and research, work up to any valid generalizations which I could." A year after he came to Atlanta, he delivered a paper before the American Academy of Political and Social Science entitled "The Study of the Negro Problems." As organizer of the Annual Atlanta Studies of the Negro Problem, and editor of their Annual Publications, Dr. Du Bois carried into effect many of the themes stressed in his paper.

The present period in the development of sociological study is a trying one; it is the period of observation, research and comparison—work always wearisome, often aimless, without well-settled principles and guiding lines, and subject ever to the pertinent criticism: What, after all, has been accomplished? To this the one positive answer which years of research and speculation have been able to return is that the phenomena of society are worth the most careful and systematic study, and whether or not this study may eventually lead to a systematic body of knowledge deserving the name of science, it cannot in any case fail to give the world a mass of truth worth the knowing.

Being then in a period of observation and comparison, we must confess to ourselves that the sociologists of few nations have so good an opportunity for observing the growth and evolution of society as those of the United States. The rapid rise of a young country, the vast social changes, the wonderful economic development, the bold political experiments, and the contact of varying moral standards—all these make for American students crucial tests of social action, microcosmic reproductions of long centuries of world history, and rapid—even violent— repetitions of great social problems. Here is a field for the sociologist—a field rich, but little worked, and full of great possibilities. European scholars envy our opportunities and it must be said to our credit that great interest in the observation of social phenomena has been aroused in the last decade—an interest of which much is ephemeral and superficial, but which opens the way for broad scholarship and scientific effort.

In one field, however—and a field perhaps larger than any other single domain of social phenomena, there does not seem to have been awakened as yet a fitting realization of the opportunities for scientific inquiry. This is the group of social phenomena arising from the presence in this land of eight million persons of African descent.

It is my purpose in this paper to discuss certain considerations concerning the study of the social problems affecting American Negroes; first, as to the historical development of these problems; then as to the necessity for their careful systematic study at the present time; thirdly, as to the results of scientific study of the Negro up to this time; fourthly, as to the scope and method which future scientific inquiry should take, and lastly, regarding the agencies by which this work can best be carried out.

1. Development of the Negro Problems

A social problem is the failure of an organized social group to realize its group ideals, through the inability to adapt a certain desired line of action to given conditions of life. If, for instance, a government founded on universal manhood suffrage has a portion of its population so igno-

rant as to be unable to vote intelligently, such ignorance
becomes a menacing social problem. The impossibility of
economic and social development in a community where a
large percent of the population refuse to abide by the
social rules of order makes a problem of crime and lawlessness. Prostitution becomes a social problem when the
demands of luxurious homelife conflict with marriage
customs.

Thus a social problem is ever a relation between conditions and action, and as conditions and actions vary and
change from group to group from time to time and from
place to place, so social problems change, develop and
grow. Consequently, though we ordinarily speak of the
Negro problem as though it were one unchanged question,
students must recognize the obvious facts that this problem,
like others, has had a long historical development, has
changed with the growth and evolution of the nation;
moreover, that it is not *one* problem, but rather a plexus
of social problems, some new, some old, some simple,
some complex; and these problems have their one bond of
unity in the fact that they group themselves about those
Africans whom two centuries of slave-trading brought into
the land.

In the latter part of the seventeenth and early in the
eighteenth centuries, the central and all-absorbing economic need of America was the creation of a proper labor
supply to develop American wealth. This question had
been answered in the West Indies by enslaving Indians
and Negroes. In the colonies of the mainland it was answered by the importation of Negroes and indented servants. Immediately then there arose the question of the
legal status of these slaves and servants; and dozens of
enactments, from Massachusetts to Georgia, were made
"for the proper regulation of slaves and servants." Such
statutes sought to solve problems of labor and not of race
or color. Two circumstances, however, soon began to
differentiate in the problem of labor, problems which concerned slaves for life from those which concerned servants
for limited periods; and these circumstances were the eco-

nomic superiority of the slave system, and the fact that the slaves were neither of the same race, language nor religion as the servants and their masters. In laboring classes thus widely separated there naturally arose a difference in legal and social standing. Colonial statutes soon ceased to embrace the regulations applying to slaves and servants in one chapter, and laws were passed for servants on the one hand and for Negro slaves on the other.

As slave labor, under the peculiar conditions of colonial life, increased in value and efficiency, the importations of Africans increased, while those of indented servants decreased; this gave rise to new social problems, namely, those of protecting a feeble civilization against an influx of barbarism and heathenism. Between 1750 and 1800 an increasing number of laws began to form a peculiar and systematic slave code based on a distinct idea of social caste. Even, as this slave code was developing, new social conditions changed the aspect of the problems. The laws hitherto had been made to fit a class distinguished by its condition more than by its race or color. There arose now, however, a class of English-speaking Negroes born on American soil, and members of Christian churches; there sprang from illicit intercourse and considerable intermarriage with indented servants, a number of persons of mixed blood; there was also created by emancipation and the birth of black sons of white women a new class of free Negroes: all these developments led to a distinct beginning of group life among Negroes.

Repeated attempts at organized insurrection were made; wholesale running away, like that which established the exiles in Florida, was resorted to; and a class of black landholders and voters arose. Such social movements brought the colonists face to face with new and serious problems; which they sought at first to settle in curious ways, denying the rite of baptism, establishing the legal presumption that all Negroes and mulattoes were slaves, and finally changing the Slave Code into a Black Code, replacing a caste of condition by a caste of race, harshly stopping legal sexual intercourse, and seeking to prevent further complications by restricting and ever suppressing the slave trade.

This concerted and determined action again changed the character of the Negro problems, but they did not cease to be grave. The inability of the Negro to escape from a servile caste into political freedom turned the problems of the group into problems of family life. On the separated plantations and in households the Negro became a constituent member of the family, speaking its language, worshiping in its church, sharing its traditions, bearing its name, and sometimes sharing its blood; the talented slaves found large freedom in the intimate intercourse with the family which they enjoyed; they lost many traditions of their fatherland, and their ideals blended with the ideals of their new country.

Some men began to see in this development a physical, economic and moral danger to the land, and they busied themselves with questions as to how they might provide for the development of white and black without demoralizing the one or amalgamating with the other. The solution of these difficulties was sought in a widespread attempt to eliminate the Negro from the family, as he had formerly been eliminated from the state, by a process of emancipation that made him and his sons not even half-free, with the indefinite notion of colonizing the anomalous serfs thus created. This policy was carried out until one-half the land and one-sixth of the Negroes were quasi-freemen.

Just as the nation was on the point of realizing the futility of colonization, one of those strange incalculable world movements began to be felt throughout civilized states — a movement so vast that we call it the economic revolution of the nineteenth century. A world demand for crops peculiarly suited to the South, substituted in Europe the factory system for the house industry, and in America the large plantation slave system for the family patriarchy; slavery became an industrial system and not a training school for serfdom; the Black Codes underwent a sudden transformation which hardened the lot of the slave, facilitated the slave trade, hindered further emancipation and rendered the condition of the free Negroes unbearable. The question of race and color in America assumed a new and peculiar importance when it thus lay at the basis of some of the world's greatest industries.

The change in industrial conditions, however, not only affected the demands of a world market, but so increased the efficiency of labor, that a labor system, which in 1750 was eminently successful, soon became under the altered conditions of 1850 not only an economic monstrosity, but a political menace, and so rapidly did the crisis develop that the whole evolution of the nation came to a standstill, and the settlement of our social problems had to be left to the clumsy method of brute force.

So far as the Negro race is concerned, the Civil War simply left us face to face with the same sort of problems of social condition and caste which were beginning to face the nation a century ago. It is these problems that we are today somewhat helplessly — not to say carelessly — facing, forgetful that they are living, growing social questions whose progeny will survive to curse the nation, unless we grapple with them manfully and intelligently.

2. The Present Negro Problems

Such are some of the changes of condition and social movement which have, since 1619, altered and broadened the social problems grouped about the American Negro. In this development of successive questions about one center, there is nothing peculiar to American history. Given any fixed condition or fact — a river Nile, a range of Alps, an alien race, or a national idea — and problems of society will at every stage of advance group themselves about it. All social growth means a succession of social problems — they constitute growth, they denote that laborious and often baffling adjustment of action and condition which is the essence of progress, and while a particular fact or circumstance may serve in one country as a rallying point of many intricate questions of adjustment, the absence of that particular fact would not mean the absence of all social problems. Questions of labor, caste, ignorance and race were bound to arise in America; they were simply complicated here and intensified there by the presence of the Negro.

Turning now from this brief summary of the varied phases of these questions, let us inquire somewhat more carefully into the form under which the Negro problems present themselves today after 275 years of evolution. Their existence is plainly manifested by the fact that a definitely segregated mass of eight millions of Americans do not wholly share the national life of the people, are not an integral part of the social body. The points at which they fail to be incorporated into this group life constitute the particular Negro problems, which can be divided into two distinct but correlated parts, depending on two facts:

First — Negroes do not share the full national life because as a mass they have not reached a sufficiently high grade of culture.

Secondly — They do not share the full national life because there has always existed in America a conviction — varying in intensity, but always widespread — that people of Negro blood should not be admitted into the group life of the nation no matter what their condition might be.

Considering the problems arising from the backward development of Negroes, we may say that the mass of this race does not reach the social standards of the nation with respect to

a. Economic condition.

b. Mental training.

c. Social efficiency.

Even if special legislation and organized relief intervene, freedmen always start life under an economic disadvantage which generations, perhaps centuries, cannot overcome. Again, of all the important constituent parts of our nation, the Negro is by far the most ignorant; nearly half of the race are absolutely illiterate, only a minority of the other half have thorough common-school training, and but a remnant are liberally educated. The great deficiency of the Negro, however, is his small knowledge of the art of organized social life — that last expression of human culture. His development in group life was abruptly broken off by the slave ship, directed into abnormal channels and dwarfed by the Black Codes, and suddenly wrenched anew by the Emancipation Proclamation. He finds himself, therefore, peculiarly weak in that nice adaptation of individual life to the life of the group which is the essence of civilization. This is shown in the grosser forms of sexual immorality, disease and crime, and also in the difficulty of race organization for common ends in economic or in intellectual lines.

For these reasons the Negro would fall behind any average modern nation, and he is unusually handicapped in the midst of a nation which excels in its extraordinary economic development, its average of popular intelligence and in the boldness of its experiments in organized social life.

These problems of poverty, ignorance and social degradation differ from similar problems the world over in one important particular, and that is the fact that they are complicated by a peculiar environment. This constitutes the second class of Negro problems, and they rest, as has been said, on the widespread conviction among Americans that no persons of Negro descent should become constituent members of the social body. This feeling gives rise to economic problems, to educational problems, and nice questions of social morality; it makes it more difficult for black men to earn a living or spend their earnings as they will; it gives them poorer school facilities and restricted contact with cultured classes; and it becomes, throughout the land, a cause and excuse for discontent, lawlessness, laziness and injustice.

3. The Necessity of Carefully Studying These Problems

Such, barely stated, are the elements of the present Negro problems. It is to little purpose however to name the elements of a problem unless we can also say accurately to what extent each element enters into the final result:

whether, for instance, the present difficulties arise more largely from ignorance than from prejudice, or vice versa. This we do not know, and here it is that every intelligent discussion of the American Negro comes to a standstill. Nearly a hundred years ago Thomas Jefferson complained that the nation had never studied the real condition of the slaves and that, therefore, all general conclusions about them were extremely hazardous. We of another age can scarcely say that we have made material progress in this study. Yet these problems, so vast and intricate, demanding trained research and expert analysis, touching questions that affect the very foundation of the republic and of human progress, increasing and multiplying year by year, would seem to urge the nation with increasing force to measure and trace and understand thoroughly the underlying elements of this example of human evolution.

Now first we should study the Negro problems in order to distinguish between the different and distinct problems affecting this race. Nothing makes intelligent discussion of the Negro's position so fruitless as the repeated failure to discriminate between the different questions that concern him. If a Negro discusses the question, he is apt to discuss simply the problem of race prejudice; if a southern white man writes on the subject he is apt to discuss problems of ignorance, crime and social degradation; and yet each calls the problem he discusses *the* Negro problem, leaving in the dark background the really crucial question as to the relative importance of the many problems involved. Before we can begin to study the Negro intelligently, we must realize definitely that not only is he affected by all the varying social forces that act on any nation at his stage of advancement, but that in addition to these there is reacting upon him the mighty power of a peculiar and unusual social environment which affects to some extent every other social force.

In the second place we should seek to know and measure carefully all the forces and conditions that go to make up these different problems, to trace the historical development of these conditions, and discover as far as possible the probable trend of further development. Without doubt this would be difficult work, and it can with much truth be objected that we cannot ascertain, by the methods of sociological research known to us, all such facts thoroughly and accurately. To this objection it is only necessary to answer that however difficult it may be to know all about the Negro, it is certain that we can know vastly more than we do, and that we can have our knowledge in more systematic and intelligible form.

As things are, our opinions upon the Negro are more matters of faith than of knowledge. Every schoolboy is ready to discuss the matter, and there are few men that have not settled convictions. Such a situation is dangerous. Whenever any nation allows impulse, whim or hasty conjecture to usurp the place of conscious, normative, intelligent action, it is in grave danger. The sole aim of any society is to settle its problems in accordance with its highest ideals, and the only rational method of accomplishing this is to study those problems in the light of the best scientific research.

Finally, the American Negro deserves study for the great end of advancing the cause of science in general. No such opportunity to watch and measure the history and development of a great race of men ever presented itself to the scholars of a modern nation. If they miss this opportunity — if they do the work in a slipshod, unsystematic manner — if they dally with the truth to humor the whims of the day, they do far more than hurt the good name of the American people; they hurt the cause of scientific truth the world over, they voluntarily decrease human knowledge of a universe of which we are ignorant enough, and they degrade the high end of truth-seeking in a day when they need more and more to dwell upon its sanctity.

4. The Work Already Accomplished

It may be said that it is not altogether correct to assert that few attempts have been made to study these problems or to put the nation in possession of a body of truth in accordance with which it might act intelligently. It is far from my purpose to disparage in any way the work already done by students of these questions; much valuable effort has without doubt been put upon the field, and yet a careful survey of the field seems but to emphasize the fact that the work done bears but small proportion to the work still to be done. [1]

Moreover the studies made hitherto can as a whole be justly criticized in three particulars: (1) They have not been based on a thorough knowledge of details; (2) they have been unsystematical; (3) they have been uncritical.

In few subjects have historians been more content to go on indefinitely repeating current traditions and uninvestigated facts. We are still gravely told that the slave trade ceased in 1808, that the docility of Africans made slave insurrections almost unknown, and that the Negro never developed in this country a self-conscious group life before 1860. In the hasty endeavor to cover a broad subject when the details were unknown, much superficial work has been current, like that, for instance, of a newspaper reporter who spent "the odd intervals of leisure in active newspaper work" for "nearly eighteen months," in the District of Columbia, and forthwith published a study of 80,-000 Negroes, with observations on their institutions and development.

Again, the work done has been lamentably unsystematic and fragmentary. Scientific work must be subdivided, but conclusions which affect the whole subject must be based on a study of the whole. One cannot study the Negro in freedom and come to general conclusions about his destiny without knowing his history in slavery. A vast set of problems having a common center must, too, be studied according to some general plan, if the work of different students is to be compared or to go toward building a unified body of knowledge. A plan once begun must be carried out, and not like that of our erratic census reports, after allowing us to follow the size of farms in the South for three decades, suddenly leave us wondering as to the relation of farms and farm families. Students of Black Codes should not stop suddenly with 1863, and travelers and observers whose testimony would be of great value if arranged with some system and reasonably limited in time and space, must not ramble on without definite plan or purpose and render their whole work of doubtful value.

Most unfortunate of all, however, is the fact that so much of the work done on the Negro question is notoriously uncritical; uncritical from lack of discrimination in the selection and weighing of evidence; uncritical in choosing the proper point of view from which to study these problems, and, finally, uncritical from the distinct bias in the minds of so many writers.

To illustrate, the layman who does not pretend to first-hand knowledge of the subject and who would learn of students is today woefully puzzled by absolutely contradictory evidence. One student declares that Negroes are advancing in knowledge and ability; that they are working, establishing homes, and going into business, and that the problem will soon be one of the past. Another student of equal learning declares that the Negro is degenerating — sinking into crime and social immorality, receiving little help from education, still in the main a menial servant, and destined in a short time to settle the problem by dying entirely out. Such and many other contradictory conclusions arise from the uncritical use of material. A visitor to a great Negro school in the South catches the inspiration of youth, studies the work of graduates, and imbibes the hopes of teachers and immediately infers from the situation of a few hundred the general condition of a population numbering twice that of Holland. A college graduate sees the slums of a southern city, looks at the plantation field hands, and has some experience with Negro servants, and from the laziness, crime and disease which he finds, draws conclusions as to eight millions of people, stretched from Maine to Texas and from Florida to Washington.

We continually judge the whole from the part we are familiar with; we continually assume the material we have at hand to be typical; we reverently receive a column of figures without asking who collected them, how they were arranged, how far they are valid and what chances of error they contain; we receive the testimony of men without asking whether they were trained or ignorant, careful or careless, truthful or given to exaggeration, and, above all, whether they are giving facts or opinions. It is so easy for a man who has already formed his conclusions to receive any and all testimony in their favor without carefully weighing and testing it, that we sometimes find in serious scientific studies very curious proof of broad conclusions. To cite an extreme case, in a recently published study of the Negro, a part of the argument as to the physical condition of all these millions is made to rest on the measurement of fifteen black boys in a New York reformatory.

The widespread habit of studying the Negro from one point of view only, that of his influence on the white inhabitants, is also responsible for much uncritical work. The slaves are generally treated as one inert changeless mass, and most studies of slavery apparently have no conception of a social evolution and development among them. The slave code of a state is given, the progress of anti-slavery sentiment, the economic results of the system and the general influence of man on master are studied, but of the slave himself, of his group life and social institutions, of remaining traces of his African tribal life, of his amusements, his conversion to Christianity, his acquiring of the English tongue — in fine, of his whole reaction against his environment, of all this we hear little or nothing, and would apparently be expected to believe that the Negro arose from the dead in 1863. Yet all the testimony of law and custom, of tradition and present social condition, shows us that the Negro at the time of emancipation had passed through a social evolution which far separated him from his savage ancestors.

The most baneful cause of uncritical study of the Negro

is the manifest and far-reaching bias of writers. Americans are born in many cases with deep, fierce convictions on the Negro question, and in other cases imbibe them from their environment. When such men come to write on the subject, without technical training, without breadth of view, and in some cases without a deep sense of the sanctity of scientific truth, their testimony, however interesting as opinion, must of necessity be worthless as science. Thus too often the testimony of Negroes and their friends has to be thrown out of court on account of the manifest prejudice of the writers; on the other hand, the testimony of many other writers in the North and especially in the South has to be received with reserve on account of too evident bias.

Such facts make the path of students and foreign observers peculiarly thorny. The foreigner's views, if he be not exceptionally astute, will depend largely on his letters of introduction; the home student's views, on his birthplace and parentage. All students are apt to fail to recognize the magnitude and importance of these problems, and to succumb to the vulgar temptation of basing on any little contribution they make to the study of these problems general conclusions as to the origin and destiny of the Negro people in time and eternity. Thus we possess endless final judgments as to the American Negro emanating from men of influence and learning, in the very face of the fact known to every accurate student, that there exists today no sufficient material of proven reliability, upon which any scientist can base definite and final conclusions as to the present condition and tendencies of the eight million American Negroes; and that any person or publication purporting to give such conclusions simply makes statements which go beyond the reasonably proven evidence.

5. A Program of Future Study

If we admit the deep importance of the Negro problems, the necessity of studying them, and certain shortcomings in work done up to this time, it would seem to be the clear duty of the American people, in the interests of scientific knowledge and social reform, to begin a broad and systematic study of the history and condition of the American Negroes. The scope and method of this study, however, need to be generally agreed upon beforehand in its main outlines, not to hinder the freedom of individual students, but to systematize and unify effort so as to cover the wide field of investigation.

The scope of any social study is first of all limited by the general attitude of public opinion toward truth and truth-seeking. If in regard to any social problem there is for any reason a persistent refusal on the part of the people to allow the truth to be known, then manifestly that problem cannot be studied. Undoubtedly much of the unsatisfactory work already done with regard to the Negro is due to this cause; the intense feeling that preceded and followed the war made a calm balanced research next to impossible. Even today there are certain phases of this question which we cannot hope to be allowed to study dispassionately and thoroughly, and these phases, too, are naturally those uppermost in the public mind. For instance, it is extremely doubtful if any satisfactory study of Negro crime and lynching can be made for a generation or more, in the present condition of the public mind, which renders it almost impossible to get at the facts and real conditions. On the other hand, public opinion has in the last decade become sufficiently liberal to open a broad field of investigation to students, and here lies the chance for effective work.

The right to enter this field undisturbed and untrammeled will depend largely on the attitude of science itself. Students must be careful to insist that science as such — be it physics, chemistry, psychology, or sociology — has but one simple aim: the discovery of truth. Its results lie open for the use of all men — merchants, physicians, men of letters, and philanthropists, but the aim of science itself is simple truth. Any attempt to give it a double aim, to make social reform the immediate instead of the mediate object of a search for truth, will inevitably tend to defeat both objects. The frequent alliance of sociological research with various panaceas and particular schemes of reform has resulted in closely connecting social investigation with a good deal of groundless assumption and humbug in the popular mind. There will be at first some difficulty in bringing the southern people, both black and white, to conceive of an earnest, careful study of the Negro problem which has not back of it some scheme of race amalgamation, political jobbery, or deportation to Africa. The new study of the American Negro must avoid such misapprehensions from the outset by insisting that historical and statistical research has but one object, the ascertainment of the facts as to the social forces and conditions of one-eighth of the inhabitants of the land. Only by such rigid adherence to the true object of the scholar can statesmen and philanthropists of all shades of belief be put into possession of a reliable body of truth which may guide their efforts to the best and largest success.

In the next place, a study of the Negro, like the study of any subject, must start out with certain generally admitted postulates, We must admit, for instance, that the field of study is large and varying, and that what is true of the Negro in Massachusetts is not necessarily true of the Negro in Louisiana; that what was true of the Negro in 1850 was not necessarily true in 1750; and that there are many distinct social problems affecting the Negro. Finally, if we would rally to this common ground of scientific inquiry all partisans and advocates, we must explicitly admit what all implicitly postulate — namely, that the Negro is a member of the human race, and as one who, in the light of history and experience, is capable to a degree of improvement and culture, is entitled to have his interests considered according to his numbers in all conclusions as to the common weal.

With these preliminary considerations we may say that the study of the Negro falls naturally into two categories, which though difficult to separate in practice, must for

the sake of logical clearness, be kept distinct. They are
(*a*) the study of the Negro as a social group, (*b*) the
study of his peculiar social environment.

The study of the Negro as a social group may be, for
convenience, divided into four not exactly logical but
seemingly most practicable divisions, viz.:

1. Historical study.
2. Statistical investigation.
3. Anthropological measurement.
4. Sociological interpretation.

The material at hand for historical research is rich and
abundant; there are the colonial statutes and records,
the partially accessible archives of Great Britain, France
and Spain, the collections of historical societies, the vast
number of executive and congressional reports and documents, the state statutes, reports and publications, the reports of institutions and societies, the personal narratives
and opinions of various observers and the periodical
press covering nearly three centuries. From these sources
can be gathered much new information upon the economic
and social development of the Negro; upon the rise and
decline of the slave trade; the character, distribution and
state of culture of the Africans; the evolution of the slave
codes as expressing the life of the South; the rise of such
peculiar expressions of Negro social history, as the Negro
church; the economics of plantation life; the possession of
private property by slaves; and the history of the oft-for-
gotten class of free Negroes. Such historical research must
be subdivided in space and limited in time by the nature
of the subject, the history of the different colonies and
groups being followed and compared, the different periods of development receiving special study, and the whole
subject being reviewed from different aspects.

The collection of statistics should be carried on with
increased care and thoroughness. It is no credit to a great
modern nation that so much well-grounded doubt can be
thrown on our present knowledge of the simple matters
of number, age, sex and conjugal condition in regard to

our Negro population. General statistical investigations should avoid seeking to tabulate more intricate social conditions than the ones indicated. The concrete social status of the Negro can only be ascertained by intensive studies carried on in definitely limited localities, by competent investigators, in accordance with one general plan. Statistical study by groups is apt to be more accurately done and more easily accomplished, and able to secure more competent and responsible agents than any general census. General averages in so complicated a subject are apt to be dangerously misleading.

This study should seek to ascertain by the most approved methods of social measurement the size and condition of families, the occupations and wages, the illiteracy of adults and education of children, the standard of living, the character of the dwellings, the property owned and rents paid, and the character of the organized group life. Such investigations should be extended until they cover the typical group life of Negroes in all sections of the land and should be so repeated from time to time in the same localities and with the same methods, as to be a measure of social development.

The third division of study is anthropological measurement, and it includes a scientific study of the Negro body. The most obvious peculiarity of the Negro — a peculiarity which is a large element in many of the problems affecting him — is his physical unlikeness to the people with whom he has been brought into contact. This difference is so striking that it has become the basis of a mass of theory, assumption and suggestion which is deep-rooted and yet rests on the flimsiest basis of scientific fact. That there are differences between the white and black races is certain, but just what those differences are is known to none with an approach to accuracy. Yet here in America is the most remarkable opportunity ever offered of studying these differences, of noting influences of climate and physical environment, and particularly of studying the effect of amalgamating two of the most diverse races in the world — another subject which rests under a cloud of ignorance.

The fourth division of this investigation is sociological interpretation; it should include the arrangement and interpretation of historical and statistical matter in the light of the experience of other nations and other ages; it should aim to study those finer manifestations of social life which history can but mention and which statistics cannot count, such as the expression of Negro life as found in their hundred newspapers, their considerable literature, their music and folklore and their germ of aesthetic life — in fine, in all the movements and customs among them that manifest the existence of a distinct social mind.

The second category of studies of the Negro has to do with his peculiar social environment. It will be difficult, as has been intimated, to separate a study of the group from a study of the environment, and yet the group action and the reaction of the surroundings must be kept clearly distinct if we expect to comprehend the Negro problems. The study of the environment may be carried on at the same time with a study of the group, only the two sets of forces must receive distinct measurement.

In such a field of inquiry it will be found difficult to do more than subdivide inquiry in time and space. The attempt should be made to isolate and study the tangible phenomena of Negro prejudice in all possible cases; its effect on the Negro's physical development, on his mental acquisitiveness, on his moral and social condition, as manifested in economic life, in legal sanctions and in crime and lawlessness. So, too, the influence of that same prejudice on American life and character would explain the otherwise inexplicable changes through which Negro prejudice has passed.

The plan of study thus sketched is, without doubt, long, difficult and costly, and yet is not more than commensurable with the size and importance of the subject with which it is to deal. It will take years and decades to carry out such a plan, with the barest measure of success, and yet there can be no doubt but that this plan or something similar to it, points to the quickest path toward the ultimate solution of the present difficulties.

6. *The Proper Agents for This Work*

In conclusion it will not be out of place to suggest the agencies which seem best fitted to carry out a work of this magnitude. There will, without doubt, always be room for the individual working alone as he wills; if, however, we wish to cover the field systematically, and in reasonable time, only organized and concerted efforts will avail; and the requisite means, skill and preparation for such work can be furnished by two agencies alone: the government and the university.

For simple, definite inquiries carried out periodically on a broad scale we should depend on the national and state governments. The decennial census properly organized under civil-service rules should be the greatest single agency for collecting general information as to the Negro. If, however, the present Congress cannot be induced to organize a census bureau under proper civil-service rules, and in accordance with the best expert advice, we must continue for many years more to depend on clumsy and ignorant methods of measurement in matters demanding accuracy and trained technique. It is possible also for the different national bureaus and for the state governments to study certain aspects of the Negro question over wide areas. A conspicuous example of this is the valuable educational statistics collected by Commissioner Harris, and the series of economic studies just instituted by the Bureau of Labor.

On the whole it may be laid down as axiomatic that government activity in the study of this problem should confine itself mainly to the ascertainment of simple facts covering a broad field. For the study of these social problems in their more complicated aspects, where the desideratum is intensive study, by trained minds, according to the best methods, the only competent agency is the university. Indeed, in no better way could the American university repay the unusual munificence of its benefactors than by placing before the nation a body of scientific truth in the light of which they could solve some of their most vexing social problems.

It is to the credit of the University of Pennsylvania that she has been the first to recognize her duty in this respect, and insofar as restricted means and opportunity allowed, has attempted to study the Negro problems in a single definite locality. [2] This work needs to be extended to other groups, and carried out with larger system; and here it would seem is the opportunity of the southern Negro college. We hear much of higher Negro education, and yet all candid people know there does not exist today in the center of Negro population a single first-class fully-equipped institution devoted to the higher education of Negroes; not more than three Negro institutions in the South deserve the name of *college* at all; and yet what is a Negro college but a vast college settlement for the study of a particular set of peculiarly baffling problems? What more effective or suitable agency could be found in which to focus the scientific efforts of the great universities of the North and East, than an institution situated in the very heart of these social problems, and made the center of careful historical and statistical research? Without doubt the first effective step toward the solving of the Negro question will be the endowment of a Negro college which is not merely a teaching body, but a center of sociological research, in close connection and cooperation with Harvard, Columbia, Johns Hopkins and the University of Pennsylvania.

In this direction the Negro conferences of Tuskegee and Hampton are tending; and there is already inaugurated an actual beginning of work at Atlanta University. In 1896 this university brought into correspondence about one hundred southern college-bred men and laid before them a plan of systematic investigation into certain problems of Negro city life, as, for instance, family conditions, dwellings, rents, ownership of homes, occupations, earnings, disease and death rates. Each investigator took one or more small groups to study, and in this way fifty-nine groups, aggregating 5,000 people in various parts of the country, were studied, and the results have been published by the United States Bureau of Labor. Such purely scientific work, done with an eye single to ascertaining true conditions, marks an era in our conception of the place of the Negro college, and it is certainly to be desired that Atlanta University may be enabled to continue this work as she proposes to do.

Finally the necessity must again be emphasized of keeping clearly before students the object of all science, amid the turmoil and intense feeling that clouds the discussion of a burning social question. We live in a day when in spite of the brilliant accomplishments of a remarkable century there is current much flippant criticism of scientific work; when the truth-seeker is too often pictured as devoid of human sympathy, and careless of human ideals. We are still prone in spite of all our culture to sneer at the heroism of the laboratory while we cheer the swagger of the street broil. At such a time true lovers of humanity can only hold higher the pure ideals of science, and continue to insist that if we would solve a problem we must study it, and that there is but one coward on earth, and that is the coward that dares not know.

Annals of the American Academy of Political and Social Science (Publications #219), 1898, Vol. XI, pp. 1-23.

5

ADDRESS TO THE NATIONS
OF THE WORLD

While discussing "The Concept of Race" in Dusk of Dawn, *subtitled* An Essay toward an Autobiography of a Race Concept, *Dr. Du Bois wrote: "Africa is of course my father-land. . . . On this vast continent were born and lived a large portion of my direct ancestors going back a thousand years or more." But he added that "the physical bond is least and the badge of color relatively unimportant save as a badge; the real essence of this kinship is its social heritage of slavery; the discrimination and insult; and this heritage binds together not simply the children of Africa, but extends through yellow Asia and into the South Seas. It is this unity that draws me to Africa." And it was this "unity" that brought him to the First Pan-African Conference in London, at the turn of the twentieth century, and led to his prominent and continuing role in this vitally important movement.*

The call for the first Pan-African Conference was issued by Henry Sylvester-Williams, a barrister at law from Trinidad. Thirty-two delegates responded and assembled in London at Westminster Hall on July 23-25, 1900. The Conference, among other things, appointed a Committee on Address to the Nations of the World with Dr. Du Bois as its chairman. The "Address" was drawn up by Du Bois and when he read it to the Conference it was adopted and "sent to the sovereigns in whose realms are subjects of African descent."

While the meeting did not lead to immediate action, it,

*in Du Bois's words, "attracted attention, put the word
'Pan-African' in the dictionaries for the first time." It also
produced in the "Address to the Nations of the World"
the first reference to one of Dr. Du Bois's most famous
statements: "The problem of the twentieth century is the
problem of the color line, the question as to how far differences of race—which show themselves chiefly in the
color of the skin and the texture of the hair—will hereafter be made the basis of denying to over half the world
the right of sharing to their utmost ability the opportunities
and privileges of modern civilization."*

In the metropolis of the modern world, in this the closing
year of the nineteenth century, there has been assembled
a congress of men and women of African blood, to deliberate solemnly upon the present situation and outlook of
the darker races of mankind. The problem of the twentieth century is the problem of the color line, the question
as to how far differences of race—which show themselves
chiefly in the color of the skin and the texture of the hair—
will hereafter be made the basis of denying to over half the
world the right of sharing to their utmost ability the opportunities and privileges of modern civilization.

To be sure, the darker races are today the least advanced in culture according to European standards. This
has not, however, always been the case in the past, and
certainly the world's history, both ancient and modern,
has given many instances of no despicable ability and
capacity among the blackest races of men.

In any case, the modern world must remember that in
this age when the ends of the world are being brought so
near together the millions of black men in Africa, America,
and the Islands of the Sea, not to speak of the brown and
yellow myriads elsewhere, are bound to have a great influence upon the world in the future, by reason of sheer
numbers and physical contact. If now the world of culture
bends itself towards giving Negroes and other dark men
the largest and broadest opportunity for education and

self-development, then this contact and influence is bound
to have a beneficial effect upon the world and hasten human progress. But if, by reason of carelessness, prejudice,
greed and injustice, the black world is to be exploited and
ravished and degraded, the results must be deplorable, if
not fatal—not simply to them, but to the high ideals of
justice, freedom and culture which a thousand years of
Christian civilization have held before Europe.

And now, therefore, to these ideals of civilization, to the
broader humanity of the followers of the Prince of Peace,
we, the men and women of Africa in world congress assembled, do now solemnly appeal:

Let the world take no backward step in that slow but
sure progress which has successively refused to let the
spirit of class, of caste, of privilege, or of birth, debar
from life, liberty and the pursuit of happiness a striving
human soul.

Let not color or race be a feature of distinction between
white and black men, regardless of worth or ability.

Let not the natives of Africa be sacrificed to the greed
of gold, their liberties taken away, their family life debauched, their just aspirations repressed, and avenues of
advancement and culture taken from them.

Let not the cloak of Christian missionary enterprise be
allowed in the future, as so often in the past, to hide the
ruthless economic exploitation and political downfall of
less developed nations, whose chief fault has been reliance
on the plighted faith of the Christian church.

Let the British nation, the first modern champion of
Negro freedom, hasten to crown the work of Wilberforce,
and Clarkson, and Buxton, and Sharpe, Bishop Colenso,
and Livingstone, and give, as soon as practicable, the
rights of responsible government to the black colonies of
Africa and the West Indies.

Let not the spirit of Garrison, Phillips, and Douglass
wholly die out in America; may the conscience of a great
nation rise and rebuke all dishonesty and unrighteous
oppression toward the American Negro, and grant to
him the right of franchise, security of person and property,

and generous recognition of the great work he has accomplished in a generation toward raising nine millions of human beings from slavery to manhood.

Let the German Empire, and the French Republic, true to their great past, remember that the true worth of colonies lies in their prosperity and progress, and that justice, impartial alike to black and white, is the first element of prosperity.

Let the Congo Free State become a great central Negro state of the world, and let its prosperity be counted not simply in cash and commerce, but in the happiness and true advancement of its black people.

Let the nations of the world respect the integrity and independence of the free Negro states of Abyssinia, Liberia, Haiti, and the rest, and let the inhabitants of these states, the independent tribes of Africa, the Negroes of the West Indies and America, and the black subjects of all nations take courage, strive ceaselessly, and fight bravely, that they may prove to the world their incontestible right to be counted among the great brotherhood of mankind.

Thus we appeal with boldness and confidence to the Great Powers of the civilized world, trusting in the wide spirit of humanity, and the deep sense of justice of our age, for a generous recognition of the righteousness of our cause.

ALEXANDER WALTERS (Bishop)
  President Pan-African Association
HENRY B. BROWN
  Vice-President
H. SYLVESTER-WILLIAMS
  General Secretary
W. E. BURGHARDT DU BOIS
  Chairman Committee on Address

Alexander Walters, *My Life and Work,* New York, 1917, pp. 257-260.

6

ON BOOKER T. WASHINGTON

Dr. Du Bois's great work, The Souls of Black Folk, *published in 1903, and which Henry James called "the only Southern book of distinction published in many years," contains so many significant chapters and sections that it is almost impossible to select one that is of special importance. Yet, it was the chapter entitled, "On Booker T. Washington and Others" which aroused the widest attention. Most of what was in the chapter had already been presented by Dr. Du Bois in speeches before the book appeared, but none of these were published so that the appearance in print of his explicit indictment of Washington created a sensation. Here is the essence of that indictment.*

In the history of nearly all other races and peoples the doctrine preached has been that manly self-respect is worth more than lands and houses, and that a people who voluntarily surrender such respect, or cease striving for it, are not worth civilizing.

In answer to this, it has been claimed that the Negro can survive only through submission. Mr. Washington distinctly asks that black people give up, at least for the present, three things: —

First, political power,

Second, insistence on civil rights,

Third, higher education of Negro youths, —

and concentrate all their energies on industrial education,

the accumulation of wealth, and the conciliation of the South. As a result of this tender of the palm-branch, what has been the return? In these years since Booker T. Washington's Atlanta speech on 1895[1] there have occurred:

1. The disfranchisement of the Negro.

2. The legal creation of a distinct status of civil inferiority.

3. The steady withdrawal of aid from institutions for the higher training of the Negro.

These movements are not, to be sure, direct results of Mr. Washington's teachings; but his propaganda has, without a shadow of doubt, helped their speedier accomplishment. The question then comes: Is it possible, and probable, that nine millions of men can make effective progress in economic lines if they are deprived of political rights, made a servile caste, and allowed only the most meager chance for developing their exceptional men? If history and reason give any distinct answer to these questions, it is an emphatic NO.

The growing spirit of kindliness and reconciliation between the North and South after the frightful difference of a generation ago ought to be a source of deep congratulation to all, but if that reconciliation is to be marked by the industrial slavery and civic death of black men, with permanent legislation into a position of inferiority, then those black men, if they are really men, are called upon by every consideration of patriotism and loyalty to oppose such a course by all civilized methods, even though such opposition involves disagreement with Mr. Booker T. Washington. We have no right to sit silently by while the inevitable seeds are sown for a harvest of disaster to our children, black and white.

W. E. B. Du Bois, *The Souls of Black Folk,* Chicago, 1903, pp. 43-46.

7

THE TRAINING OF NEGROES

FOR SOCIAL POWER

Following the publication of his criticism of Booker T. Washington in The Souls of Black Folk, *Dr. Du Bois was invited to lecture at numerous institutions to explain still further his differences with the philosophy of the leading American Negro. One aspect of the differences between the two men was especially of concern to black Americans: the part that industrial education should play in the training of young Negroes. Washington placed his entire faith for the future of the Negro in industrial training, but Dr. Du Bois, while making it clear that industrial education must occupy an important place in the solution of America's Negro problem, felt that overemphasis of industrial training to the detriment of other forms of education was dangerous to the well-being of black Americans.*

In his speech, "The Training of Negroes for Social Power," Dr. Du Bois set forth clearly and fully his views at the time of the type of education he felt was essential for his people. The speech was originally published in The Outlook *of October 17, 1903, and reprinted in* The Colored American Magazine *as the seventh article in a series entitled, "Industrial Education— Will It Solve the Negro Problem?" The question, the magazine informed its readers, would be "answered each month by the greatest thinkers of the Black Race."*

The responsibility for their own social regeneration ought to be placed largely upon the shoulders of the Negro

people. But such responsibility must carry with it a grant
of power; responsibility without power is a mockery and
a farce. If, therefore, the American people are sincerely
anxious that the Negro shall put forth his best efforts to
help himself, they must see to it that he is not deprived
of the freedom and power to strive. The responsibility
for dispelling their own ignorance implies that the power
to overcome ignorance is to be placed in black men's
hands; the lessening of poverty calls for the power of
effective work, and one responsibility for lessening crime
calls for control over social forces which produce crime.

Such social power means, assuredly, the growth of initiative among Negroes, the spread of independent thought,
the expanding consciousness of manhood; and these things
today are looked upon by many with apprehension and
distrust, and there is systematic and determined effort
to avoid this inevitable corollary of the fixing of social
responsibility. Men openly declare their design to train
these millions as a subject caste, as men to be thought
for, but not to think; to be led, but not to lead themselves.
Those who advocate these things forget that such a solution flings them squarely on the other horn of the dilemma;
such a subject child-race could never be held accountable
for its own misdeeds and shortcomings; its ignorance
would be part of the nation's design, its poverty would
arise partly from the direct oppression of the strong and
partly from thriftlessness which such oppression breeds;
and, above all, its crime would be the legitimate child
of that lack of self-respect which caste systems engender.
Such a solution of the Negro problem is not one which
the saner sense of the nation for a moment contemplates;
it is utterly foreign to American institutions, and is unthinkable as a future for any self-respecting race of men.
The sound afterthought of the American people must come
to realize that the responsibility for dispelling ignorance
and poverty and uprooting crime among Negroes cannot be put upon their own shoulders unless they are given
such independent leadership in intelligence, skill, and mo-

rality as will inevitably lead to an independent manhood which cannot and will not rest in bonds.

Let me illustrate my meaning particularly in the matter of educating Negro youth.

The Negro problem, it has often been said, is largely a problem of ignorance — not simply of illiteracy, but a deeper ignorance of the world and its ways, of the thought and experience of men; an ignorance of self and the possibilities of human souls. This can be gotten rid of only by training; and primarily such training must take the form of that sort of social leadership which we call education. To apply such leadership to themselves, and to profit by it, means that Negroes would have among themselves men of careful training and broad culture, as teachers and teachers of teachers. There are always periods of educational evolution when it is deemed proper for pupils in the fourth reader to teach those in the third. Such a method, wasteful and ineffective at all times, is peculiarly dangerous when ignorance is widespread and when there are few homes and public institutions to supplement the work of the school. It is, therefore, of crying necessity among Negroes that the heads of their educational system — the teachers in the normal schools, the heads of high schools, the principals of public systems, should be unusually well-trained men; men trained not simply in common-school branches, not simply in the technique of school management and normal methods, but trained beyond this, broadly and carefully, into the meaning of the age whose civilization it is their peculiar duty to interpret to the youth of a new race, to the minds of untrained people. Such educational leaders should be prepared by long and rigorous courses of study similar to those which the world over have been designed to strengthen the intellectual powers, fortify character, and facilitate the transmission from age to age of the stores of the world's knowledge.

Not all men — indeed, not the majority of men, only the exceptional few among American Negroes or among any other people—are adapted to this higher training, as, indeed, only the exceptional few are adapted to higher training in any line; but the significance of such men is not to be measured by their numbers, but rather by the numbers of their pupils and followers who are destined to see the world through their eyes, hear it through their trained ears, and speak to it through the music of their words.

Such men, teachers of teachers and leaders of the untaught, Atlanta University and similar colleges seek to train. We seek to do our work thoroughly and carefully. We have no predilections or prejudices as to particular studies or methods, but we do cling to those time-honored sorts of discipline which the experience of the world has long since proven to be of especial value. We sift as carefully as possible the student material which offers itself, and we try by every conscientious method to give to students who have character and ability such years of discipline as shall make them stronger, keener, and better for their peculiar mission. The history of civilization seems to prove that no group or nation which seeks advancement and true development can despise or neglect the power of well-trained minds; and this power of intellectual leadership must be given to the talented tenth among American Negroes before this race can seriously be asked to assume the responsibility of dispelling its own ignorance. Upon the foundation stone of a few well-equipped Negro colleges of high and honest standards can be built a proper system of free common schools in the South for the masses of the Negro people; any attempt to found a system of public schools on anything less than this—on narrow ideals, limited or merely technical training—is to call blind leaders for the blind.

The very first step toward the settlement of the Negro problem is the spread of intelligence. The first step toward wider intelligence is a free public-school system; and the first and most important step toward a public-school system is the equipment and adequate support of a sufficient number of Negro colleges. These are first steps, and they involve great movements: first, the best of the existent colleges must not be abandoned to slow atrophy and death, as the tendency is today; secondly, systematic attempt must be made to organize secondary education. Below the colleges and connected with them must come the normal and high schools, judiciously distributed and carefully manned. In no essential particular should this system of common and secondary schools differ from educational systems the world over. Their chief function is the quickening and training of human intelligence; they can do much in the teaching of morals and manners incidentally, but they cannot and ought not to replace the home as the chief moral teacher; they can teach valuable lessons as to the meaning of work in the world, but they cannot replace technical schools and apprenticeship in actual life, which are the real schools of work. Manual training can and ought to be used in these schools, but as a means and not as an end—to quicken intelligence and self-knowledge and not to teach carpentry; just as arithmetic is used to train minds and not to make skilled accountants.

Whence, now, is the money coming for this educational system? For the common schools, the support should come from local communities, the state governments, and the United States government; for secondary education, support should come from local and state governments and private philanthropy; for the colleges, from private philanthropy and the United States government. I make no apology for bringing the United States government in thus conspicuously. The general government must give aid to southern education if illiteracy and ignorance are to cease threatening the very foundations of civilization within any reasonable time. Aid to common-school education could be appropriated to the different states on the basis of illiteracy. The fund could be administered by state officials, and the results and needs reported upon by United States educational inspectors under the Bureau of Education. The states could easily distribute the funds so as to encourage local taxation and enterprise and not result in pauperizing the communities. As to higher training, it must be remembered that the cost of a single battleship like the *Massachusetts* would endow all the distinctively college work necessary for Negroes during the next half-century; and it is without doubt true that the unpaid balance from bounties withheld from Negroes in the Civil War would, with interest, easily supply this sum.

But spread of intelligence alone will not solve the Negro problem. If this problem is largely a question of ignorance, it is also scarcely less a problem of poverty. If Negroes are to assume the responsibility of raising the standards of living among themselves, the power of intelligent work and leadership toward proper industrial ideals must be placed in their hands. Economic efficiency depends on intelligence, skill, and thrift. The public-school system is designed to furnish the necessary intelligence for the ordinary worker, the secondary school for the more gifted worker, and the college for the exceptional few. Technical knowledge and manual dexterity in learning branches of the world's work are taught by industrial and trade schools, and such schools are of prime importance in the training of colored children. Trade-teaching cannot be effectively combined with the work of the common schools because the primary curriculum is already too crowded, and thorough common-school training should precede trade-teaching. It is, however, quite possible to combine some of the work of the secondary schools with purely technical training, the necessary limitations being matters of time and cost: the question whether the boy can afford to stay in school long enough to add parts of a high-school course to the trade course, and particularly the question whether the school can afford or ought to afford to give trade-training to high-school students who do not intend to become artisans. A system of trade schools, therefore, supported by state and private aid, should be added to the secondary-school system.

An industrial school, however, does not merely teach technique. It is also a school — a center of moral influence and of mental discipline. As such it has peculiar problems in securing the proper teaching force. It demands broadly trained men: the teacher of carpentry must be more than a carpenter, and the teacher of the domestic arts more than a cook; for such teachers must instruct, not simply in manual dexterity, but in mental quickness and moral habits. In other words, they must be teachers as well as artisans. It thus happens that college-bred men and men from other higher schools have always been in demand in technical schools, and it has been the high privilege of Atlanta University to furnish during the thirty-six years of its existence a part of the teaching force of nearly every Negro industrial school in the United States, and today our graduates are teaching in more than twenty such institutions. The same might be said of Fisk University and other higher schools. If the college graduates were today withdrawn from the teaching force of the chief Negro industrial schools, nearly every one of them would have to close its doors. These facts are forgotten by such advocates of industrial training as oppose the higher schools. Strong as the argument for industrial school is — and its strength is undeniable — its cogency simply increases the urgency of the plea for higher training-schools and colleges to furnish broadly educated teachers.

But intelligence and skill alone will not solve the southern problem of poverty. With these must go that combination of homely habits and virtues which we may loosely call thrift. Something of thrift may be taught in school, more must be taught at home; but both these agencies are helpless when organized economic society denies to workers the just reward of thrift and efficiency. And this has been true of black laborers in the South from the time of slavery down through the scandal of the Freedmen's Bank[1] to the peonage and crop-lien system of today. If the southern Negro is shiftless, it is primarily because over large areas a shiftless Negro can get on in the world about as well as an industrious black man. This is not universally true in the South, but it is true to so large an extent as to discourage striving in precisely that class of Negroes who most need encouragement. What is the remedy? Intelligence — not simply the ability to read and write or to sew — but the intelligence of a society permeated by that larger division of life and broader tolerance which are fostered by the college and university. Not that all men must be college-bred, but that some men, black and white, must be, to leaven the ideals of the lump. Can any serious student of the economic South doubt that this today is her crying need?

Ignorance and poverty are the vastest of the Negro problems. But to these later years have added a third — the problem of Negro crime. That a great problem of social morality must have become eventually the central problem of emancipation is as clear as day to any student of history. In its grosser form as a problem of serious crime it is already upon us. Of course it is false and silly to represent that white women in the South are in daily danger of black assaulters. On the contrary, white womanhood in the South is absolutely safe in the hands of ninety-five percent of the black men — ten times safer than black womanhood is in the hands of white men. Nevertheless, there is a large and dangerous class of Negro criminals, paupers, and outcasts. The existence and growth of such a class, far from causing surprise, should be recognized as the natural result of that social disease called the Negro problem; nearly every untoward circumstance known to human experience has united to increase Negro crime: the slavery of the past, the sudden emancipation, the narrowing of economic opportunity, the lawless environment of wide regions, the stifling of natural ambition, the curtailment of political privilege, the disregard of the sanctity of black men's homes, and above all, a system of treatment for criminals calculated to breed crime far faster than all other available agencies could repress it. Such a combination of circumstances

is as sure to increase the numbers of the vicious and out-
cast as the rain is to wet the earth. The phenomenon calls
for no delicately drawn theories of race differences; it is
a plain case of cause and effect.

But, plain as the causes may be, the results are just
as deplorable, and repeatedly today the criticism is made
that Negroes do not recognize sufficiently their responsibility in this matter. Such critics forget how little power
today Negroes have over their own lower classes. Before the black murderer who strikes his victim today, the
average black man stands far more helpless than the
average white, and, too, suffers ten times more from the
effects of the deed. The white man has political power,
accumulated wealth, and knowledge of social forces; the
black man is practically disfranchised, poor, and unable to discriminate between the criminal and martyr.
The Negro needs the defense of the ballot, the conserving
power of property, and, above all, the ability to cope
intelligently with such vast questions of social regeneration and moral reform as confront him. If social reform
among Negroes be without organization or trained leadership from within, if the administration of law is always for the avenging of the white victim and seldom
for the reformation of the black criminal, if ignorant black
men misunderstand the functions of government because
they have had no decent instruction, and intelligent black
men are denied a voice in government because they are
black — under such circumstances to hold Negroes responsible for the suppression of crime among themselves
is the cruelest of mockeries.

On the other hand, a sincere desire among the American people to help the Negroes undertake their own social regeneration means, first, that the Negro be given
the ballot on the same terms as other men, to protect
him against injustice and to safeguard his interests in
the administration of law; secondly, that through education and social organization he be trained to work, and
save, and earn a decent living. But these are not all;

wealth is not the only thing worth accumulating; experience and knowledge can be accumulated and handed down, and no people can be truly rich without them. Can the Negro do without these? Can this training in work and thrift be truly effective without the guidance of trained intelligence and deep knowledge — without that same efficiency which has enabled modern peoples to grapple so successfully with the problems of the submerged tenth? There must surely be among Negro leaders the philanthropic impulse, the uprightness of character and strength of purpose, but there must be more than these: philanthropy and purpose among blacks as well as among whites must be guided and curbed by knowledge and mental discipline — knowledge of the forces of civilization that make for survival, ability to organize and guide those forces, and realization of the true meaning of those broader ideals of human betterment which may in time bring heaven and earth a little nearer. This is social power — it is gotten in many ways — by experience, by social contact, by what we loosely call the chances of life. But the systematic method of acquiring and imparting it is by the training of the youth to thought, power, and knowledge in the school and college. And that group of people whose mental grasp is by heredity weakest, and whose knowledge of the past is for historic reasons most imperfect, that group is the very one which needs above all, for the talented of its youth, this severe and careful course of training; especially if they are expected to take immediate part in modern competitive life, if they are to hasten the slower courses of human development, and if the responsibility for this is to be in their own hands.

Three things American slavery gave the Negro — the habit of work, the English language, and the Christian religion; but one priceless thing it debauched, destroyed, and took from him, and that was the organized home. For the sake of intelligence and thrift, for the sake of work and morality, this homelife must be restored and

regenerated with newer ideals. How? The normal method would be by actual contact with a higher homelife
among his neighbors, but this method the social separation of white and black precludes. A proposed method is by schools of domestic arts, but, valuable as these
are, they are but subsidiary aids to the establishment of
homes; for real homes are primarily centers of ideals
and teaching and only incidentally centers of cooking.
The restoration and raising of home ideals must, then,
come from social life among Negroes themselves; and
does that social life need no leadership? It needs the best
possible leadership of pure hearts and trained heads, the
highest leadership of carefully trained men.

Such are the arguments for the Negro college, and such
is the work that Atlanta University and a few similar
institutions seek to do. We believe that a rationally arranged college course of study for men and women able
to pursue it is the best and only method of putting into
the world Negroes with ability to use the social forces
of their race so as to stamp out crime, strengthen the
home, eliminate degenerates, and inspire and encourage
the higher tendencies of the race not only in thought and
aspiration, but in everyday toil. And we believe this, not
simply because we have argued that such training ought
to have these effects, or merely because we hoped for such
results in some dim future, but because already for years
we have seen in the work of our graduates precisely such
results as I have mentioned: successful teachers of teachers, intelligent and upright ministers, skilled physicians,
principals of industrial schools, businessmen, and, above
all, makers of model homes and leaders of social groups,
out from which radiate subtle but tangible forces of uplift and inspiration. The proof of this lies scattered in every
state of the South, and, above all, in the half-unwilling
testimony of men disposed to decry our work.

Between the Negro college and industrial school there
are the strongest grounds for cooperation and unity. It
is not a matter of mere emphasis, for we would be glad
to see ten industrial schools to every college. It is not

a fact that there are today too few Negro colleges, but rather that there are too many institutions attempting to do college work. But the danger lies in the fact that the best of the Negro colleges are poorly equipped, and are today losing support and countenance, and that, unless the nation awakens to its duty, ten years will see the annihilation of higher Negro training in the South. We need a few strong, well-equipped Negro colleges, and we need them now, not tomorrow; unless we can have them and have them decently supported, Negro education in the South, both common-school and the industrial, is doomed to failure, and the forces of social regeneration will be fatally weakened, for the college today among Negroes is, just as truly as it was yesterday among whites, the beginning and not the end of human training, the foundation and not the capstone of popular education.

Strange, is it not, my brothers, how often in America those great watchwords of human energy—"Be strong!" "Know thyself!" "Hitch your wagon to a star!"—how often these die away into dim whispers when we face these seething millions of black men? And yet do they not belong to them? Are they not their heritage as well as yours? Can they bear burdens without strength, know without learning, and aspire without ideals? Are you afraid to let them try? Fear rather, in this our common fatherland, lest we live to lose those great watchwords of liberty and opportunity which yonder in the eternal hills their fathers fought with your fathers to preserve.

The Colored American Magazine, May 1904, pp. 333-39.

8

CREDO

Du Bois's "Credo" was, next to The Souls of Black Folk, *the most well known of his writings. Originally used in his speeches, it appeared in print first in the New York periodical,* The Independent, *in October 1904 and was immediately widely reprinted, especially in the Negro press. It was later published in scroll form, framed, and hung in Negro homes throughout the country.*

I believe in God who made of one blood all races that dwell on earth. I believe that all men, black and brown, and white, are brothers, varying, through Time and Opportunity, in form and gift and feature, but differing in no essential particular, and alike in soul and in the possibility of infinite development.

Especially do I believe in the Negro Race; in the beauty of its genius, the sweetness of its soul, and its strength in that meekness which shall inherit this turbulent earth.

I believe in pride of race and lineage itself; in pride of self so deep as to scorn injustice to other selves; in pride of lineage so great as to despise no man's father; in pride of race so chivalrous as neither to offer bastardy to the weak nor beg wedlock of the strong, knowing that men may be brothers in Christ, even though they be no brothers-in-law.

I believe in Service—humble reverent service, from the blackening of boots to the whitening of souls; for Work is Heaven, Idleness Hell, and Wages is the "Well done!" of the Master who summoned all them that labor and are heavy laden, making no distinction between the black sweating cotton-hands of Georgia and the First Families of Virginia, since all distinction not based on deed is devilish and not divine.

I believe in the Devil and his angels, who wantonly work to narrow the opportunity of struggling human beings, especially if they be black; who spit in the faces of the fallen, strike them that cannot strike again, believe the worst and work to prove it, hating the image which their Maker stamped on a brother's soul.

I believe in the Prince of Peace. I believe that War is Murder. I believe that armies and navies are at bottom the tinsel and braggadocio of oppression and wrong; and I believe that the wicked conquest of weaker and darker nations by nations white and stronger but foreshadows the death of that strength.

I believe in Liberty for all men; the space to stretch their arms and their souls; the right to breathe and the right to vote; the freedom to choose their friends, enjoy the sunshine and ride on the railroads, uncursed by color; thinking, dreaming, working as they will in a kingdom of God and love.

I believe in the training of children black even as white; the leading out of little souls into the green pastures and beside the still waters, not for pelf truth; lest we forget, and the sons of the fathers, like Esau, for mere meat barter their birthright in a mighty nation.

Finally, I believe in Patience—patience with the weakness of the Weak and the strength of the Strong, the prejudice of the Ignorant and the ignorance of the Blind; patience with the tardy triumph of Joy and the chastening of Sorrow—patience with God.

The Independent, New York, October 6, 1904.

9

THE NIAGARA MOVEMENT

Following the launching of the Niagara Movement in July 1905, Dr. Du Bois, its founder and general secretary, delivered a number of speeches explaining the Movement and its purposes. The following address was published in The Voice of the Negro, *a publication issued in Atlanta by J. Max Barber, a charter member of the Niagara Movement.*

What is the Niagara Movement? The Niagara Movement is an organization composed at present of fifty-four men resident in eighteen states of the United States. These men having common aspirations have banded themselves together into an organization. This organization was perfected at a meeting held at Buffalo, N. Y., July 11, 12 and 13, 1905, and was called "The Niagara Movement." The present membership, which of course we hope to enlarge as we find others of like thought and ideal, consists of ministers, lawyers, editors, businessmen and teachers. The honor of founding the organization belongs to F. L. McGhee, who first suggested it; C. C. Bentley, who planned the method of organization and W. M. Trotter, who put the backbone into the platform.

The organization is extremely simple and is designed for effective work. Its officers are a general secretary and treasurer, a series of state secretaries and a number of secretaries of specific committees. Its membership in each state constitutes the state organization under the state secretary.

Why this organization is needed. The first exclamation of anyone hearing of this new movement will naturally be: "Another!" Why, we may legitimately be asked, should men attempt another organization after the failures of the past? We answer soberly but earnestly, "For that very reason." Failure to organize Negro-Americans for specific objects in the past makes it all the more imperative that we should keep trying until we succeed. Today we have no organization devoted to the general interests of the African race in America. The Afro-American Council, while still in existence, has done practically nothing for three years, and is today, so far as effective membership and work is concerned, little more than a name.[1] For specific objects we have two organizations, the New England Suffrage League and the Negro Business League.[2] There is, therefore, without the slightest doubt room for a larger national organization. What now is needed for the success of such an organization? If the lessons of the past are read aright, there is demanded:

1. Simplicity of organization.
2. Definiteness of aim.

The country is too large, the race too scattered and the rank and file too unused to organized effort to attempt to impose a vast machine-like organization upon a wavering, uncertain constituency. This has been the mistake of several efforts at united work among us. Effective organization must be simple — a banding together of men on lines essentially as simple as those of a village debating club. What is the essential thing in such organization. Manifestly it is like-mindedness. Agreement in the object to be worked for, or in other words, *definiteness of aim.*

Among ten million people enduring the stress under which we are striving there must of necessity be great and far-reaching differences of opinions. It is idle, even nonsensical, to suppose that a people just beginning self-

mastery and self-guidance should be able from the start
to be in perfect accord as to the wisdom or expediency
of certain policies. And some universal agreement is impossible. The best step is for those who agree to unite
for the realization of those things on which they have
reached agreement. This is what the Niagara Movement
has done. It has simply organized and its members agree
as to certain great ideals and lines of policy. Such people as are in agreement with them it invites to cooperation and membership. Other persons it seeks to convert
to its way of thinking; it respects their opinion, but believes thoroughly in its own. This the world teaches us
is the way of progress.

What the Niagara Movement proposes to do. What now
are the principles upon which the membership of the Niagara Movement are agreed? As set forth briefly in the constitution they are as follows:

    a. Freedom of speech and criticism.

    b. An unfettered and unsubsidized press.

    c. Manhood suffrage.

    d. The abolition of all caste distinctions based simply on
race and color.

    e. The recognition of the principle of human brotherhood
as a practical present creed.

    f. The recognition of the highest and best training as the
monopoly of no class or race.

    g. A belief in the dignity of labor.

    h. United effort to realize these ideals under wise and
courageous leadership.

All these things we believe are of great and instant importance; there has been a determined effort in this country to stop the free expression of opinion among black
men; money has been and is being distributed in considerable sums to influence the attitude of certain Negro papers;
the principles of democratic government *are* losing ground,
and caste distinctions are growing in all directions. Human
brotherhood is spoken of today with a smile and a sneer;
effort is being made to curtail the educational opportunities

of the colored children; and while much is said about money-making, not enough is said about efficient, self-sacrificing toil of head and hand. Are not all these things worth striving for? *The Niagara Movement* proposes to gain these ends.

All this is very well, answers the objector, but the ideals are impossible of realization. We can never gain our freedom in this land. To which we reply: We certainly cannot unless we try. If we expect to gain our rights by nerveless acquiescence in wrong, then we expect to do what no other nation ever did. What must we do then? We must complain. Yes, plain, blunt complaint, ceaseless agitation, unfailing exposure of dishonesty and wrong — this is the ancient, unerring way to liberty, and we must follow it. I know the ears of the American people have become very sensitive to Negro complaints of late and profess to dislike whining. Let that worry none. No nation on earth ever complained and whined so much as this nation has, and we propose to follow the example. Next we propose to work. These are the things that we as black men must try to do:

To press the matter of stopping the curtailment of our political rights.

To urge Negroes to vote intelligently and effectively.

To push the matter of civil rights.

To organize business cooperation.

To build schoolhouses and increase the interest in education.

To open up new avenues of employment and strengthen our hold on the old.

To distribute tracts and information in regard to the laws of health.

To bring Negroes and labor unions into mutual understanding.

To study Negro history.

To increase the circulation of honest, unsubsidized newspapers and periodicals.

To attack crime among us by all civilized agencies. In

fact to do all in our power by word or deed to increase
the efficiency of our race, the enjoyment of its manhood,
rights and the performance of its just duties.

This is a large program. It cannot be realized in a
short time. But something can be done and we are going
to do something. It is interesting to see how the platform
and program has been received by the country. In not a
single instance has the justice of our demands been denied.
The *Law Register* of Chicago acknowledges openly that
"the student of legal and political history is aware that
every right secured by men either individually or as a nation has been won only after asserting the right and sometimes fighting for it. And when a people begin to voice
their demand for a right and keep it up, they ultimately
obtain the right as a rule." The *Mail and Express* says that
this idea is "that upon which the American white man has
founded his success." All this *but—* and then have come the
excuses: The *Outlook* thinks that "A child should use other
language." It is all right for the white men says the *Mail
and Express,* but black men — well they had better "work."
Complaint has a horrible and almost a treasonable sound
to the *Tribune* while the *Chicago Record-Herald* of course
makes the inevitable discovery of "social equality." Is not
this significant? Is justice in the world to be finally and
definitely labeled white and that with your apathetic consent? Are we not men enough to protest, or shall the
sneer of the *Outlook* and its kind be proven true that out
of ten millions there are only a baker's dozen who will
follow these fifty Negro-Americans and dare to stand up
and be counted as demanding every single right that belongs to free American citizens? This is the critical time,
black men of America; the staggering days of emancipation, of childhood, are gone.

> "God give us men! A time like this demands
> Strong minds, great hearts, true faith, and ready hands;
> Men whom lust of office does not kill;
> Men whom the spoils of office cannot buy;
> Men who possess opinions and a will;
> Men who have honor, men who will not lie;

Men who can stand before a demagogue,
And damn his treacherous flatterers without winking.
Tall men, sun-crowned, who live above the fog
In public duty and private thinking.
For when the rabble, with their thumb-worn creeds,
Their large professions and their little deeds,
Mingle in selfish strife — lo, Freedom weeps,
Wrong rules the land, and waiting Justice sleeps.

The Voice of the Negro, Atlanta, September 1905, pp. 619-22.

10

THE ECONOMIC FUTURE
OF THE NEGRO

At the 1906 session of the American Economic Association, Dr. Du Bois delivered an important paper on "The Economic Future of the Negro." Nowhere at that time was there a more thorough or thoughtful analysis of the economic conditions of black Americans, the problems they faced in seeking to earn a living in American society, and the obstacles in the path of their obtaining economic independence. Most of what Dr. Du Bois noted was to remain true for decades to come. Apart from the importance of the paper as an analysis of the economic problems of American Negroes, it is also significant in revealing Dr. Du Bois's early interest in economic organization and cooperation among Negroes to achieve control of their own communities.

The object of this paper is to note the historic rise of economic classes among Negro Americans and to seek by a study of present conditions to forecast the economic future of this class of American citizens. As has been many times pointed out, the slaves consisted of a mass of field hands and a smaller number of selected servants and a few artisans. When this mass of labor was suddenly transmuted into a body of laborers more or less free, there ensued a struggle for economic independence which is still going on. When now we discuss the economic future of this group of ten millions, we must first of all not fall into the prevalent error of speaking of these persons as though they formed one essentially homogeneous group. This was not true even in slavery times, and it is so false today that any theories built on such a conception are false from the start.

The Negro American after slavery made four distinct and different efforts to reach economic safety. The first effort was through the preferment of the selected house servant class; the second was by means of competitive industry; the third was by means of landholding; and the fourth by means of what I am going to call the group economy — a phrase which I shall later explain.

1. The effort of the house servant.

The one person who under the slavery regime came nearest escaping from the toils of the system and disabilities of the caste was the favorite house servant. This arose from four reasons:

a. The house servant was brought into closest contact with the culture of the master's family.

b. He had more often the advantages of town and city life.

c. He was able to gain at least some smattering of an education.

d. He was usually a blood relative of the master class.

For this reason the natural leadership of the emancipated race fell to this class, the brunt of the burden of reconstruction fell on their shoulders and when the history of this period is written according to truth and not according to our prejudices it will be clear that no group of men ever made a more tremendous fight against more overwhelming odds.

It seemed natural at this time that this leading class of upper servants would step into the economic life of the nation from this vantage ground and play a leading role. This they did in several instances: the most conspicuous being the barber, the caterer, and the steward. For the most part however economic society refused to admit the black applicant on his merits to any place of authority or advantage; he held his own in the semi-servile work of

barber until he met the charge of color discrimination from
his own folk and the strong competition of Germans and
Italians; while the caterer was displaced by the palatial
hotel in which he could gain no foothold. On the whole
then the mass of house servants found the doors of advancement closed in their faces; the better tenth both themselves and through their better-trained children escaped into
the professions and thus found economic independence.
The mass of servants remained servants or turned toward
industry.

2. In lines of industrial cooperation the second attempt
of the freedmen was made. It was a less ambitious attempt
than that of the house servants and comprehended larger
numbers; it was characterized by a large migration to
cities and towns and entrance into work as teamsters, railway section hands, miners, sawmill employees, porters,
hostlers, etc.

This class met and joined in the towns the older class of
artisans, most of them connected with the building trades
and together this class attempted economic advance. Outside the farmers it is this class that has attracted most
attention, that has met all the brunt of the economic battle,
and that are usually referred to in studies of this sort.
What the outcome of this second attempt at economic freedom will be can only be divined by calling attention to the
third method by which the Negro has sought the way of
life.

3. Meantime, however, the freedmen had started forward by a third way, that of land ownership. Most of
those who got any start became share-tenants and a fourth
of these succeeded in buying land. Those who bought land
approximated economic independence, forming the closed
plantation economy of the olden times but with colored
owner, colored laborers, and colored tenants. In an increasing number of cases the colored store came in to help
them and we have a complete system of what I have
called the group economy.

4. The group economy. This fourth method is of strik-

ing importance but outside the country districts is little understood. It consists of such a cooperative arrangement of industries and services within the Negro group that the group tends to become a closed economic circle largely independent of the surrounding white world. The recognition of this fact explains many of the anomalies which puzzle the student of the Negro American — pardon me, I should not say puzzle; nothing ever puzzles a student of the Negro — but that which makes our conclusions so curiously incoherent.

You used to see numbers of colored barbers; you are tempted to think they are all gone — yet today there are more Negro barbers in the United States than ever before, but at the same time a larger number than ever before cater solely to colored trade where they have a monopoly. Because the Negro lawyer, physician, and teacher serve almost exclusively a colored clientage, their very existence is half forgotten. The new Negro businessmen are not successors of the old; there used to be Negro businessmen in New York, Philadelphia, and Baltimore, catering to white trade. The new Negro businessman caters to colored trade. So far has this gone that today in every city of the United States with a considerable Negro population, the colored group is serving itself with religious ministration, medical care, legal advice, and education of children: to a growing degree with food, houses, books, and newspapers. So extraordinary has been this development that it forms a large and growing part in the economy in the case of fully one-half of the Negroes of the United States, and in the case of something between 50,000 and 100,000 town and city Negroes, representing at least 300,000 persons, the group economy approaches a complete system. To these may be added the bulk of the 200,-000 Negro farmers who own their farms. They form a natural group economy and are increasing the score of it in every practical way. This then is the fourth way in which the Negro has sought economic salvation.

Having reviewed now historically these four sets of

efforts let us ask next: What are the questions in the present problem of economic status? They may be summed
up in four groups:

1. The relation of the Negro to city and country.

2. The relation of the Negro to group and national
economy.

3. The influence of race prejudice.

4. The question of efficiency.

1. City and country. A fact of great importance in regard
to the economic condition of the Negro is his rush city-
ward so that today nearly a fourth of the colored population lives in cities and towns.[1] This means an intensify-
ing of the urban economic problem. The group of over
two million town Negroes represents preeminently all of
the economic problems outside of those connected with
landholding and agriculture.

Moreover the city Negroes contain probably a third
of the intelligent Negroes, and have a rate of illiteracy
of probably less than 33 percent. Here it is then in the
city that the more intricate problems of economic life and
race contact are going to be fought out. On the other
hand, the very presence of seven million Negroes in the
country districts makes the economic problem there, though
simpler in quality, of tremendous proportions in quantity
and of added significance when we see how the country
is feeding the city problems.

2. The group and national economy. Present conditions
show that while the force of competition from without is
of tremendous economic importance in the economic development of the Negro, it is not by any means final;
in an isolated country the industry of the inhabitants could
be supported and developed by means of a protective tariff, until the country was able to enter into international
trade with fully developed resources; that a similar kind
of thing could be accomplished in a group not isolated
but living scattered among more numerous and richer
neighbors is often forgotten. There is therefore a double
question in regard to the Negroes' economic advance; the
first question is: how far is the Negro likely to gain a

foothold as one of the economic factors in the nation's industrial organization? The second is: how far can the Negro develop a group economy which will break the force of race prejudice until his right and ability to enter the national economy are assured?

3. The influence of race prejudice. This brings us to a consideration of the kind of retarding prejudice which the Negro meets in the economic world. This may be stated briefly as follows: outside of all question of ability, an American of Negro descent will find more or less concerted effort on the part of his white neighbors:

a. To keep him from all positions of authority.

b. To prevent his promotion to higher grades.

c. To exclude him entirely from certain lines of industry.

d. To prevent him from competing upon equal terms with white workingmen.

e. To prevent his buying land.

f. To prevent his defense of his economic rights and status by the ballot.

These efforts have had varying success and have been pressed with varying degrees of emphasis. Yet they must all be taken into account; strikes have repeatedly occurred against Negro foremen, of whose ability there was no complaint; the white office boy, errand boy, section hand, locomotive firemen, all have before them the chance to become clerk or manager or to rise in the railway service. The Negro has few such openings. Fully half of the trade unions of the United States, counted by numerical strength, exclude Negroes from membership and thus usually prevent them from working at the trade. Another fourth of the unions, while admitting a few black men here and there, practically exclude most of them.[2] Only in a few unions, mostly unskilled, is the Negro welcomed as in the case of the miners[3]; in a few others the economic foothold of the Negro was good enough to prevent his expulsion as in some of the building trades. Agitation to prevent the selling of land to Negroes has always been spread over large districts in the South and is spreading, and in a recent campaign in Atlanta the most telling cartoon for the influencing of white voters was one which repre-

sented the house of the candidate being built by black
men. The black vote was of course disfranchised in this
contest.

4. The last element in the economic condition of the
Negro is the great question: how efficient a laborer is
the Negro, and how efficient can he become with intelligence, technical training, and encouragement? That the
average Negro laborer today is less efficient than the
average European laborer is certain. When, however, you
take into account the Negro's ignorance, his past industrial
training, and the social atmosphere in which he works,
it is not so easy to say offhand what his possible worth
is. Certainly increasing intelligence has made him increasingly discontented with his conditions of work; the determined withdrawing of responsibility from the Negro has
not increased his sense of responsibility; the systematic
exploiting of black labor has hurt its steadiness and reliability; notwithstanding all this, there never were before in
the world's history so many black men steadily engaged
in common and skilled labor as in the case of the American Negro; nor is there a laboring force, which judiciously guided, seems capable of more remarkable development.

Having now glanced at the historic development and the
present elements of the problem, let us take each economic
group of Negroes and consider its present condition and
probable future.

1. The 250,000 independents. This group includes 200,-
000 farmers, 20,000 teachers, 15,000 clergymen, 10,000
merchants, and numbers of professional men of various
sorts. They are separated sharply into a rural group of
farmers and an urban group. They are characterized by
the fact that with few exceptions they live by an economic
service done their own people. This is least true in regard
to the farmers but even in their case it is approximately
true; they, more than any other group of Negro farmers,
raise their own supplies, and use their cotton as a surplus
crop; through this alone usually do they come into the
national economy. This group is the one that feels the force
of outward competition and prejudice least in its economic
life and most in the spiritual life. It is the head and front

of the group-economy movement, comprehends the spiritual as well as economic leaders and is bound in the future to have a large and important development, limited only by the ability of the race to support it.

In some respects it is of course vulnerable. Many of the teachers for instance, depend upon educational boards elected by white voters, and upon philanthropy. There has been concerted action in the rural districts of the South to drive out the best Negro teachers and even in the cities the way of the independent black teacher who dares think his own thought is made difficult, the teachers too in the great philanthropic foundations are being continually warned that their bread and butter depend on their agreeing with present public opinion in regard to the Negro. There is growing up however silently almost unnoticed a distinct Negro private school system officered, taught, attended, and supported by Negroes. Such private schools have today at least 25,000 pupils and are growing rapidly.

If we regard now the city group exclusively we find this is true:

The best class of this group is fully abreast in education and morality with the great middle class of Americans, their physical record in the thirty-four great life insurance companies is far better than the record of the Irish and as good as that of German-Americans. They have furnished notable names in literature, art, business, and professional life and have repeatedly in Boston, New York, Philadelphia, Chicago, Washington, and in other great centers proved their right to be treated as American citizens on a plane of perfect equality with other citizens.

Despite this, and despite the fact that this group is numerically small and without much inherited wealth, it has been struggling under two overwhelming burdens: first upon this group has been laid the duty and responsibility of the care, guidance, and reformation of the great stream of immigrants from the rural South simply because they are of the same race; there is no claim or vestige of a claim that this small city group of risen Negroes is responsible for the degradation of the plantation, yet the whole community partly by thoughtless transference of ideas and largely by deliberate intention has said, for instance, that

when between 1840 and 1900, 50,000 strangers, ignorant,
mistrained, careless, and sometimes vicious — that when this
group precipitated itself on a city like Philadelphia that
practically the whole responsibility of their training and
uplifting be placed not upon the half million Philadelphians
but upon a small group of 10,000 persons in that city
who were related to them by ties of blood. This was a hard
thing to ask and an unfair requirement, and yet if it is
asked that Irish see to poor Irish immigrants, and Jews
to poor Jews, at least this is always done: the helpers are
given all aid and sympathy in their undertakings and
their hands are upheld. In the case of the Negro, however,
every disability, every legal, social and economic bar
placed before the new immigrant must be endured by the
city group on whom they were dumped. And that group
must be judged continually and repeatedly by the worst
class of those very immigrants whose uplift was calmly
shifted to their shoulders by the city at large.

What could be the result of this? It could only be the
submerging of the talented tenth under the wave of immigration. This has happened repeatedly in great cities; New
York had in the forties as intelligent a group of well-to-
do thrifty and skilled Negroes as the nation has ever seen.
Forty thousand strangers dropped on them. The city
stimulated by white southerners formed a cordon around
them and not only cut off every avenue of economic and
social escape, but narrowed, beat, and crowded back the
better class out of their vantage ground which men like
my grandfather helped them gain by work and diligence
and desert, and this group was literally drowned and suf-
focated beneath the deluge of immigrants and has never
wholly recovered itself to this day. In Philadelphia this
rise and choking to death has taken place three distinct
times within a single century. In Chicago today a silent
battle of this sort to the death is taking place; there is
a city where in law, medicine, and dentistry men of Negro
blood have repeatedly stood in the foremost ranks of their
profession, where Negroes have risen in economic cooperation to positions of authority and preferment, today
when 25,000 strangers trained partially in the Mississippi

delta of which my good friend, Mr. Stone, will tell you, when these men have been precipitated on Chicago a desperate effort is being made to level every Negro in the city by treatment and discrimination down to the disabilities and limitations of the least deserving of the group.

In the South the beating back of the leading group has not awaited the excuse of immigration. On the general ground of impudence or indolence this class of economic and social leaders have been repeatedly driven out of the smaller towns, while in the larger cities every possible combination and tool from the Jim Crow laws to the secret society and the boycott have been made time and time again to curtail the economic advantages of this class and to make their daily life so intolerable that they would either leave or sink into listless aquiescence. I know a Negro businessman worth $50,000 in a southern city. He has a white clientele and he tells me that he dare not buy a horse and buggy lest the white people may think he's getting rich and boycott him; a barber in another city built a fine house on a corner lot and in a single year his white trade was gone. A black businessman in a country town of Alabama, where I made some studies preparatory to this paper, underbid his white fellow merchant in buying cotton seed and was shot down for his shrewdness.

What then can this town group do in self defense? It can organize the Negroes about it into a self-supplying group. This organization is going on. So far has it gone that in cities like Washington, Richmond, and Atlanta a colored family which does not employ a colored physician is in danger of social ostracism; in the North this is extending to grocery stores; in Atlanta when I went there eight years ago the whole business of insurance for sickness and accident was in the hands of white companies. Today fully one-half of it has passed to black companies. This year I saw organized such a company with $12,000 cash capital and this company today is taking $700 a week in dues.

There are persons who see nothing but the advantages of this course. But it has its disadvantages. It intensifies prejudice and bitterness. The white collectors of Atlanta

insurance companies for fear of white opinion would not
take off their hats when they entered Negro homes. The
black companies have harped on this, published it, called
attention to it, and actually capitalized it into cold cash.
Then too this movement narrows the activity of the best
class of Negroes, withdraws them from much helpful competition and contact, perverts and cheapens their ideals—
in fact provincializes them in thought and deed. Yet it is
today the only path of economic escape for the most
gifted class of black men, and the development in this
line which you and I will live to see is going to be enormous.

Turning now to the rural group of this independent
class, we come to the Negro landowners. Here first we
run flat against one of those traditional statements which
pass for truth because unchallenged: namely, that it is
easy for the southern Negro to buy land. The letter of
this statement is true, but the spirit of it is false. There
are vast tracts of land in the South that anybody black or
white can buy for little or nothing for the simple reason
that they are worth little or nothing. Eventually these
lands will become valuable. But they are nearly valueless
today. For the Negro, land to be of any value must
have present value—he is too poor to wait. Moreover it
must be:

1. Land which he knows how to cultivate.
2. Land accessible to a market.
3. Land so situated as to afford the owner protection.

There are certain crops which the Negro farmer knows
how to cultivate: to these can be added certain food supplies. Gradually intensive cultivation can be taught but this
takes a long time. It is idle to compare the South with
Belgium or France. The agricultural economy of their
lands is the result of centuries of training aided by a rising
market and by law and order. The present agricultural
economy of the South is but a generation removed from
the land-murder of a slave regime. No graduate of that
school knows how to make the desert bloom and the
process of teaching must be long and tedious. Meantime
he must live on such crops as he knows how to cultivate.
Moreover bad roads, comparatively few railroads, and

few navigable rivers throw much of this land out of usefulness. But even more important than all this: the black farmer must seek the protection of some community life with his own people and he finds that in the black belt.

But it is precisely in this black belt that it is most difficult to buy land; here it is that the capitalistic culture of cotton with a system of labor peonage is so profitable that land is high; moreover, in many of these regions it is considered bad policy to sell Negroes land because a fever of landowning "demoralizes" the labor system so that in the densest black belt of the South the percentage of landholding is often least among Negroes — a fact that has led to curious moralizing on the shiftlessness of black men. The country does not yet realize that the cutting up of southern plantations has ceased, and that under the new slavery of Negro labor there has begun an astounding and dangerous concentration of landholding in the South; this is shown not simply by the increase of the average size of farms in the central South from 144 to 155 acres in the last decade but these figures must be modified enormously by the fact that these farms do not belong to single owners but are owned in groups of as high as 40 or 50 by great landed proprietors. In the South there are 185,000 owners who hold from 2 to 50 farms each and there are 5,000 owners who have over 20 farms apiece. In the South Central states alone 800 men own a tract of land larger than Massachusetts, Rhode Island, and Connecticut combined, and but a few days ago I stood on the land of a white Alabama landowner who held 50 square miles and would not sell a single acre to a black man. This land is the best land of these regions. There are still other regions in the South, and large regions, where black men can buy land at reasonable terms but it is usually land poorly situated as regards market, or unhealthful in climate, or so placed as to afford the owner poor schools and lawless and overbearing white neighbors.

Now add to this fact the realization of the training and character of the Negro American farmer. We continually discuss and criticize these farmers as though they were responsible trained men who carelessly or viciously neglect their economic opportunity. They are on the contrary unlettered men, trained consciously and carefully to irresponsibility, to whom all concepts of modern property and saving are new and who need benevolent guardianship in their upward striving. Such guardianship they have in some cases received from former masters and in this way a considerable number of the present landowners first got their land.

In the great majority of cases, however, this guardianship has consisted in deliberately taking the earning of the Negro farmer and appropriating them to the use of the landlord. The argument was this: "These Negroes do not need this money — if I give it to them they'll squander it or leave the plantation; therefore give them just enough to be happy and keep them with me. In any case their labor rightfully belongs to me and my fathers and was illegally taken from us." On the strength of this argument and by such practices it is a conservative estimate to say that three-fourth of the stipulated wages and shares of crops which the Negro has earned on the farm since emancipation has been illegally withheld from him by the white landlords, either on the plea that this was for his own good or without any plea.

Would this wealth have been wasted if given the laborer? I waive the mere question of the right of any employer to withhold wages — and take the purely economic question: is the community richer by such practices? It is not. The South is poorer. The best Negroes would have squandered much at first and most would have squandered all, but this would have been more than offset by the increased responsibility and efficiency of the resulting Negro landholders. Nor is this mere pious opinion.

There is in the South in the middle of the black belt, a county of some 700 square miles. Lowndes County, Alabama; it contained in 1900 31,000 Negroes and 6,000 whites. It was the seat of the most strenuous type of American slavery — with absentee owners, living at ease in Montgomery, great stretches of plantation with 500 to 1,000 slaves on each driven by overseers and riders. There was no communication with the outside world, little passing between plantations and even today a forty-eight hours rain turns half the county into an impassible bog. The Negroes were slothful and ignorant—even today forty years after emancipation the illiteracy among those over ten is nearly 70 percent, and of the males of voting age over 72 percent. I know something of the South from ten years' residence and study, and outside of some sections of the Mississippi and Red River valley, I do not think it would be easy to find a place where conditions were on the whole more unfavorable to the rise of the Negro. The white element was lawless, the Negroes thoroughly cowed, and up until recent times the body of a dead Negro did not even call for an arrest.

In this county, during the last ten years there has been carried on a scheme of cooperative land buying under the Calhoun School. It was asked for by a few Negroes who could not get land; it was engineered by a Negro graduate of Hampton; it was made possible by the willingness of a white landlord to sell his plantation and actively further the enterprise by advice and goodwill. It was capitalized by white northerners and inspired by a New England woman. Here was every element in partnership and the experiment began in 1897. It involved the buying of 3,000 acres by 100 men. It encountered all sorts of difficulties: the character and training of the men involved; the enmity of the surrounding white population with a few notable exceptions; the natural suspicion of the black population born of a regime of cheating; the low price of cotton until the last two years, and several years of alternate flood and drought; and the attempts of neighboring whites to secure the homesteads through mortgages.

And yet what are the results? Nine years ago not one of the 100 men had a deed to a single acre of land; today they hold 77 warranty deeds conveying to them over 3,000 acres of absolutely unencumbered land. Of the 100 men who tried to buy land 7 gave up and 18 were sent away after trial—25 in all. Seven are still paying for their land but owe only small sums. Of the men who tried to buy land 29 were born in slavery, 37 in Reconstruction times, and the rest since 1875. I rode over that land a week ago with the black man who managed the enterprise.

He knew every farm, and every person, and their personal
history. All around pretty three or four-room painted
cottages were arising. Twenty-three one-room cabins still
remain, but there are 34 two-room houses and 29 of three
or more rooms. The Negroes round about call this the
"Free Land"—there are no overseers and riders roaming
about whipping the workers and seducing their wives and
daughters; there is an eight months' school in their midst,
a pretty new church, monthly conferences, a peculiar system
of self-government, and a family life untainted in a single
instance.

And yet: if ten years ago a planter from Lowndes County
had appeared here he would have told you of a lazy shiftless set of Negroes who had to be driven to work, who
squandered their money in whiskey and gambling, who
did not buy land because they did not want to. He would
have told you that, and what's more he would have sincerely believed every word he said. Yet in this very place
comes an experiment which calls out, selects and chooses in
one small corner of this county out of a neighborhood of
perhaps 400 families, some 75, who in ten years have been
transmuted into a respectable peasantry paying taxes on
$25,000 worth of property. Nor does this exhaust the
possibilities of this community; if the land were available
the same experiment could be repeated—men are clamoring
for a trial but it is doubtful if they will get it for one man
owns 50 square miles about there and he doesn't sell to
Negroes.

My honest belief is that what has been done in Lowndes
County under the Calhoun School and the sensible far-seeing guardianship of John Lemon, Pitt Dillingham, and
Charlotte Thorn, could be duplicated in every single black-
belt county of the South.

That it will be done to some extent is my hope, and on
that hope is based my faith in the economic future of this
rural group.

I have dwelt upon this group of 250,000 independent
men because in them lies the real economic future of the
Negro. They are the examples, the leaders, the test. Let us
now turn to the class which I call the *struggling;* they
include the artisans, the industrial helpers, the servants, and

the farm tenants. This group is characterized by five things:

1. It is sharply divided into a city and a country group.

2. While it has a large significance in the group economy of the Negro American — its overwhelming meaning is for the industry of the nation as a whole.

3. Its great hindrance is the necessity of group substitution in the place of individual promotion.

4. Its greatest enemy is the trade union.

5. Its greatest danger is immigration.

We may briefly review these points. The rural group consists of farm tenants. In a large number of cases farm tenancy has been an aid to land buying; in many cases farm tenancy has been a school of thrift and saving; in the majority of cases it was the only available system after the war, so long as the nation refused to do its bounden duty and furnish free land; and yet, when all this is said, it remains true that the system of farm tenancy as practiced over the larger part of the South today is a direct encouragement to cheating and peonage, a source of debauching labor, and a feeder of crime and vagrancy. It demands for its support a system of mortgage and contract laws and a method of administration which are a disgrace to twentieth century civilization, and for every man which the system has helped into independence it has pushed ten back into slavery.

It is claimed that honest and benevolent employers have made this system a means of uplift, development, and growth. This is perfectly true in thousands of cases as I can testify from personal knowledge; but at the same time it remains true, and terribly true that any system of free labor where the returns of the laborer, the settlement of all disputes, the drawing of the contract, the determination of the rent, the expenditures of the employees, the prices they pay for living, the character of the houses they live in, and their movements during and after work — any system of free labor where all these things are left practically to the unquestionable power of one man who owns the land and profits by the labor and is in the exercise of his power practically unrestrained by public opinion or the courts and has no fear of ballots in the hands of the laborers or of their friends — any such system is inherently wrong, and if men complain of its results being listlessness, shiftlessness, and crime, they have themselves to thank.

To the man that declares that he is acting justly and treating his men even better than they treat themselves, it is a sufficient answer to say that he is an exception to the rule; that the majority of the landholders are as indifferent to the welfare of their men as employers the world over, and that a large minority consciously oppress and cheat them. The best employer suffers therefore from the sins of the average. The only future of these tenants which means salvation is landholding and this is coming slowly. However shiftless and imprudent the Negroes of Mississippi can be proven to be, some of them somehow in one generation have bought 20,000 farms worth 18 millions of dollars. If they had been encouraged by such economic leadership as is found in Lowndes County, this record could have been multiplied by ten.

The city group of this class of workers consists of perhaps 125,000 skilled artisans, 575,000 semiskilled and ordinary industrial helpers, and 500,000 servants. The servant class have lost their best representatives because it offers a narrower and narrower method of uplift, because of foreign competition, and because the temptations to Negro girls in house service are greater than in any single industry. It must be remembered that the mulatto is the product of house service in the South. With the skilled and semiskilled workers the industrial history has been this: groups of Negroes have been excluded entirely from certain trades and admitted to others. They held the second set by working for lower wages and they forced themselves into certain industries from which they were excluded by the same lever of low wages. This gave the trade unions a chance to fight Negroes as scabs. In some battles the unions won and kept excluding Negroes. In other cases the Negroes won and were admitted to the unions. Even in the union, however, they were and are discriminated against in many cases. On the whole in the last ten years the Negroes have forced back the color line, but undoubtedly increased the color prejudice of workingmen by so doing.

In the near future this class of Negro American workingmen are going to have the struggle of their lives and the outlook indicates that by the fulcrum of low wages and the group economy, coupled with increasing efficiency, they will win. This means that the Negro is to be admitted to the national economy only by degrading labor conditions. The alternative offered is shameful and could be easily avoided if color prejudice did not insist on group substitution for Negroes in industry. I mean by this that a single individual or a few men of Negro descent cannot gain admittance to an industry usually. Only when they can supply workmen enough to supply the whole industry or the particular enterprise the black can be admitted. And immediately this substitution is made the occasion of a change in labor conditions — less wages, longer hours, worse treatment, etc. Thus often by refusing to work beside a single black man, workingmen in an industry suffer a general lowering of wages and conditions.

The real question of questions then in the South is how long will race prejudice supply a more powerful motive to white workingmen of the South than decent wages and industrial conditions. Today the powerful threat of Negro labor is making child labor and fourteen-hour days possible in southern factories. How long will it be before the white workingman discovers that the interests that bind him to his black brother in the South are greater than those that artificially separate them? The answer is easy: that discovery will not be made until the present wave of extraordinary prosperity and exploitation passes and the ordinary everyday level of economic struggle begins. If the Negro can hold his own until then, his development is certain.

I now come to the final group of two million common laborers. A million and a quarter are farm laborers, 500,-000 are laborers of other sorts, and the other quarter million are washerwomen. This group includes half the breadwinners of the race and its condition is precarious. In the southern country districts the laws as to contracts and wages and vagrancy are continually forcing the lower half of the laborers into crime and pauperism. In most southern states the breaking of a contract to work made between an ignorant farmhand and a landowner and covering a year's

time is enforced to the letter and its breaking on the part of
the laborer is a penitentiary offense. My observation is that
three-fourths of the homicides in country districts in which
Negroes are the killed or the killers arise from disputes
over wage settlement.

The condition of the country laborer in the South has become so intolerable that he is running away to the cities. A
demand for immigrants to fill his place is being heard and
I am curious to see the result. Certainly no immigrants
can stand the present contract and crop-lien system[4] and
above all they cannot stand the lawlessness of the country
districts where every white man is a law unto himself and
no Negro has any rights which the worst white is bound
to respect. So bad has this lawlessness been in parts of the
Gulf states that concerted and commendable action has been
taken against Whitecappers, and a few peonage cases
brought to court.[5] But these efforts have but scratched the
surface of the real trouble.

On the whole there are four general cures for the economic submersion of this class of Negro Americans: first, the
classes above must be given every facility to rise so as not
to bear down upon them from above; secondly, the system
of law and courts in the South by which it is practically
impossible in the country districts and improbable even in
cities for a black laborer to force justice from a white employer must be changed. Thirdly, Negro children must be
given common-school training. The states are not doing it
today, the tendency is in my state to do less, and the
United States government must step in and give black
children common-school training.

Finally, the black laborer must have a vote. For any
set of intelligent men like you, to think that a mass of two
million laborers can be thrust into modern competitive
industry and maintain themselves, when the state refuses
their children decent schools and allows them no voice or
influence in the making of the laws or their interpretation
or administration, is to me utterly inconceivable. I have
told you of those seventy-five landholders in Lowndes
County — owning $25,000 worth of land, building new and
better houses and working steadily and saving. And yet,
gentlemen, not a single one of those men under the new

constitution of Alabama has the right to vote: they cannot say a word as to the condition of the roads that pass their farms, the situation of the schools, the choice of teachers, the kind of county officers or the rate of taxation. They are just as absolutely disfranchised as the worst criminal in the penitentiary and as I am in Georgia. You can twist this matter up and down and apologize for it and reason it out—it's wrong, and unjust, and economically unsound, and you know it.

To sum up then the conclusions of this paper: half the Negro breadwinners of the nation are partially submerged by a bad economic system, an unjust administration of the laws, and enforced ignorance. Their future depends on common schools, justice, and the right to vote. A million and three quarters of men just above these are fighting a fierce battle for admission to the industrial ranks of the nation— for the right to work. They are handicapped by their own industrial history which has made them often shiftless and untrustworthy but they can, by means of wise economic leadership, be made a strong body of artisans and landowners. A quarter of a million men stand economically at the head of the Negroes, and by a peculiar self-protecting group economy are making themselves independent of prejudice and competition. This group economy is extending to the lower economic strata.

Publications of the American Economic Association, vol. VII, 1906, pp. 219-42.

11

WE CLAIM OUR RIGHTS

The second annual meeting of the Niagara Movement was held in Harper's Ferry, West Virginia, in homage to John Brown, August 16, 1906. Here the delegates made a pilgrimage at dawn barefooted, to the scene of Brown's martyrdom, and here they heard Dr. Du Bois read the Niagara Address to the Nation, one of the most important statements in the history of the Negro liberation movement.

The men of the Niagara Movement coming from the toil of the year's hard work and pausing a moment from the earning of their daily bread turn toward the nation and again ask in the name of ten million the privilege of a hearing. In the past year the work of the Negro-hater has flourished in the land. Step by step the defenders of the rights of American citizens have retreated. The work of stealing the black man's ballot has progressed and the fifty and more representatives of stolen votes still sit in the nation's capital. Discrimination in travel and public accommodation has so spread that some of our weaker brethren are actually afraid to thunder against color discrimination as such and are simply whispering for ordinary decencies.

Against this the Niagara Movement eternally protests. We will not be satisfied to take one jot or tittle less than our full manhood rights. We claim for ourselves every single right that belongs to a freeborn American, political, civil and social; and until we get these rights we will never cease to protest and assail the ears of America. The battle we wage is not for ourselves alone but for all true Americans. It is a fight for ideals, lest this, our common fatherland, false to its founding, become in truth the land of the thief and the home of the slave — a byword and a hissing among the nations for its sounding pretensions and pitiful accomplishment.

Never before in the modern age has a great and civilized folk threatened to adopt so cowardly a creed in the treatment of its fellow citizens born and bred on its soil. Stripped of verbiage and subterfuge and in its naked nastiness, the new American creed says: Fear to let black men even try to rise lest they become the equals of the white. And this is the land that professes to follow Jesus Christ. The blasphemy of such a course is only matched by its cowardice.

In detail, our demands are clear and unequivocal. First, we would vote; with the right to vote goes everything: freedom, manhood, the honor of your wives, the chastity of your daughters, the right to work, and the chance to rise, and let no man listen to those who deny this.

We want full manhood suffrage, and we want it now, henceforth and forever.

Second. We want discrimination in public accommodation to cease. Separation in railway and street cars, based simply on race and color, is un-American, undemocratic, and silly. We protest against all such discrimination.

Third. We claim the right of freemen to walk, talk, and be with them that wish to be with us. No man has a right to choose another man's friends, and to attempt to do so is an impudent interference with the most fundamental human privilege.

Fourth. We want the laws enforced against rich as well as poor; against capitalist as well as laborer; against white as well as black. We are not more lawless than the white race: we are more often arrested, convicted and mobbed. We want justice even for criminals and outlaws. We want the Constitution of the country enforced. We want Congress to take charge of Congressional elections. We want the Fourteenth Amendment carried out to the letter and every state disfranchised in Congress which attempts to disfran-

chise its rightful voters. We want the Fifteenth Amendment
enforced and no state allowed to base its franchise simply
on color.

The failure of the Republican Party in Congress at the
session just closed to redeem its pledge of 1904 with reference to suffrage conditions at the South seems a plain,
deliberate, and premeditated breach of promise, and
stamps that party as guilty of obtaining votes under false
pretense.

Fifth. We want our children educated. The school system
in the country districts of the South is a disgrace, and in
few towns and cities are the Negro schools what they ought
to be. We want the national government to step in and
wipe out illiteracy in the South. Either the United States
will destroy ignorance or ignorance will destroy the United
States.

And when we call for education we mean real education.
We believe in work. We ourselves are workers, but work
is not necessarily education. Education is the development
of power and ideal. We want our children trained as intelligent human beings should be, and we will fight for all
time against any proposal to educate black boys and girls
simply as servants and underlings, or simply for the use
of other people. They have a right to know, to think, to
aspire.

These are some of the chief things which we want. How
shall we get them? By voting where we may vote, by persistent, unceasing agitation, by hammering at the truth,
by sacrifice and work.

We do not believe in violence, neither in the despised
violence of the raid nor the lauded violence of the soldier,
nor the barbarous violence of the mob, but we do believe
in John Brown, in that incarnate spirit of justice, that
hatred of a lie, that willingness to sacrifice money, reputation, and life itself on the altar of right. And here on the
scene of John Brown's martyrdom we reconsecrate ourselves, our honor, our property to the final emancipation
of the race which John Brown died to make free.

Our enemies, triumphant for the present, are fighting
the stars in their courses. Justice and humanity must prevail. We live to tell these dark brothers of ours — scattered

in counsel, wavering and weak—that no bribe of money or notoriety, no promise of wealth or fame, is worth the surrender of a people's manhood or the loss of a man's self-respect. We refuse to surrender the leadership of this race to cowards and trucklers. We are men; we will be treated as men. On this rock we have planted our banners. We will never give up, though the trump of doom find us still fighting.

And we shall win. The past promised it, the present foretells it. Thank God for John Brown! Thank God for Garrison and Douglass! Sumner and Phillips, Nat Turner and Robert Gould Shaw,[1] and all the hallowed dead who died for freedom! Thank God for all those today, few though their voices be, who have not forgotten the divine brotherhood of all men, white and black, rich and poor, fortunate and unfortunate.

We appeal to the young men and women of this nation, to those whose nostrils are not yet befouled by greed and snobbery and racial narrowness: stand up for the right, prove yourselves worthy of your heritage and whether born North or South dare to treat men as men. Cannot the nation that has absorbed ten million foreigners into its political life without catastrophe absorb ten million Negro Americans into that same political life at less cost than their unjust and illegal exclusion will involve?

Courage, brothers! The battle for humanity is not lost or losing. All across the skies sit signs of promise. The Slav is rising in his might,[2] the yellow millions are tasting liberty, the black Africans are writhing toward the light, and everywhere the laborer, with ballot in his hand, is voting open the gates of opportunity and peace. The morning breaks over blood-stained hills. We must not falter, we may not shrink. Above are the everlasting stars.

Herbert Aptheker, editor, *Documentary History of the Negro People in the United States*, New York, 1951, pp. 907-10. Dr. Du Bois wrote the preface to Dr. Aptheker's work.

12

THE VALUE OF AGITATION

*"We claim for ourselves every single right that belongs
to a freeborn American, political, civil and social; and
until we get these rights we will never cease to protest
and assail the ears of America," Du Bois wrote in the
Niagara Address of 1906. The militant tone of the statement alarmed and annoyed large sections of the press
accustomed to the accommodating language of Booker
T. Washington, and Du Bois was denounced as "an agitator." His reply came nearly a year later, and is as valid
today as when it first appeared.*

There are those people in the world who object to agitation and one cannot wholly blame them. Agitation after
all is unpleasant. It means that while you are going on
peaceably and joyfully on your way some half-mad person insists upon saying things that you do not like to
hear. They may be true but you do not like to hear them.
You would rather wait till some convenient season; or you
take up your newspaper and instead of finding pleasant
notices about your friends and the present progress of
the world, you read of some restless folks who insist on
talking about wrong and crime and unpleasant things.
It would be much better if we did not have to have agitation; if we had a world where everything was going so
well and it was unnecessary often to protest strongly,
even wildly, of the evil and the wrong of the universe.
    As a matter of fact, however, no matter how unpleasant
the agitator is, and no matter how inconvenient and un-

reasonable his talk, yet we must ever have him with us. And why? Because this is a world where things are not all right. We are gifted with human nature which does not do the right or even desire the right always. So long as these things are true, then we are faced by this dilemma: either we must let the evil alone and refuse to hear of it or listen to it or we must try and right it. Now, very often it happens that the evil is there, the wrong has been done, and yet we do not hear of it — we do not know about it. Here then comes the agitator. He is the herald — he is the prophet — he is the man that says to the world: "There are evils which you do not know, but which I know and you must listen to them." Now, of course, there may be agitators who are telling the truth and there may be agitators who are telling untruths. Those who are not telling the truth may be lying or they may be mistaken. So that agitation in itself does not necessarily mean always the right and always reform.

Here then is some one who thinks that he has discovered some dangerous evil and wants to call the attention of good men of the world to it. If he does not persevere, we may perhaps pass him by. If he is easily discouraged, we may perhaps think that the evil which he thought he saw has been cured. But if he is sincere and if he is persistent, then there is but one thing for a person to do who wants to live in a world worth living in; that is, listen to him carefully, prove his tale and then try and right the wrong.

If we remember the history of all great reform movements, we remember that they have been preceded by agitation. Take for instance, the suppression of the slave trade. It was in a day when slavery could not be successfully attacked. But there was no doubt of the horrors of the slave trade. The best and worst of people alike admitted that. Here came a young man just graduated from college. By writing a prize essay he found himself interested in this great evil. He began to know and learn of things which other people did not know. Not that they knew nothing about them, but they had not brought together all the facts. One isolated person knew that fact and one knew this fact, but no one person knew both facts in

juxtaposition. When they did become acquainted with all
the facts he was sure that they must be moved to act.
What then must he do? He must agitate. It was not pleasant—it was putting himself in jeopardy; he was called
upon to lose friends in some cases, and in all cases to
make himself unpleasant, insistent, persistent, telling of
things that people did not want to hear about, because
they were not interested in them. He must interest people
in things in which they were not interested before, which
is a hard task in this busy world; and yet, nevertheless,
if Clarkson had not persisted, we would have much less
than a chance to agitate for human rights today.[1]

So it is with all great movements. They must be preceded by agitation. In the present status of the Negro
it is particularly necessary that we today make the world
realize what his position is—make them realize that he
is not merely insisting on ornamental rights and neglecting
plain duties, but that the rights we want are the rights
that are necessary, inevitable before we can rightly do
our duties.

Mrs. Gilman has a poem somewhere, where she speaks
of that rule which is to be laid down in the great future
state, "Unless a man works, he may not eat," and she
says very aptly that "The cart is before the horse," because "unless a man eats he cannot work."[2] So to those
people who are saying to black men today, "Do your
duties first and then clamor for rights," we have a right
to answer and to answer insistently: that the rights we
are clamoring for are those that will enable us to do
our duties. That we cannot possibly be asked to do any
partial measure of our duty even, unless we can have
those rights and have them now. We realize this. The
great mass of people in the United States do not realize
it. What then are we to do? We may sit in courteous and
dumb self-forgetting silence until other people are interested and come to our rescue. But is it reasonable to
suppose that this is going to happen before degeneration
and destruction overtake us? This is a busy world. People are attending to their own affairs as they ought to

The man that has a grievance is supposed to speak
for himself. No one can speak for him—no one knows

the thing as well as he does. Therefore it is reasonable to say that if the man does not complain that it is because he has no complaint. If a man does not express his needs, then it is because his needs are filled. And it has been our great mistake in the last decade that we have been silent and still and have not complained when it was our duty not merely to ourselves but to our country and to humanity in general to complain and to complain loudly. It is then high time that the Negro agitator should be in the land.

It is not a pleasant role to play. It is not always pleasant to nice ears to hear a man ever coming with his dark facts and unpleasant conditions. Nevertheless it is the highest optimism to bring forward the dark side of any human picture. When a man does this he says to the world: "Things are bad but it is worthwhile to let the world know that things are bad in order that they may become better. The real crushing pessimism takes hold of the world when people say things are so bad that they are not worth complaining of because they cannot be made better.

It is manifest that within the last year the whole race in the United States has awakened to the fact that they have lost ground and must start complaining and complain loudly. It is their business to complain.

This complaint should be made with reason and with strict regard to the truth, but nevertheless it should be made. And it is interesting to find even those persons who were deriding complaint a few years ago joining in the agitation today.

We of the Niagara Movement welcome them. We are glad of help from all sources. We are confirmed in our belief that if a man stand up and tell the thing he wants and point out the evil around him, that this is the best way to get rid of it. May we not hope then that we are going to have in the next century a solid front on the part of colored people in the United States, saying we want education for our children and we do not have it today in any large measure; we want full political rights and we never have had that; we want to be treated as human beings; and we want those of our race who stand on the threshold and within the veil of crime to be treated not as beasts, but as men who can be reformed or as children who can be prevented from going further in their career.

If we all stand and demand this insistently, the nation must listen to the voice of ten millions.

The Voice of the Negro, Atlanta, vol. IV, March 1907.

13

IS RACE SEPARATION
PRACTICABLE?

On December 30, 1907, Alfred Holt Stone read a paper before the American Sociological Society at Madison, Wisconsin, entitled, "Is Race Friction Between Blacks and Whites in the United States Growing and Inevitable?" Dr. Du Bois was asked by the Society, which had hitherto ignored his significant contributions in sociology, to comment on Stone's paper. He was unable to attend the meeting and his comments did not reach Madison in time to be read at the gathering. However, they were inserted in the American Journal of Sociology *following Stone's paper because, the* Journal *explained, "Dr. Du Bois presents the views of a distinguished Negro educator. . . ." The final section of Du Bois's comments reflects his firm belief at this stage in his life that racial separation was both impractical and impossible.*

I think we may all of us agree in the main with Mr. Stone's very careful presentation of the real significance of racial distinctions today, and also his explanation of the differing attitude of white men toward Negroes North and South and the role of slavery in making race contact practicable. There remain, then, three pressing questions: first, is the old status of acknowledged superiority and inferiority between the white and black races in America longer possible? Secondly, are the race differences in this case irreconcilable? And thirdly, is racial separation practicable?

Taking up the first question as to the possibility of a

continuance of the old status of acknowledged superiority
and inferiority between white and black races, it is certain
that physical slavery was a failure, not because it mistook
altogether the relative endowment of most of the men who
were enslavers and most of those who were the enslaved,
but because it denied growth or exception on the part
of the enslaved and kept up that denial by physical force.

Emancipation was simply the abolition of the grosser
forms of that physical force. The Negro freedman, just
as the freedman of Rome or Germany, stepped out of a
world of physical restraint into a spiritual world. In this
thought-world there is still slavery of ideas and customs;
and given men as they are, this is probably fortunate.
Yet we all hope for gradual emancipation in thought and
custom, and it is peculiarly dangerous for a people of
today, who expect to keep up with modern civilization,
to base their hope of peace and prosperity on the ignorance of their fellows or the lack of aspiration among
workingmen — on the survival of such virtues for instance
as we expect and cultivate in dogs but not in men. Moreover, even if a people like those in the South do hope that
the Negro is not going to aspire and not going to demand
equal rights and fair treatment, then they are bound to
disappointment. There is today in the South growing protest from the mass of Negroes, protest to which whites
are yielding today and must yield. These matters are not
yet, to be sure, the greater matters of voting and freedom
of travel, but they are the more pressing matters of wages
and personal treatment, of housing and property-holding.
Protest is not confined to a few leaders, it is not confined
to the North; it is not confined to mulattoes. Daily and
yearly it is growing. And it is that growing which makes
the Negro problem today; without it there would be no
race problem.

Mr. Stone refers to the meetings in Boston, the Nell
meeting and the last Protest, and notes their similarity.[1]
He might, however, have noted very distinct differences.
The Nell meeting represented four million people, over
nine-tenths of whom were physically owned by the whites,
and the rest of whom were largely ignorant and without
property; while the meeting this year represented ten mil-

lions of people whose property runs into the hundreds of millions, most of whom can read and write and some of whom are well educated (indeed, the leader in the last meeting was a *magna cum laude* bachelor of Harvard, and member of the Phi Beta Kappa).[2] In the Nell meeting the leading moving force was after all the white friends of the Negro; in this meeting the Negro was leading himself and the whites assisted. The attitude of men toward Nell was that of tolerant contempt or amusement or irritation; the attitude toward his descendants is that of consternation and perplexity and more or less veiled dislike. Such a change in fifty years is not only significant. It is tremendous, and only those unacquainted with the deeds of time can discount it.

Have we then today the old case of the irresistible force and the immovable body? If we assume the white South as planted immovably on the proposition that most human beings are to be kept in absolute and unchangeable serfdom and inferiority to the Teutonic world; and if we assume that not only the Negroes of America but those of Africa and the West Indies — not only Negroes, but Indians, Malays, Chinese, and Japanese, not to mention the Mediterranean lands — are determined to contest this absurd stand to the death, then the world has got some brisk days ahead, and race friction will inevitably grow and not only in the United States but the world over. But if, as seems more reasonable, we have in the South the beginning of a set of honest reasonable people, beset with hard social questions, but determined to think them through with reason and not with rope, and if we have a set of aspiring and rising serfs determined to be free, but willing to be patient, then race friction need not grow and meantime the nation can calmly scrutinize and answer the second of our queries:

How great is this incompatibility and repugnancy of qualities between white and black Americans? And here we find ourselves facing a field of science rather than opinion. As I have often said before, it is a matter of serious disgrace to American science that with the tremendous opportunity that it has had before it for the study of race differences and race development, race intermingling and contact among the most diverse of human kinds right here at its doors, almost nothing has been done.

When we at Atlanta University say that we are the only institution in the United States that is making any serious study of the race problems in the United States, we make no great boast because it is not that we are doing so much, but rather that the rest of the nation is doing nothing, and that we can get from the rest of the nation very little encouragement, cooperation, or help in this work. It has been my dream for many years that we could in the United States begin at a small Negro college a movement for the scientific study of race differences and likenesses which should in time revolutionize the knowledge of the world.

If for instance the dictum of Professor Boas of Columbia University [3] be true, namely, "that an unbiased estimate of the anthropological evidence so far brought forward does not permit us to countenance the belief in a racial inferiority, which would unfit an individual of the Negro race to take his part in modern civilization. We do not know of any demand made on the human body or mind in modern life that anatomical or ethnological evidence would prove to be beyond the powers of the Negro"—if this dictum be true (and there is certainly strong scientific backing for it), then how different an aspect this would put upon race differences in the United States than would be the case if it were proven that really black men and white men were of such differing powers and possibilities that they could not be treated as belonging to the same great branch of humanity. As I have said, this is primarily a scientific question, a matter of scientific measurement and observation; and yet the data upon which the mass of men, and even intelligent men, are basing their conclusions today, the basis which they are putting back of their treatment of the Negro, is a most ludicrous and harmful conglomeration of myth, falsehood, and desire. It would certainly be a most commendable thing if this and other learned societies would put themselves on record as favoring a most thorough and unbiased scientific study of the race problem in America.

Meantime, in the absence of such scientific basis for our conclusions, there are certain antecedent probabilities in the case which we have a right to take into account: we remember for instance that not many generations ago the very same arguments that are brought to prove the impossibility of white men and Negroes living together, except as inferior and superior, were also brought to prove that white men of differing rank and birth could not possibly exist in the same physical environment without similar subordination. And in still nearer time it was proved to the absolute satisfaction of certain economic philosophers that the conflict between capitalists and laborers was an inevitable conflict which must lead to poverty and social murder of the masses.

Today what seems to many of us an exactly similar fight is being made on the subject of race. Not only is it assumed without proof that here, as in the matter of birth and work, substantial equality of treament is impossible, but it is also assumed that the physical conditions of life and social contact are today practically what they were in former ages. But this is not so today; a physical living together of differing groups and kinds of individuals is possible today to a degree which was unthinkable one, two, and three centuries ago. Indeed when the bars between aristocrat and peasant were broken down, it did not mean that the aristocrats disappeared or that the peasants all became dukes; it simply meant that men lived and mingled together and rose and fell freely according to their individual desert, without artificial prop or bars. A spiritual world took the place of the strait walls and ghettos of their former physical environment. So in the race problem in America, we may ask with regard to this question of incompatibility of whites and blacks: just what degree of social compatibility is absolutely essential to group contact today? And in answering this question we must realize that not only does the modern world spell increased and increasing contact of groups and nations and races, but that indeed race or group segregation is impossible.

This brings us to our third question, is race separation practicable? People say very often with regard to the Negro that the Pilgrims of England found a place for liberty

when they could not get it at home; why then does not the
Negro do the same of his own motion and will? And then
they explain it by a shrug and a reminder that one set of
people were English and the others are Negroes. Flattering
as this is to the sayers, yet this does not explain all. Today
we have in the world growing race contact. The world is
shrinking together; it is finding itself neighbor to itself in
strange, almost magic degree. No one has done more for
increasing this contact of the nations than we here in
America. We not only brought Negroes here in defiance of
law, right, and religion, but we have pounded masterfully,
almost impudently, at the gates of China and Japan. Europe
has insisted upon the opening of Africa. Now when the
world suddenly appears open, with chance of access for all
to all parts, we find ourselves standing amazed before a
curious exemplification of the old adage, "What's sauce for
the goose is sauce for the gander"! If the world can enter
Asia, why cannot Asiatics enter the world? We could of
course in case of a helpless nation like China chivalrously
refuse to answer the question and bar out Chinese. But
when it comes to a question of Japan and Japanese guns,
the dilemma before the modern world is somewhat startling.
Just so with the Philippines. Here is a group of colored
folks half a world away, yet the United States is not content
until it goes, annexes them, and rules them according to its
own ideas.[4]

Now if these things are so, what chance is there for a
new nation to establish itself, especially if it be a colored
nation, on any spot in the world worth having? And is it
going to be possible in the future for races to remain
segregated or to escape contact or domination simply by
retiring to themselves? Certainly it is not. Race segregation
in the future is going to be impossible primarily because
these races are needed more and more in the world's economy. Mr. Stone has often expressed the cheerful hope that
the Negro would be supplanted by the white man as worker in the South. But the thing does not happen. On the
contrary there are today more Negroes working steadily
and efficiently than ever before in the world's history. The
world is beginning to work for the world. This work is
necessary. A new standard of national efficiency is coming.

And that efficiency is marked by the way in which a great modern advanced nation can be neighborly to the rest of the world. It is the counterpart to the sort of rivalry for the world empire that went on when France and England made a hundred years' struggle for empire in America and India.

And while we in America may sneer at neighbors, who are neither as rich or impudent or lucky as we, we can also, if we will, remark that the English again are learning certain things in advance of the rest of the world. They are learning how to get on in peace and amity with colored races; how to treat them as men and gain their friendship and gain the results of their work and skill and brain. And if the United States expects to take her place among the new nations beside England and France, the nations which first are going to solve this problem of race contact, then certainly she has got right here in her own land to find out how to live in peace and prosperity with her own black citizens. If she does that, she will gain an advantage over the rest of the world in the development of the earth which will be simply inestimable in the new commerce and in the new humanity. If she does not, she will always have in her contact with the rest of the world not only the absolute dislike and distrust of the darker two-thirds, but a tremendous moral handicap such as she met when she asked Russia to stop her atrocities and it was answered with perfect truth that they did not compare with the barbarities committed right here in the land of the free.[5]

We may therefore justly conclude, first, that the Negro is not going to submit any longer than he must to the present serfdom and the disgraceful and humiliating discrimination; secondly, that while we do not know as much of race differences as we may know if we study this problem as we ought, we certainly do know that the chances are that most men in this world can be civilized, and that the world of races, just as the world of individuals, does not consist of a few aristocrats and chosen people and a mass of dark serfs and slaves. And that thirdly, any dream of separating the races in America or of separating the races of the world is at present not only impracticable but is against the whole trend of the age, and that what we ought to do in America is to seek to bind the races together rather than to accen-

tuate differences. No part of the world could play a greater
role in the future moral development of the world than the
South, if it would. And while today there are few signs that
the South realizes this, yet may we not hope that this will
be the case before another generation passes? Finally,
rhetoric like that quoted by Mr. Stone is not in itself of
particular importance, except when it encourages those
Philistines who really believe that Anglo-Saxons owe their
preeminence in some lines to lynching, lying, and slavery,
and the studied insult of the helpless neighbors.

God save us from such social philosophy!

American Journal of Sociology, vol. XIII, May 1908,
pp. 834-38.

14

POLITICS AND INDUSTRY

In 1909 the interracial National Negro Committee, later to take the name National Association for the Advancement of Colored People, called a conference to be held in New York City, May 31, 1909, at which the key issues facing the Negro people would be discussed. Papers were read by black and white scholars and activists, two of them by a Columbia University anthropologist and a Cornell University zoologist which, in Du Bois's opinion, "left no doubt in the minds of listeners that the whole argument by which Negroes were pronounced absolutely and inevitably inferior to whites was utterly without scientific basis."

Du Bois addressed the conference twice, the first time delivering a paper on "Politics and Industry." Boldly criticizing Booker T. Washington's willingness to surrender the right to vote for the time being, he argued that Negroes would find it more difficult to achieve the franchise as long as demands for the ballot were played down. His main point was that the aspirations of a voteless group of workers could be destroyed by laborers who were permitted to vote since economic competition stimulated race prejudice and white men equipped with the franchise could make occupational discrimination permanent.

In discussing Negro suffrage, we must remember that, in the three hundred years between the settlement of this country and the present, there never has been a time when it was not legal for a Negro to vote in some considerable part of this land. From 1700 to 1909, Negroes have probably cast their ballots at some time in every single state of the Union, and all the time in some states; and there has been no period in the history of the land when all Negroes were disfranchised.

The early movement for disfranchisement came in two waves: the first, early in the eighteenth century, when Negro freedmen first appeared with required qualifications for voting. In this case Negroes, along with Jews and Catholics, were deprived of a vote. This initial movement was persisted in only in South Carolina and Georgia. In all other states, South and North, it subsided, and Negroes regularly voted in nearly every other state. Then came a second wave of disfranchisement in the North, about the beginning of the nineteenth century, which had the same object as the disfranchising clauses in the western states early in the next century: namely, to discourage and drive out free Negroes. The third wave of disfranchisement came in the South about 1830 and marked the end of the abolition movement there, and the beginning of the Cotton Kingdom. The population of free Negroes began to decrease, and the complete subjection of the black race was in sight.

The last wave of disfranchisement began in 1890 in Mississippi and now embraces Virginia, North Carolina, and the Gulf states excepting Florida and Texas. These states have adopted four kinds of qualifications: (1) educational qualifications; (2) property qualifications; (3) qualifications of birth; (4) other miscellaneous qualifications, the effect of which depends entirely on local election officials. These qualifications have been proposed with two reasons: (*a*) to keep the Negroes from voting, and (*b*) to eliminate the ignorant electorate.

Against both these excuses there were strong arguments, but at the time they were gathering force and momentum, there came a counterargument that practically stopped all effective opposition to the disfranchisement laws. This argument was that the economic development of the Negro in right lines demanded his exclusion from the right of suffrage at least for the present. This proposition has been insisted on so strenuously and advocated by Negroes of such prominence that it simply took the wind out of the sails of those who had proposed defending his rights, and today so deeply has this idea been driven that to most readers' minds the Negroes of the land are divided into two great parties — one asking no political rights but giving all attention to economic growth, and the other wanting votes, higher education and all rights. Moreover, the phrase "take the Negro out of politics" has come to be regarded as synonymous with industrial training and property getting by the black men.

I want in this short paper to show that, in my opinion, both these propositions are wrong and mischievous. In the first place there is no such division of opinion among Negroes as is assumed. They are practically a unit in their demand for the ballot. The real difference of opinion comes as to how the ballot is to be gained. One set of opinions favors open, frank agitation. The other favors influence and diplomacy; and the result, curious to say, is that the latter party has today an organized political machine which dictates the distribution of offices among black men and sometimes among southern whites. It is not too much to say that today the political power of the black race in America is in certain restricted lines very considerable. But those of us who oppose this party hold that this kind of political development by secrecy and machine methods is both dangerous and unwholesome and is not leading toward real democracy. It may, and undoubtedly does, put a large number of black men in office and it lessens momentary friction, but it is encouraging a coming economic conflict which will threaten the South and the Negro race.

And this brings me to the second proposition: that political power in the hands of the Negro would hinder economic development. It is untrue that any appreciable number of black men today forget or slur over the tremendous importance of economic uplift among Negroes. Every intelligent person knows that the most pressing problem of any people suddenly emancipated from slavery is the problem of regular work and accumulated property. But this problem of work and property is no simple thing — it is complicated of many elements. It is not simply a matter of manual dexterity but includes the spirit and the ideal back of that dexterity.

We who want to build and build firmly the strong foundations of a racial economy believe in vocational training,
but we also believe that the vocation of a man in a modern, civilized land includes not only the technique of his
actual work but intelligent comprehension of his elementary
duties as a father, citizen, and maker of public opinion, as
a possible voter, a conservor of the public health, an intelligent follower of moral customs, and one who can at
least appreciate, if not partake of, something of the higher
spiritual life of the world. We do not pretend that all of this
can be taught each individual in school but it can be put
into his social environment, and the more that environment
is curtailed and restricted, the more emphatic is the demand
that some part at least of the group shall be trained and
trained thoroughly in these higher matters of human development, if—and here is the crucial question—if they are
going to be able to share the surrounding civilization.

This brings us to the matter of voting. It is possible—
easily possible—to train a working class who shall have
no right to participate in the government. Most of the manual workers in the history of the world have been so
trained. It is also possible, and the modern world thinks
desirable, to train a working class who shall also have the
right to vote—both these things are possible although the
overwhelming trend of modern thought is toward making
workers voters. But the one thing that is impossible and
proven so again and again is to train two sets of workers
side by side in economic competition and make one set
voters and deprive the other set of all participation in
government. To attempt this is madness. It invites conflict
and oppression. A nation cannot exist half slave and half
free. Either the slave will rise through blood or the freeman
will sink.

So far, tremendous effort in the South has been put forth
to keep down economic competition between the races by
confining the Negroes by law and custom to certain vocations. But, for two reasons, this effort is bound to break
down: first there is no caste of ability corresponding with
the caste of color, and secondly because if every Negro in
the South worked twenty-four hours a day at the kinds of
work which are tacitly assigned him, he could not fill the

demand for that kind of labor. Economic competition is therefore inevitable, as facts like these show: in Alabama there are 94,000 Negro farm laborers and 82,000 whites. In Georgia there are 1,100 Negro barbers and 275 white barbers. In Florida there are 2,100 Negroes employed on railroads and 1,500 whites. In Tennessee there are 1,000 white masons and 1,200 black masons. And so on — we might go through endless figures showing that economic competition among whites and blacks was not only existent but growing.

Moreover the schools that increase the competition are the industrial schools, and this is both natural and proper. Negro professional men, teachers, physicians and artists come very seldom in competition with the whites. But farmers, masons, painters, carpenters, seamstresses and shoe-repairers work at the same work as whites and largely under like conditions. This competition accentuates race prejudice; when a whole community, a whole nation, pours contempt on a fellowman, it seems a personal insult for that man to work beside me or at the same kind of work. Thus one of the first results of the denial of civil rights is industrial jealousy and hatred. Here is a man whom all my companions say is unworthy and dangerous as a companion on the streetcar or steam car, as a fellow listener at a concert, theater or lecture, as a table companion in the same house or restaurant, often as a dweller in the same neighborhood and always as a worshiper in the same church or occupant of the same graveyard. If all this is so — and this the southern white workingman is industriously taught from the cradle to the grave — if this is so then why should I be forced to work at the same job or be engaged in similar kinds of work, or receive the same wages? If we cannot play together, why should we work together?

Not only is there this feeling but there is also power to act. After the Atlanta riot,[1] the police and militia searched the houses of colored people and took away guns and ammunition, while the sheriff almost gave away guns to some of the very men who had composed the mob. We think this monstrous, but it is but a parallel of the action of the whole nation. They have put the ballot in the hands of the white workingmen of the South and taken it away

from the black fellow-workmen. The result is that the white
workman can enforce his feeling of prejudice and repulsion.
Other things being equal, the employer is forced to dis-
charge the black man and hire the white man—public
opinion demands it, the administrators of government,
including police, magistrates, etc., render it easier, since by
preferring the white, many intricate questions of social
contact are avoided and political influence is vastly increased.

Under such circumstances there is nothing for the Negro
to do but to bribe the employer by underbidding his white
fellow; to work not only for less money wages, but for
longer hours and under worse conditions. No sooner does
he do this than he is mocked as a "scab" from Mexico to
Canada, and visited with all the consequent penalties. He
is said to be taking bread from others' mouths—and he
may be, but his excuse is tremendous: he is dragging others
down to keep himself from complete submergence, and he
is taking some of the bread from others' mouths lest his
children starve. Does he *want* to do this? Does he like long
hours? Ignorant as he is as a mass, has he not intelligence
enough to perceive the value of the labor unions and the
meaning of the labor movement? No, it is not because the
black man is a fool but because he is a victim that he
drags labor down.

Faced by this situation, the next step of the white workmen is to enforce by law and administration that which
they cannot gain by competition. In the past these laws
have been laws to separate and humiliate the blacks, but
more aggressive laws are demanded today and will be in
the future. The Alabama child labor law excepts from its
operation children in domestic service and in agriculture—
i.e., Negro children. *They* may grow up in absolute ignorance so far as the law is concerned. The Alabama law
makes the breaking of a contract to work by a farm laborer a felony punishable by a penitentiary sentence. Such a
breaking of law in other industries is a misdemeanor punishable by a fine.

Certain oppressive labor regulations in many southern
states are only applicable to such counties as vote their
enforcement. Counties with white workmen vote it down.

Counties with disfranchised black workmen vote it in. In the state civil service no Negro can be employed at any job which any white man wants, for obvious reasons. More than that, no white man whose business depends on public approbation or political concession can dare to hire Negroes or, if he hires them, promote them as they deserve. He must often be content with a distinctly inferior grade of white help.

Judges and juries in the South are at the absolute mercy of the white voters. Few ordinary judges would dare oppose the momentary whim of the white mob, and practically only now and then will a jury convict a white man for aggression on a Negro. This is true not only in criminal but also in civil suits, so much so that it is a widespread custom among Negroes of property never to take a civil suit to court but to let the white complainant settle it. In all public benefits like schools and parks and gatherings and institutions, Negroes are regularly taxed for what they cannot enjoy. I am taxed for the Carnegie Public Library of Atlanta, where I cannot enter to draw my own books. The Negroes of Memphis are taxed for public parks where they cannot sit down. . . .

Even in serving his own people and organizing his own business, the Negro is at the absolute mercy of the white voters. It is often said grandiloquently: let the Negroes organize their own theaters, transport their own passengers, organize their own industrial companies; but such kinds of businesses are almost absolutely dependent on public license and taxation requirements. A theater built and equipped could by a single vote be refused a license, a transportation company could get no franchise, and an industrial enterprise could be taxed out of existence. This is not always done, but it is done just as soon as any white man or group of white men begin to feel the competition. Then the voters proceed to put the industrial screws on the disfranchised.

Witness the strike of the white locomotive firemen in Georgia today.[2] Negro firemen get from fifty cents to one dollar a day less than the white firemen and have to do menial work and cannot become engineers. They can, however, by good service and behavior be promoted to the

best runs by the rule of seniority. Even this the white firemen now object to and say in a manifesto: the "white people
of this state refuse to accept Negro equality. This is worse
than that." The other day the white automobile drivers of
Atlanta made a frantic appeal in the papers for persons to
stop hiring black drivers. The black drivers replied, "We
have had fewer accidents than you and get less wages," but
the whites simply said, "This ought to be a white man's
job."

This sort of thing is destined to grow and develop. The
fear of Negro competition in all lines is increasing in the
South. The demand of tomorrow is going to be increasingly
not to protect white people from ignorance and degradation
but from knowledge and efficiency — that is, to so arrange
the matter by law and custom as to make it possible for the
inefficient and lazy white workman to be able to crush and
keep down his black competitor at all hazards, and so
that no black man shall be allowed to do his best if his
success lifts him to any degree out of the place in which
millions of Americans are being taught he ought to stay.

This is bad enough but this is not all. The voteless Negro is a provocation, an invitation to oppression, a play-
thing for mobs and a bonanza for demagogues. They serve
always to distract attention from real issues and to ride
fools and rascals into political power. The political campaign in Georgia before the last was avowedly and openly
a campaign not against Negro crime and ignorance but
against Negro intelligence and property-owning and industrial competition as shown by an 83 percent increase in
their property in ten years.

It swept the state, and if it had not culminated in riot
and bloodshed and thus scared capital, it would still be
triumphant. As it is, the end is not yet. The political power
of a mass of active working people thus without votes is
greater for harm, manipulation and riot than the power of
the same people with votes could possibly be, with the
additional fact that voters would learn to vote intelligently
by voting. Fourteen years ago Mississippi began disfranchising Negroes. You were promised that the result would
be to settle the Negro problem. Is it settled? No, and it
never will be until you give black men the power to be men,

until you give them the power to defend that manhood. When the Negro casts a free and intelligent vote in the South, then and not until then will the Negro problem be settled.

Proceedings of the National Negro Conference, New York, May 31 and June 1, 1909, pp. 79-86.

15

THE EVOLUTION OF THE

RACE PROBLEM

The second paper delivered by Dr. Du Bois at the National Negro Conference was entitled "The Evolution of the Race Problem."

Those who complain that the Negro problem is always with us and apparently insoluble must not forget that under this vague and general designation are gathered many social problems and many phases of the same problem; that these problems and phases have passed through a great evolutionary circle and that today especially one may clearly see a repetition, vaster but similar, of the great cycle of the past.

That problem of the past, so far as the black American was concerned, began with caste — a definite place preordained in custom, law and religion where all men of black blood must be thrust. To be sure, this caste idea as applied to blacks was no sudden, full-grown conception, for the enslavement of the workers was an idea which America inherited from Europe and was not synonymous for many years with the enslavement of the blacks, although the blacks were the chief workers. Men came to the idea of exclusive black slavery by gradually enslaving the workers, as was the world's long custom, and then gradually conceiving certain sorts of work and certain colors of men as necessarily connected. It was, when once set up definitely in the southern slave system, a logically cohering whole which the simplest social philosopher could easily grasp and state. The difficulty was it was too simple to be either just or true. Human nature is not simple and any classification that roughly divides men into good and bad, superior and inferior, slave and free, is and must ever be ludicrously untrue and universally dangerous as a permanent exhaustive classification. So in the southern slave system the thing that from the first damned it was the free Negro—the Negro legally free, the Negro economically free and the Negro spiritually free.

How was the Negro to be treated and conceived of who was legally free? At first with perfect naturalness he was treated as a man—he voted in Massachusetts and in South Carolina, in New York and Virginia; he intermarried with black and white, he claimed and received his civil rights—all this until the caste of color was so turned as to correspond with the caste of work and enslave not only slaves but black men who were not slaves. Even this system, however, was unable to ensure complete economic dependence on the part of all black men; there were continually artisans, foremen and skilled servants who became economically too valuable to be slaves. In vain were laws hurled at Negro intelligence and responsibility; black men continued to hire their time and to steal some smattering of knowledge, and it was this fact that became the gravest menace to the slave system. But even legal and economic freedom was not so dangerous to slavery as the free spirit which continually cropped out among men fated to be slaves: they thought, they dreamed, they aspired, they resisted. In vain were they beaten, sold south and killed, the ranks were continually filled with others and they either led revolt at home or ran away to the North, and these by showing their human qualities continually gave the lie to the slave assumption. Thus it was the free Negro in these manifold phases of his appearance who hastened the economic crisis which killed slavery and who made it impossible to make the caste of work and the caste of color correspond, and who became at once the promise and excuse of those who forced the critical revolution.

Today in larger cycle and more intricate detail we are passing through certain phases of a similar evolution. Today we have the caste idea—again not a sudden full-grown conception but one being insidiously but consciously and persistently pressed upon the nation. The steps toward it which are being taken are: first, political disfranchisement, then vocational education with the distinct idea of narrowing to the uttermost of the vocations in view, and finally a curtailment of civil freedom of travel, association, and entertainment, in systematic effort to instill contempt and kill self-respect.

Here then is the new slavery of black men in America — a new attempt to make degradation of social condition correspond with certain physical characteristics — not to be sure fully realized as yet, and probably unable for reasons of social development ever to become as systematized as the economic and physical slavery of the past — and yet realized to an extent almost unbelievable by those who have not taken the pains to study the facts — to an extent which makes the lives of thinking black men in this land a perpetual martyrdom.

But right here, as in the past, stands in the path of this idea the figure of this same thinking black man — this new freedman. This freedman again, as in the past, presents himself as free in varying phases: there is the free black voter of the North and border states whose power is far more tremendous than even he dare think so that he is afraid to use it; there is the black man who has accomplished economic freedom and who by working himself into the vast industrial development of the nation is today accumulating property at a rate that is simply astounding. And finally there is the small but growing number of black men emerging into spiritual freedom and becoming participators and freemen of the kingdom of culture around which it is so singularly difficult to set metes and bounds, and who in art, science and literature are making their modest but ineffaceable mark.

The question is what is the significance of this group of men for the future of the caste program and for the future social development of America? In order to answer this question intelligently let us retrace our steps and follow more carefully the details of the proposed program of renewed caste in America. This program when one comes to define and state it is elusive. There are even those who deny its existence as a definite consciously conceived plan of action. But, certain it is, there is growing unanimity of a peculiar sort on certain matters. And this unanimity is centering about three propositions:

1. That it was a mistake to give Negroes the ballot.
2. That Negroes are essentially an inferior race.
3. That the only permanent settlement of the race problem will be open and legal recognition of this inferiority.

When now a modern nation condemns ten million of its fellows to such a fate it would be supposed that this conclusion has been reluctantly forced upon them after a careful study and weighing of the facts. This, however, is not the case in the Negro problem. On the contrary there has been manifest a singular reluctance and indisposition carefully to study the Negro problem. Ask the average American: why should the ballot have been withheld from the Negro, and he will answer: "Because he wasn't fit for it." But that is not a sufficient answer: first, because few newly enfranchised groups of the most successful democracies have been fit for the ballot when it was first given, and secondly, because there were Negroes in the United States fit for the ballot in 1870.

Moreover the political philosophy that condemns out of hand the Fifteenth Amendment does not often stop to think that the problem before the American nation 1865-1870 was not a simple problem of fixing the qualifications of voters. It was, on the contrary, the immensely more complicated problem of enforcing a vast social and economic revolution on a people determined not to submit to it. Whenever a moral reform is forced on a people from without there ensue complicated and tremendous problems, whether that reform is the correction of the abuse of alcohol, the abolition of child labor or the emancipation of slaves. The enforcement of such a reform will strain every nerve of the nation and the real question is not: is it a good thing to strain the framework of the nation but rather: is slavery so dangerous a thing that sudden enfranchisement of the ex-slaves is too great a price to pay for its abolition?

To be sure there are those who profess to think that the white South of its own initiative after the war, with

the whole of the wealth, intelligence and lawmaking power
in its hands, would have freely emancipated its slaves in
obedience to a decree from Washington, just as there are
those who would entrust the regulation of the whiskey
traffic to saloon keepers and the bettering of the conditions
of child labor to the employers. It is no attack on the
South or on saloon keepers or on employers to say that
such a reform from such a source is unthinkable. It is
simply human nature that men trained to a social system
or condition should be the last to be entirely entrusted
with its reformation.

It was, then, not the Emancipation Proclamation but the
Fifteenth Amendment that made slavery impossible in
the United States and those that object to the Fifteenth
Amendment have simply this question to answer: which
was best, slavery or ignorant Negro voters? The answer
is clear as day: Negro voters never did anything as bad
as slavery. If they were guilty of all the crimes charged
to them by the wildest enemies, even then what they did
was less dangerous, less evil and less cruel than the system of slavery whose death knell they struck. And when
in addition to this we remember that the black voters of
the South established the public schools, gave the poor
whites the ballot, modernized the penal code and put on
the statute books of the South page after page of legislation that still stands today — when we remember this, we
have a right to conclude that the Fifteenth Amendment
was a wise and far-sighted piece of statesmanship.

But today the men who oppose the right of Negroes to
vote are no longer doing so on the ground of ignorance,
and with good reason, for today a majority and an appreciable majority of the black men of the South twenty-one
years of age and over can read and write. In other words,
the bottom has been clean knocked out of their ignorance
argument and yet the fact has elicited scarcely a loud remark.

Indeed we black men are continually puzzled by the easy
almost unconscious way in which our detractors change
their ground. Before emancipation it was stated and reiterated with bitter emphasis and absolute confidence that a
free Negro would prove to be a shiftless scamp, a bar-

barian and a cannibal reverting to savagery and doomed to death. We forget today that from 1830 to 1860 there was not a statement made by the masters of slaves more often reiterated than this, and more dogmatically and absolutely stated. After emancipation, for twenty years and more, so many people looked for the fulfillment of the prophecy that many actually saw it and we heard and kept hearing and now and then still hear that the Negro today is worse off than in slavery days. Then, as this statement grew less and less plausible, its place came to be taken by other assumptions. When a Louisiana senator saw the first Negro school he stopped and said: "This is the climax of foolishness!" The Negro could not be educated—he could imitate like a parrot but real mental development was impossible.

Then, when Negroes did learn some things, it was said that education spoiled them; they can learn but it does them no practical good; the young educated Negroes become criminals—they neither save nor work, they are shiftless and lazy. Now today are coming uncomfortable facts for this theory. The generation now working and saving is post-bellum and yet no sooner does it come on the stage than accumulated property goes on at an accelerated pace so far as we have measurements. In Georgia the increase of property among Negroes in the last ten years has been 83 percent.

But no sooner do facts like these come to the fore than again the ground of opposition subtly shifts and this last shifting has been so gradual and so insidious that the Negro and his friends are still answering arguments that are no longer being pushed. The most subtle enemies of democracy and the most persistent advocates of the color line admit almost contemptuously most that their forebears strenuously denied: the Negroes have progressed since slavery, they are accumulating some property, some of them work readily and they are susceptible of elementary training; but, they say, all thought of treating black men like white men must be abandoned. They are an inferior stock of men, limited in attainment by nature. You cannot legislate against nature, and philanthropy is powerless against deficient cerebral development.

To realize the full weight of this argument recall to
mind a character like John Brown and contrast his attitude with the attitude of today. John Brown loved his
neighbor as himself. He could not endure, therefore, to
see his neighbor poor, unfortunate or oppressed. This
natural sympathy was strengthened by a saturation in
Hebrew religion which stressed the personal responsibility
of every man's soul to a just God. To this religion of
equality and sympathy with misfortune was added the
strong influence of the social doctrines of the French
Revolution with its emphasis on freedom and power in
political life. And on all this was built John Brown's
own inchoate but growing belief in a juster and more
equal distribution of property. From all this John Brown
concluded — and acted on that conclusion — that all men
were created free and equal and that the cost of liberty
was less than the price of repression.

Up to the time of John Brown's death this doctrine
was a growing, conquering social thing. Since then there
has come a change and many would rightly find reason for that change in the coincidence that the year John
Brown suffered martyrdom was the year that first published the *Origin of Species*. Since that tremendous scientific and economic advance has been accompanied by
distinct signs of moral change in social philosophy; strong
arguments have been made for the fostering of war, the
social utility of human degradation and disease, and the
inevitable and known inferiority of certain classes and races
of men. While such arguments have not stopped the efforts
of the advocates of peace, the workers of social uplift
and the believers in human brotherhood, they have, it
must be confessed, often made their voices falter and
tinged their arguments with apology.

Why is this? It is because the splendid scientific work
of Darwin, Weissman, Galton and others has been widely and popularly interpreted as meaning that there is
such essential and inevitable inequality among men and
races of men as no philanthropy can or ought to eliminate;
that civilization is a struggle for existence whereby the
weaker nations and individuals will gradually succumb
and the strong will inherit the earth. With this interpreta-

tion has gone the silent assumption that the white European stock represents the strong surviving peoples and that the swarthy, yellow and black peoples are the ones rightly doomed to eventual extinction.

One can easily see what influence such a doctrine would have on the nation. Those that stepped into the pathway marked by the early abolitionists faltered and large numbers turned back. They said: they were good men—even great, but they have no message for us today—John Brown was a "belated covenanter," William Lloyd Garrison was an anachronism in the age of Darwin—men who gave their lives to lift not the unlifted but the unliftable. We have, consequently, the present reaction—a reaction which says in effect: keep these black people in their places, and do not attempt to treat a Negro simply as a white man with a black face; to do this would mean moral deterioration of the race and nation—a fate against which a divine racial prejudice is successfully fighting. This is the attitude of the larger portion of the thinking nation today.

It is not, however, an attitude that has brought mental rest or social peace. On the contrary, it is today involving a degree of moral strain and political and social anomaly that gives the wisest pause. The chief difficulty has been that the natural place in which, by scientific law, the black race in America should stay cannot easily be determined. To be sure, the freedmen did not, as the philanthropists of the sixties apparently expected, step in forty years from slavery to nineteenth-century civilization. Neither, on the other hand, did they, as the ex-masters confidently predicted, retrograde and die.

Contrary to both these views, they chose a third and apparently quite unawaited way: from the great, sluggish, almost imperceptibly moving mass they sent off larger and larger numbers of faithful workmen and artisans, some merchants and professional men, and even men of educational ability and discernment. They developed in a generation no world geniuses, no millionaires, no captains of industry, no artists of first rank; but they did in forty years get rid of the larger part of their illiteracy, accumulate a half billion of property in small

homesteads and gained now and then respectful attention
in the world's ears and eyes. It has been argued that
this progress of the black man in America is due to the
exceptional men among them and does not measure the
ability of the mass. Such admission is, however, fatal to
the whole argument. If the doomed races of men are
going to develop exceptions to the rule of inferiority then
no law, scientific or moral, should or can proscribe the
race as such.

To meet this difficulty in racial philosophy a step has
been taken in America fraught with the gravest social
consequences to the world and threatening not simply
the political but the moral integrity of the nation: that
step is to deny in the case of black men the validity of
those evidences of culture, ability and decency which are
accepted unquestionably in the case of other people, and
by vague assertion, unprovable assumption, unjust emphasis, and now and then by deliberate untruth, to secure
not only the continued proscription of these people, but
by caste distinction to shut in the faces of their rising
classes many of the paths to further advance.

When a social policy based on a supposed scientific
sanction leads to such a moral anomaly it is time to
examine rather carefully the logical foundations of the
argument. And so soon as we do this many things are
clear. First, assuming that there are certain stocks of
human beings whose elimination the best welfare of the
world demands; it is certainly questionable if these stocks
include the majority of mankind and it is indefensible
and monstrous to pretend that we know today with any
reasonable certainty which these stocks are. We can point
to degenerate individuals and families here and there
among all races, but there is not the slightest warrant
for assuming that there do not exist among the Chinese
and Hindus, the African Bantus and American Indians
as lofty possibilities of human culture as any European
race has ever exhibited. It is, to be sure, puzzling to know
why the Sudan should linger a thousand years in culture behind the valley of the Seine, but it is no more
puzzling than the fact that the valley of the Thames was
miserably backward as compared with the banks of the

Tiber. Climate, human contact, facilities of communication, and what we call accident have played greater part in the rise of culture among nations: to ignore these and to assert dogmatically that the present distribution of culture is a fair index of the distribution of human ability and desert is to make an assertion for which there is not the slightest scientific warrant.

What the age of Darwin has done is to add to the eighteenth-century idea of individual worth the complementary idea of physical immortality of the human race. And this, far from annulling or contracting the idea of human freedom, rather emphasizes its necessity and eternal possibility—the boundlessness and endlessness of possible human achievement. Freedom has come to mean not individual caprice or aberration but social self-realization in an endless chain of selves, and freedom for such development is not the denial but the central assertion of the revolutionary theory. So, too, the doctrine of human equality passed through the fire of scientific inquiry not obliterated but transfigured; not equality of present attainment but equality of opportunity for unbounded future attainment is the rightful demand of mankind.

What now does the present hegemony of the white races threaten? It threatens by the means of brute force a survival of some of the worst stocks of mankind. It attempts to people the best part of the earth and put in absolute authority over the rest not only, and indeed not mainly, the culture of Europe, but its greed and degradation—not only some representatives of the best stocks of the West End of London, upper New York and the Champs Elysées but also, and in as large, if not larger, numbers, the worst stocks of Whitechapel, the East Side and Montmartre; and it attempts to make the slums of white society in all cases and under all circumstances the superior of any colored group, no matter what its ability or culture; it attempts to put the intelligent, property-holding, efficient Negroes of the South under the heels and at the absolute mercy of such constituencies as Tillman, Vardaman[1] and Jeff Davis represent.

To be sure, this outrageous program of wholesale human degeneration is not outspoken yet save in the back-

ward civilizations of the southern United States, South
Africa and Australia. But its enunciation is listened to
with respect and tolerance in England, Germany and the
northern states and nowhere with more equanimity than
right here in New York by those very persons who accuse
philanthropy with seeking to degenerate white blood by
an infiltration of colored strains. And the average citizen
is voting ships and guns to carry out this program.

This movement gathered force and strength during the
latter half of the nineteenth century and reached its culmination when France, Germany and England and Russia began the partition of China and the East. With
the sudden self-assertion of Japan its wildest dreams collapsed, but it is still today a living, virile, potent force
and motive, and the most subtle and dangerous enemy
of world peace and the dream of human brotherhood.
It has a whole vocabulary of its own: the strong races,
superior peoples, race preservation, the struggle for survival and a peculiar use of the word "white." And by
this it means the right of white men of any kind to club
blacks into submission, to make them surrender their
wealth and the use of their women, and to submit to the
dictation of white men without murmur, for the sake of
being swept off the fairest portions of the earth or held
there in perpetual serfdom or guardianship. Ignoring
the fact that the era of physical struggle for survival
has passed away among human beings and that there
is plenty of room accessible on earth for all, this theory
makes the possession of Krupp guns the main criterion
of mental stamina and moral fitness.

Even armed with this morality of the club and every
advaйtage of modern culture, the white races have been
unable to possess the earth; many signs of degeneracy
have appeared among them; their birthrate is falling,
their average ability is not increasing, their physical stamina is impaired, their social condition is not reassuring,
and their religion is a growing mass of transparent and
self-confessed hypocrisy. Lacking the physical ability to
take possession of the world, they are today fencing in
America, Australia, and South Africa and declaring that

no dark race shall occupy or develop the land which they themselves are unable to use. And all this on the plea that their stock is threatened with deterioration from without, when in fact its most dangerous fate is deterioration from within.

We are in fact today repeating in our intercourse between races all the former evils of class injustice, unequal taxation and rigid caste. Individual nations outgrew these fatal things by breaking down the horizontal barriers between classes. We are bringing them back by seeking to erect vertical barriers between races. Men were told that abolition of compulsory class distinction meant leveling down, degradation, disappearance of culture and genius, and the triumph of the mob. As a matter of fact, it has been the salvation of European civilization. Some deterioration and leveling there was, but it was more than balanced by the discovery of new reservoirs of ability and strength. So today we are told that free racial contact — or "social equality" as southern *patois* has it — means contamination of blood and lowering of ability and culture. It need mean nothing of the sort. Abolition of class distinction does not mean universal intermarriage of stocks, but rather the survival of the fittest by peaceful personal and social selection, a selection all the more effective because free democracy and equality of opportunity allow the best to rise to their rightful place.

The same is true in racial contact. The abolition of the lines of vertical race distinction and their tearing away involves fewer chances of degradation and greater opportunities of human betterment than in the case of class lines. On the other hand, the persistence in racial distinctions spells disaster sooner or later. The earth is growing smaller and more accessible. Race contact will become in the future increasingly inevitable, not only in America, Asia and Africa, but even in Europe. The color line will mean not simply a return to the absurdities of class as exhibited in the sixteenth and seventeenth centuries, but even to the caste of ancient days. This, however, the Japanese, the Chinese, the East Indian and the Negroes are going to resent in just such proportion as they gain the power; and they are gaining the power, and they cannot be kept from gaining more power. The price of repression will then be hypocrisy and slavery and blood.

This is the problem of today, and what is its mighty answer? It is this great word: the cost of liberty is less than the price of repression. The price of repressing the world's darker races is shown in a moral retrogression and economic waste unparalleled since the age of the African slave trade. What would be the cost of liberty? What would be the cost of giving the great stocks of mankind every reasonable help and incentive to self-development — opening the avenues of opportunity freely, spreading knowledge, suppressing war and cheating, and treating men and women as equals the world over whenever and wherever they attain equality? It would cost something. It would cost something in pride and prejudice, for eventually many a white man would be blacking black men's boots; but this cost we may ignore — its greatest cost would be the new problems of racial intercourse and intermarriage which would come to the front. Freedom and equal opportunity in this respect would inevitably bring some intermarriage of whites and yellows and browns and blacks. If such marriages are proven inadvisable how could they be stopped? Easily. We associate with cats and cows but we do not fear intermarriage with them even though they be given all freedom of development. So, too, intelligent human beings can be trained to breed intelligently without the degradation of such of their fellows as they may not wish to breed with. In the southern United States on the contrary it is assumed that unwise marriage can only be stopped by the degradation of the blacks, the classing of their women with prostitutes, the loading the whole race with every badge of public isolation, degradation and contempt and by burning offenders at the stake.

Is this civilization? No. The civilized method of preventing ill-advised marriage lies in the training of mankind in ethics of sex and childbearing. We cannot ensure the survival of the best blood by the public murder and degradation of unworthy suitors, but we can substitute a civilized human selection of husbands and wives which shall ensure the survival of the fittest. Not the methods of the jungle, not even the careless choices of the drawing room, but the thoughtful selection of the schools and laboratory is the ideal of future marriage. This will cost something in ingenuity, self-control, and toleration but it will cost less than forcible repression.

Not only is the cost of repression today large—it is a continually increasing cost, because of the fact that furnished the fatal moral anomaly against which physical slavery could not stand—the free Negro—the Negro who in spite of contempt, discouragement, caste and poverty has put himself on a plane where it is simply impossible to deny that he is by every legitimate measurement the equal of his average white neighbor. The former argument was as I have mentioned that no such class existed. This assertion was persisted in until it became ludicrous. Today the fashion is come to regard this class as exceptional so far as the logic of the Negro problem is concerned, dangerous so far as social peace is concerned, and its existence more than offset by an abnormal number of criminals, degenerates and defectives.

Right here, then, comes the center of the present problem, namely: What is the *truth* about this? What are the real facts? How far is Negro crime due to inherited and growing viciousness and how far to poverty, degradation and systematic oppression?

How far is Negro labor lazy and how far is it the listless victim of systematic theft?

How far is the Negro woman lewd and far the helpless victim of social custom?

How far are Negro children being educated today in the public schools of the South and how far is the effort to curtail that training increasingly successful?

How far are Negroes leaving the farms and rushing to the cities to escape work and how far to escape slavery?

How far is this race designated as Negroes the descendants of African slaves and how far is it descended from the most efficient white blood of the nation?

What does actual physical and social measurement prove as to the status of these descendants of black men?

All these are fundamental questions. Not a single valid
conclusion as to the future can be absolutely insisted upon
without definite skillful scientific answers to these questions
and yet not a single systematic effort to answer these
questions on an adequate scale has been made in these
United States from 1619 to 1909. Not only this but on all
sides opposition ranging from indifference and reluctance to
actual force is almost universal when any attempt to study
the Negro problem adequately is proposed. Yet in spite of
this universal and deliberate ignorance the demand is made
that one line of solution, which a number of good men have
assumed is safe and sane, shall be accepted by everybody
and particularly by thinking black men. The penalty for
not accepting this program is to be dubbed a radical, a
busybody, an impatient dreamer and a dangerous agitator.
Yet this program involves justification of disfranchisement,
the personal humiliation of Jim Crowism, a curtailed and
purposely limited system of education and a virtual acknowledgment of the inevitable and universal inferiority of
black men. And then in the face of this we are asked to
look pleasant and do our very best. I think it is the most
cowardly dilemma that a strong people ever thrust upon the
weak. And I for one have protested and do protest and shall
protest that in my humble opinion the assumption is an
outrageous falsehood dictated by selfishness, cowardice and
greed and for the righteousness of my cause and the proof
of my assertions, I appeal to one arbitrament and one alone
and that is: *the truth.*

Proceedings of the National Negro Conference, New York,
1909, pp. 142-58.

16

RACE PREJUDICE

Early in 1910, Dr. Du Bois was invited to discuss the subject of race prejudice at the Saturday discussion of the Republican Club of New York City. His speech, delivered March 5, 1910, is a brilliant analysis of the economic price the United States paid because of discrimination against people of color.

The more or less theoretical problem of race prejudice today enters largely into the domain of practical politics, and has become of increasing importance in the United States not only because it involves to the Negro in large sections of the country a denial of the principles of democracy, thus engendering passionate feelings against such discrimination, but on account of the unwisdom from an economic standpoint of repressing the colored races.

We have in the United States today a series of rotten boroughs or districts, the political power of which is tremendously and unfairly increased by the wholesale disfranchisement of their voters, until one man in Georgia or Mississippi often exercises as much power in the counsels of the national government as seven men in Massachusetts. Moreover, these southern voters have had their political power increased so enormously, not because of political efficiency (since they are the most illiterate part of the nation), but because strong racial prejudice has led them to deny the right to vote to the black man. There has been some pretense of letting a few competent blacks vote, but as the new senator from Missis-

sippi says boldly, "There is today no such thing as Negro
suffrage in Mississippi and never will be as long as the
white men of the state stand together."

Thus a second political complication enters. The all-pow-
erful rump of the voting population of the South cannot
today consider the merits of any political question presented
to them. They must vote always and simply to keep Negroes
down. Outside of all questions of party, such a denial of
the fundamental principles of democracy is dangerous to
the nation. It means that there are certain parts of the
country where reason cannot be applied to the settlement of
great political questions. Such weak spots in the political
body are sure to become the seat of disease, and so long as
the race prejudice in the South shows its result in such dis-
organization of government and disfranchisement of a
large part of the working class and in an unequal balance
of political power, as compared with the rest of the nation,
just so long race prejudice is bound to be a burning
question of practical politics.

The question, however, is not simply political; it is not
simply the old question of the Negro's right to vote—a
problem which has been with us so long that we are disposed to give it up in despair. Today the problem is becoming more and more economic. We are seeing arise in
the South two great groups of laborers: one white and one
black, one with the power of the ballot and one disfranchised. That the disfranchisement of the black workingmen
is practically complete there can be no reasonable doubt.
These two groups of workingmen are coming more and
more into economic competition, and the industrial education
of the Negro is bound to increase this competition. The result is a situation which is being taken advantage of by two
different kinds of selfish interests. The politician in the South
who is out of a job finds it more and more to his interest
to stir up the passions of the white workingman who has
the ballot by appealing to the grossest and worst instincts
of race prejudice, and by representing all the present and
possible economic ills of the white workingman as due to
his black competitor. We have already seen in the South
instance after instance of demagogues arising with widespread political power by these means, and we have known

the horror of the Atlanta riot as a sort of firstfruits of this newer economic race danger.

On the other hand, the exploiting capitalist is also tempted to transmute race prejudice in the coin of the realm. He says to his white laborers, "I am not in business for my health; I seek the cheapest competent labor. Larger and larger numbers of blacks are demanding work at low wages; if you are dissatisfied and continue to make trouble and demand too much, I will replace you by black men." He turns to his black laborers. "You are lazy and incompetent—unless you work harder and stop complaining, I will replace you with white men." This again leads each class to regard the other as the chief cause of low wages and unfair treatment; and the situation in the South affects the labor problem over the whole nation, and is destined to affect it more and more. The high level of wages in the North cannot entirely withstand the competition of the lower level of wages in the South, and fight as the white laborer may at once to keep up wages and to exclude the black man from his union, he is bound to lose; for he is fighting black men, while black men are fighting starvation and must consequently fight harder. So that here again we have a result of race prejudice which is bringing us face to face with a great labor problem.

But the results of race prejudice do not stop even here. The United States is today going through a great economic crisis. It is changing from being a country which raises and exports foodstuffs and imports its manufactured articles, into a country which largely consumes its own foodstuffs and exports its manufactures. Now the export of food from the United States brought us into contact with European civilization, but the export of manufactured articles is bringing us into contact with the darker world, with Asia, Africa, the West Indies and South America. In our endeavor, however, to open markets for trade in these countries and with these peoples, we are being brought face to face with the unpleasant fact that America is not liked in the darker world; she has gone out of her way to insult many of these people. She has enslaved "Niggers," sneered at "Dagos," insulted Chinese and Japanese, and found no words too contemptuous to express

her feeling for the "mongrel" races of Central and Southern America. Under such circumstances, our invasion of
the world market must be under a great moral handicap.
There can be no doubt but that a large part of our difficulty in getting South American trade is because of our
free exhibition of racial prejudice. In China and the East
our prejudices have not helped our economic campaign,
and the future is ominous.

Viewing then the situation calmly and judicially, it must
frankly be confessed that race prejudice is costing the
United States heavily; it is costing us certain fundamental
principles of democratic government, peace and development in the labor world, and enhanced difficulty of getting
a world market for our goods.

Facing now such a cost, it is reasonable to ask, why
are we paying it? What return are we getting out of it?
Is it really worthwhile? Most people when asked about
their prejudices as to race say simply: it is a matter of
personal like or dislike; some people like one kind of
people and some another, similar to a preference for one
sort of food over another. The difficulty is, however, that
human antipathies between men and men seldom remain
at this comparatively harmless stage. The preferences take
on a vitality and warmth, a value and importance that
make us not satisfied to indulge our likes and dislikes,
but to wish to force them on our neighbors, and to this
end we are nearly always driven, or think we are driven,
to use three weapons of offense, which are of tremendous
import in world history. These are: personal insult, persecution, and repression.

We forcibly keep certain men from occupying certain
positions or entering certain careers. We deliberately per-
secute some people by means, for instance, of Jim Crow
cars or other discriminations, or we heap personal insult
and ridicule upon them. It may be admitted that there
are perhaps times in this world when it is necessary and
defensible to take a human being by the throat, slowly
choke his life out and throw his dead carcass to one side;
or if we are not prepared personally to go to that extreme,
it is, I am told, at times justifiable to render the life of
certain persons so uncomfortable that they will eliminate

themselves; and finally it certainly seems to many as though personal insult was now and then necessary to repress some sorts of undesirable men; but despite all this, every civilized being hesitates and shudders at the use of these three awful weapons; and they hesitate because these weapons are dangerous things, not simply deadening, corroding, fatal to the victims, but doubly dangerous to those who get into the habit of using them.

From the use of insult grows the arrogant, overbearing nation which so often blindly misses the way of truth; from the bigotry of persecution grows the dead rot of mental death, and from war and murder come national as well as individual death. Worse than that, these weapons of race prejudice often fail to effect their object. Doubtless objectionable individuals and groups have been persecuted and insulted out of existence or simply massacred. But not always. Often with fierce persistence they have lived, directly or indirectly — consciously or unconsciously — to avenge their wrongs. At least these weapons of offense are so despicable and their efficiency so questionable that before we continue their use, ought we not to ask ourselves frankly: just what is it that we really want to accomplish in this matter of racial prejudice?

I think that most people would say upon first thought that they want to be able to live in a world which is in most respects according to their liking and according to their idea of fitness, both in persons and in things; but so soon as such a desire is expressed, it must be said plainly, without further argument, that such a consummation is largely impossible. The simplest and most exclusive club cannot in its membership suit all the people included. We must always come more or less in contact, even in intimate contact, with people whom we do not like. This is true of all ages, but it is especially true in the modern world.

A few centuries ago the world existed in such airtight compartments that groups could isolate themselves and live to themselves. Today we are demanding vociferously the policy of the Open Door.[1] We are demanding, now chiefly for economic reasons, but also in part for political and social reasons, a worldwide contact of men with men.

It is expressed today in the right of white men to go anywhere they choose and be treated with consideration and
respect. It will be expressed tomorrow in the right of the
colored races to return the visits.

Under no easily conceivable circumstances can the future
world be peopled simply with one of the present social
groups or with one of the existing races. Some people, to
be sure, dream of a future white world. A glance at any
map or newspaper will prove that this is, to say the least,
highly improbable. Today the human race throughout the
world contains a vast numerical preponderance of colored
peoples and the population among these colored races is
probably increasing faster than among the whites, so that
in the future the aggregate of the black and yellow races
may outnumber the white race.

Many people would frankly acknowledge this. They
would expect a future world of black and yellow and
white men. But they say: we wish these several races to
be kept in their places.

Here again there arise difficulties. What are the respective
places of these races? Is the easily assumed hierarchy
composed by ruling white, servile black, and docile yellow
men really the last word in social evolution? History is
not reassuring on this point, present tendencies are disconcerting, and science is helplessly spreading its hands.
Wise men acknowledge that it is perfectly possible that
black and yellow men may yet reach and surpass white
civilization. This may not seem probable but in human
history the improbable has often happened.

But let all this be as it may, certain it is that if by
natural constitution the great races of men arrange themselves in a hierarchy of ability, efficiency and development, then no such social weapons as are now used by
racial prejudice are necessary to reinforce natural law.
Education will keep the superior races from degeneracy
by intermarriage far better than organized insult; persecution will be quite unnecessary to eliminate such races
as are unable to survive under civilized conditions; and
repression of ambition and ability will be attended to by
the law of social gravity much more effectively than by
"Jim Crow" legislation. In fine, why should we threaten

the efficiency of government, the development of industry and the peace of the world by imperfect and questionable human devices?

So soon as the prejudiced are forced into this inevitable dilemma, then the real bitterness and indefensibleness of their attitude is apt to be revealed; they say bluntly that they do not care what "Niggers," "Dagos," "Chinks," or "Japs" may be capable of—they do not like them and they propose to keep such folk in a place of permanent inferiority to the white race—by peaceful policy if possible, but brute force if necessary. And when a group, a nation or a world assumes this attitude, it is handling dynamite. *There is in this world no such force as the force of a man determined to rise.* The human soul cannot be permanently chained.

Is it not then of supreme importance that here in America we refuse to aid and abet any such attempt and that we refuse to try to hold back by insult, persecution and repression those dark masses of human beings who, though beaten to their knees and bloody with blows, are still doggedly determined to be men?

In view of all this it is a matter not simply of politics but of the widest and broadest statesmanship, of economic foresight and deepest religious thought to see that race prejudice in the United States is combated and corrected and lessened.

Race Prejudice. An Address by Dr. W. E. Burghardt Du Bois, delivered at The Saturday Discussion of the Republican Club, New York, March 5, 1910, under the auspices of the Committee on National Affairs. Pamphlet issued by the Republican Club of the City of New York. (Copy in Schomburg Library.)

17

THE NEGRO PROBLEM

A conference dealing with the general relations existing between West and East was held in London from July 26 to 29, 1911. "The object of the Congress," declared the circular issued by the Executive Council, "will be to discuss, in the light of science and the modern conscience, the general relations subsisting between the peoples of the West and those of the East, between so-called white and so-called colored peoples, with a view to encouraging between them a fuller understanding, the most friendly feelings, and a heartier cooperation." The Universal Races Congress, as the gathering was called, met at the University of London. The Sixth Session was entitled "The Modern Conscience in Relation to Racial Questions (The Negro and the American Indian)." Papers were read by Sir Harry H. Johnston on "The World Position of the Negro and Negroid," by J. Tengo Jabavu on "Native Races of South Africa," by Dr. Mojola Agebibi on "The West African Problem," by Dr. Frances Hoggan on "The Negro Problem in Relation to White Women," by Dr. Charles A. Eastman on "The North American Indian," by Dr. Jean Baptiste on "The Metis, or Half-Breeds, of Brazil," and by Dr. W. E. B. Du Bois on "The Negro Race in the United States of America." For Du Bois's evaluation of the significance of the Universal Races Congress, see his article, "The First Universal Races Congress," Independent, LXXI, August 24, 1901, pp. 460-61. Du Bois's address was divided into seven sections. The first dealt with "The Slave Trade"; the second covered "Growth and Physique of the Negro-American Population,"

*with many statistical tables; the third, "Social History,"
traced briefly the history of the American Negro from the
era of Spanish explorations to the post-Reconstruction era
and the emergence of white supremacy in the South; the
fourth, "Social Condition of the Negro-American," was
again a statistical analysis; the fifth dealt with "Religion,"
and the sixth section covered "Crime." The seventh and
final section was entitled "The Negro Problem." It is this
section which is reprinted below.*

The American Negro problem is the question of the
future status of the ten million Americans of Negro descent.
It must be remembered that these persons are Americans
by birth and descent. They represent, for the most part,
four or five American-born generations, being in that respect
one of the most American groups in the land. Moreover, the
Negroes are not barbarians. They are, as a mass, poor
and ignorant; but they are growing rapidly in both wealth
and intelligence, and larger and larger numbers of them
demand the rights and privileges of American citizens as a
matter of undoubted desert.

Today these rights are largely denied. In order to realize
the disabilities under which Negroes suffer regardless of
education, wealth, or degree of white blood, we may divide
the United States into three districts: (a) the southern South,
containing 75 percent of the Negroes; (b) the border states,
containing 15 percent of the Negroes; (c) the North and
West, containing 10 percent of the Negroes.

In the southern South, by law or custom, Negroes:

1. Cannot vote, or their votes are neutralized by fraud.

2. Must usually live in the least desirable districts.

3. Receive very low wages.

4. Are, in the main, restricted to menial occupations or the
lower grades of skilled labor and cannot expect preferment
or promotion.

5. Cannot by law intermarry with whites.

6. Cannot join white churches or attend white colleges or
join white cultural organizations.

7. Cannot be accommodated at hotels and restaurants or
in any place of public entertainment.

8. Receive a distinct standard of justice in the courts and are especially liable to mob violence.

9. Are segregated so far as possible in every walk of life—in railway stations, railway trains, streetcars, lifts [elevators], etc., and usually made to pay equal prices for inferior accommodations.

10. Are often unable to protect their homes from invasion, their women from insult, and their savings from exploitation.

11. Are taxed for public facilities like parks and libraries, which they may not enter.

12. Are given meager educational facilities, and sometimes none at all.

13. Are liable to personal insult unless they appear as servants or menials or show deference to white folks by yielding the road, etc.

To many of these disabilities there are personal and local exceptions. In cities, for instance, the chance to defend the home, get an education and somewhat better wages is greater, and mob violence less frequent. Then there are always some personal exceptions—cases of help and courtesy, of justice in the courts, and of good schools. These are, however, exceptions, and, as a rule, all Negroes, no matter what their training, possessions, or desert, are subjected to the above disabilities. Within the limits of these caste restrictions there is much goodwill and kindliness between the races, and especially much personal charity and help.

The 15 percent of the Negro population living in the border states suffer a little less restriction. They have some right of voting, are better able to defend their homes, and are less discriminated against in the expenditure of public funds. In the cities their schools are much better, and public insult is less noticeable.

In the North the remaining 10 percent of the Negro population is legally undiscriminated against and may attend schools and churches and vote without restriction. As a matter of fact, however, they are made in most communities to feel that they are undesirable. They are either refused accommodation at hotels, restaurants, and theaters, or received reluctantly. Their treatment in churches and general cultural organizations is such that few join. Intermarriage with whites brings ostracism and public disfavor, and in courts Negroes often suffer undeservedly. Common labor and menial work is open to them, but avenues above this in skilled labor or professions (save as they serve their own race) are extremely difficult to enter, and there is much discrimination in wages. Mob violence has become not infrequent in later years.

There are here also many exceptional cases — instances of preferment in the industrial and political world; and there is always some little social intercourse. On the whole, however, the Negro in the North is an ostracized person who finds it difficult to make a good living or spend his earnings with pleasure.

Under these circumstances there has grown up a Negro world in America which has its own economic and social life, its churches, schools, and newpapers; its literature, public opinion, and ideals. This life is largely unnoticed and unknown even in America, and travelers miss it almost entirely.

The average American in the past made at least pretense of excusing the discrimination against Negroes on the ground of their ignorance and poverty and their tendencies to crime and disease. While the mass is still poor and unlettered, it is admitted by all today that the Negro is rapidly developing a larger and larger class of intelligent, property-holding men of Negro descent; notwithstanding this, more and more race lines are being drawn which involved the treatment of civilized men in an uncivilized manner. Moreover, the crux of the question today is not merely a matter of social eligibility. For many generations the American Negro will lack the breeding and culture which the most satisfactory human intercourse requires. But in America the discrimination against Negroes goes beyond this, to the point of public discourtesy, civic disability, injustice in the courts, and economic restriction.

The argument of those who uphold this discrimination is based primarily on race. They claim that the inherent characteristics of the Negro race show its essential inferiority and the impossibility of incorporating its descendants into the American nation. They admit that there are excep-

tions to the rule of inferiority, but claim that these but prove
the rule. They say that amalgamation of the races would be
fatal to civilization, and they advocate therefore a strict
caste system for Negroes, segregating them by occupation
and privileges and to some extent by dwelling place, to the
end that they (*a*) submit permanently to an inferior position,
or (*b*) die out, or (*c*) migrate.

This philosophy the thinking Negroes and a large number of white friends vigorously combat. They claim that
the racial differences between white and black in the United
States offer no essential barrier to the races living together
on terms of mutual respect and helpfulness. They deny, on
the one hand, that the large amalgamation of the races
already accomplished has produced degenerates, in spite
of the unhappy character of these unions; on the other
hand, they deny any desire to lose the identity of either
race through intermarriage. They claim that it should be
possible for a civilized black man to be treated as an
American citizen without harm to the republic, and that
the modern world must learn to treat colored races as
equals if it expects to advance.

They claim that the Negro race in America has more
than vindicated its ability to assimilate modern culture.
Negro blood has furnished thousands of soldiers to defend
the flag in every war in which the United States has been
engaged. They are a most important part of the economic
strength of the nation, and they have furnished a number
of men of ability in politics, literature, and art, as, for
instance, Banneker, the mathematician; Phillis Wheatley,
the poet; Lemuel Haynes, the theologian; Ira Aldridge,
the actor; Frederick Douglass, the orator; H. O. Tanner,
the artist; B. T. Washington, the educator; Granville Woods,
the inventor; Kelly Miller, the writer; Rosamond Johnson
and Will Cook, the musical composers; Dunbar, the poet;
and Chesnutt, the novelist. Many other Americans, whose
Negro blood has not been openly acknowledged, have
reached high distinction. The Negroes claim, therefore,
that a discrimination which was originally based on certain social conditions is rapidly becoming a persecution
based simply on race prejudice, and that no republic built
on caste can survive.

At the meeting of two such diametrically opposed arguments, it was natural that councils of compromise should appear, and it was also natural that a nation whose economic triumphs have been so noticeable as those of the United States should seek an economic solution to the race question. More and more in the last twenty years, the businessmen's solution of the race problem has been the development of the resources of the South. Coincident with the rise of this policy came the prominence of Mr. B. T. Washington. Mr. Washington was convinced that race prejudice in America was so strong and the economic position of the freedmen's sons so weak that the Negro must give up or postpone his ambitions for full citizenship and bend all his energies to industrial efficiency and the accumulation of wealth. Mr. Washington's idea was that eventually when the dark man was thoroughly established in the industries and had accumulated wealth, he could demand further rights and privileges. This philosophy has become very popular in the United States, both among whites and blacks.

The white South hastened to welcome this philosophy. They thought it would take the Negro out of politics, tend to stop agitation, make the Negro a satisfied laborer, and eventually convince him that he could never be recognized as the equal of the white man. The North began to give large sums for industrial training, and hoped in this way to get rid of a serious social problem.

From the beginning of this campaign, however, a large class of Negroes and many whites feared this program. They not only regarded it as a program which was a dangerous compromise, but they insisted that to stop fighting the essential wrong of race prejudice, just at the time, was to encourage it.

This was precisely what happened. Mr. Washington's program was announced at the Atlanta Exposition in 1895. Since that time four states have disfranchised Negroes, dozens of cities and towns have separated the races on streetcars, 1,250 Negroes have been publicly lynched without trial, and serious race riots have taken place in nearly every southern state and several northern states, Negro public-school education has suffered a setback, and many private schools have been forced to retrench severely or to close. On the whole, race prejudice has, during the last fifteen years, enormously increased.

This has been coincident with the rapid and substantial advance of Negroes in wealth, education, and morality, and the two movements of race prejudice and Negro advance have led to an anomalous and unfortunate situation. Some, white and black, seek to minimize and ignore the flaming prejudice in the land, and emphasize many acts of friendliness on the part of the white South, and the advance of the Negro. Others, on the other hand, point out that silence and sweet temper are not going to settle this dangerous social problem, and that manly protest and the publication of the whole truth is alone adequate to arouse the nation to its great danger.

Moreover, many careful thinkers insist that, under the circumstances, the "businessmen's" solution of the race problem is bound to make trouble: if the Negroes become good, cheap laborers, warranted not to strike or complain, they will arouse all the latent prejudice of the white workingmen whose wages they bring down. If, on the other hand, they are to be really educated as men, and not as "hands," then they need, as a race, not only industrial training, but also a supply of well-educated, intellectual leaders and professional men for a group so largely deprived of contact with the cultural leaders of the whites. Moreover, the best thought of the nation is slowly recognizing the fact that to try to educate a workingman, and not to educate the man, is impossible. If the United States wants intelligent Negro laborers, it must be prepared to treat them as intelligent men.

This countermovement of intelligent men, white and black, against the purely economic solution of the race problem, has been opposed by powerful influences both North and South. The South represents it as malicious sectionalism, and the North misunderstands it as personal dislike and envy of Mr. Washington. Political pressure has been brought to bear, and this insured a body of colored political leaders who do not agitate for Negro rights. At the same time, a chain of Negro newspapers was established to advocate the dominant philosophy.

Despite this well-intentioned effort to keep down the agitation of the Negro question and mollify the colored people, the problem has increased in gravity. The result is the present widespread unrest and dissatisfaction. Honest Americans know that present conditions are wrong and cannot last; but they face, on the one hand, the seemingly implacable prejudice of the South, and, on the other hand, the undoubted rise of the Negro challenging that prejudice. The attempt to reconcile these two forces is becoming increasingly futile, and the nation simply faces the question: are we willing to do justice to a dark race despite our prejudices? Radical suggestions of wholesale segregation or deportation of the race have now and then been suggested; but the cost in time, effort, money, and economic disturbance is too staggering to allow serious consideration. The South, with all its race prejudice, would rather fight than lose its great black laboring force, and in every walk of life throughout the nation the Negro is slowly forcing his way. There are some signs that the prejudice in the South is not immovable, and now and then voices of protest and signs of liberal thought appear there. Whether at last the Negro will gain full recognition as a man, or be utterly crushed by prejudice and superior numbers, is the present Negro problem of America.

G. Spiller, editor, *Papers on Inter-Racial Problems Communicated to the First Universal Races Congress Held at the University of London July 26-29, 1911*, pp. 360-64.

18

HOW TO CELEBRATE
THE SEMICENTENNIAL OF THE
EMANCIPATION PROCLAMATION

On January 1, 1913, the fiftieth anniversary of the Emancipation Proclamation occurred. In advance of this event, a special committee of the U.S. Senate held hearings on a planned exposition to celebrate the event. Dr. Du Bois appeared before the committee on February 2, 1912, and presented his views on what type of exposition should be prepared. For a man who was often accused of being only a scholar and with little practical talent, he amazed the committee with his detailed presentation. It is interesting to note that about the time the Encyclopedia Britannica *was asserting that Africa was a continent without a history, Dr. Du Bois was emphasizing that special attention should be paid in the exposition to the contributions of Africa to world civilization.*

In 1913 the NAACP celebrated the fiftieth anniversary of the Emancipation Proclamation with a great pageant and exposition prepared by Dr. Du Bois and featuring his historical pageant of the Negro race, "The Star of Ethiopia." Thirty thousand people visited the exposition in New York City.

I wanted to say a word to the committee about the kind of exposition we would like to have. I think a committee like this must be a little chary of expositions, because they have grown so enormous in size and they cost so much money. It has been in our minds that we could organize an exposition in this case upon a lot of new lines, distinctly educational, for the people of the United States, both for the colored people and for the white people. As a center of those exhibits it has been thought we should have a section devoted to a scheme which should be the same exhibits, something on the order of the child welfare that the committee of women have been doing — or tuberculosis, and so on — that this main scheme should try to show the condition of the colored people throughout the United States. For instance, it should have something of the African background, and in this department, and in all departments, we could make use of all the different things that can be shown to illustrate the concrete things and spiritual things which affect the colored people. For instance, maps and charts and models and mechanical figures of various sizes, and marble, pictures, and perhaps, photographs could be shown.

I presume most of you know that in nearly all of the great countries of the world there is an African exhibit. The African museums in London, Paris, and Berlin are sources in each of those cities of great educational value, and there is very little information of the sort in the United States. Something might be done to get together the things which show the wonderful mechanical genius of certain African tribes, especially their work in iron and in cloth. Then, in the second place, the question of the development of the Negro race throughout the world, and the distribution of the Negroes in the United States could be shown by relief maps with groups of figures showing this distribution, and movable figures, perhaps, showing the migration.

Then the question of the physique of the Negro could be shown. Very little has been done in this country to show what is the typical Negro physique. A great deal could be done by photographs and by plaster casts. Then the question of health and disease could be covered. My idea is that this exhibit should be a truthful exhibit. It should not be simply a thing that would be exaggerated in any way. It should be a real picture so far as possible of the condition of the Negro people, so that not only would it show the progress but also the dangers and the diseases to which they are liable.

Then the question of occupation could be covered. Of

course, that would be one of the most interesting parts of the exhibit. This could be shown perhaps by mechanical figures of correct relative size showing the occupations of the Negroes and the value of their services in a relative manner in all the different departments in which the Negro takes a considerable part.

Then the matter of education has been spoken of. We could have models and charts showing illiteracy, and conditions in cities, and photographs of institutions, and especially photographs and models showing the work of the graduates of institutions as the work of the institution filters down to the actual mass of the people. In no department has the Negro shown more genius for modern organization than in his churches, and the models of churches and of the work in churches could be shown. The younger Mr. Wright here is a representative of one of the great churches, and there is a great publishing house, as he says, in Nashville, Tennessee, and there are several other organizations. That work could be shown and a person could grasp it and it would show the tremendous development that has taken place in that line.

Then in the matter of civics — I suppose most of you would be surprised to know the number of Negro towns and quarters throughout the United States more or less organized as independent entities. Exhibits could be had showing those towns and the workings of those towns which would be of great interest. Then there would be, of course, charts and diagrams and models showing the organized life, the business life, the social life, the work of social uplift among the Negro people. There are orphan asylums and there are a good number of hospitals and homes. The family life, the interior of the homes could be shown.

And then the question of art, which has been mentioned. Negro music could be shown, and photographs of art, and other work, and a collection of Negro books. There are something like 200 weekly newspapers. And, finally, statistics of crimes and of delinquencies could be shown. In this way, it seems to me, we might build up a comparatively small central exhibit, and then around that could come the various voluntary exhibits, which are always sent to expositions of this sort. Then there could be congresses held in connection with it—congresses on agriculture and on industry, on education, on health, on music.

There should be, of course, awards and medals. Then there might be a historical pageant. I have been looking up the history of the Negro, and it is interesting indeed to know what a continuous history would show in connection with the development of the Negro from the time of the Egyptian civilization down through the Negro kingdoms in the Sudan and the migration of the Bantu tribes from North Africa to South Africa; and, as you know, the Negro has been connected with almost every event in American history. Then, finally, our idea is that this central exhibit could be kept or established as a permanent exhibit and placed in a permanent museum. Perhaps from time to time it might be moved from place to place, where people who wanted to could obtain exact information concerning the Negro in a definite form.

With these ideas it seems to me that we could have an exposition which would not be costly—and we are not asking for very much money—that would be educational, and something that we could pay for with the amount of money that we got from the government and which we could raise among ourselves.

Hearings on "Semicentennial Anniversary of Act of Emancipation," *Senate Report No. 31,* Sixty-Second Congress, Second Session.

19

DISFRANCHISEMENT

The following address was delivered by Dr. Du Bois at the 1912 Convention of the National Woman Suffrage Association and was published that same year by the Association. Here Dr. Du Bois coupled the question of disfranchisement of Negroes with the disfranchisement of women and showed his dislike for the concept of male supremacy.

The mere fact that democratic government has spread in the past and is still spreading does not prove that those concerned in its spread always realize the broader foundations of the argument that supports it. Usually nations are dealing with concrete groups whose enfranchisement is advocated and the arguments against the step fall under these categories:

 a. The persons in the group are too ignorant to vote intelligently.

 b. The persons are too inexperienced to be trusted with so great responsibility.

 c. The persons would misuse the privilege.

 d. They do not need the ballot.

 e. They do not want the right to vote.

The obvious assumptions behind these objections are that only the intelligent should have the right to vote; that voters should possess some technical knowledge of the government; that only those should have the franchise who do not misuse it for selfish or other ends, and who need the ballot for their good and are anxious to have it.

No sooner, however, do we express these qualifications

than it is manifest that these are not such qualifications as one could reasonably require. They are in reality arguments addressed to the self-interest of the present rulers and calculated to show that sharing their prerogative with another group will not disturb or prejudice their present power and perquisites.

While it is manifestly the part of practical political wisdom thus to cajole the present ruler, the weapon used is dangerous and the argument is only partially valid. The real underlying and eternally valid arguments for extending as far as possible the participation of human beings in their own government must lie deeper than these phrases and be more carefully framed. If this is done then the advance of democracy will be made easier and more effective since we can scrutinize the essential facts and not be distracted by immaterial suggestions.

What is then the essential argument for extending the right to vote? We may possibly reach it by clearing away the misapprehensions that lurk in the arguments mentioned above.

For instance, we say easily, "The ignorant ought not to vote." We mean to say, "There should be in the state, no grown person of sound mind who is not intelligent enough to vote." These two statements may seem to be essentially the same, but they have vastly different implications. In the one case we cast the ignorant aside. They ought not to vote and the implication is that it is their fault. Their interests, we assume will be looked after by others and if they are not, we acknowledge no responsibility. On the other hand, if we stress the responsibility of the state for the education of its citizens as prior to political rights, then the conclusion is that if a state allows its citizens to grow up in ignorance it ought to suffer from an ignorant ballot: that it is the threat of ignorant voters that makes good schools.

The second argument that experience is a necessary prerequisite to voting is absurd. According to this we should have no new voters, unless we assume that the capacity to rule is hereditary. Such assumptions have been made in the past with regard to certain races and one sex. It can scarcely be said, however, that any adequate proof exists which proves that only Englishmen or only persons of the male sex are capable of learning to take part in democratic government. When we consider that the civilized world today is being ruled by classes who were pronounced utterly incapable of self-rule or of being trained for self-rule a century ago, we must conclude that the ability to rule is, on the whole, a matter of individual social training and that consequently there must always be a part of the body politic without experience who must be trained by the others. In voting as in other matters we learn by doing. It is to be expected that every new voting class and every new democracy will make its costly and ridiculous mistakes — will pass through demagoguery, extravagance, "boss" rule, bribery and the like; but it is through such experience that voters learn to rule and the cost although vast is not excessive if the end is finally gained.

Thus we see that ignorance is a warning and a public responsibility rather than a permanent excuse for disfranchisement, save in the case of the small number who cannot be educated; that inexperience can only be cured by experience and is consequently no reason for disfranchisement; and that misuse of the ballot is perhaps the most effective way of teaching its right use.

There are, however, people who insist on regarding the franchise not as a necessity for the many but as the privilege of the few. They say of persons and classes, "They do not need the ballot." This is often said of women. It is argued that everything that women might do for themselves with the ballot can be done for them; that they have influence and friends "at court," and that their enfranchisement would simply double the number of ballots. So, too, we are told that Negroes can have done for them by others all that they could possibly do for themselves with the ballot, and much more because the whites are more intelligent.

Further than this it is argued that many of the disfranchised recognize this. "Women do not want the ballot," has been a very effective counter war cry; so much so that many a man has taken refuge in the declaration, "When they want to vote, why then—."

Such phrases show so curious a misapprehension of the foundations of the argument for democracy that this argument must be continually restated and emphasized. We must remember that if the theory of democracy is correct, the right to vote is not merely a privilege, not simply a method of meeting the needs of a particular group, and least of all a matter of recognized want or desire. Democracy is a method of realizing the broadest measure of justice to all human beings. The world has in the past attempted various methods of attaining this end, most of which can be summed up in three categories:

The method of the benevolent tyrant

    "   "   "   " select few

    "   "   "   " excluded groups.

The method of entrusting the government of a people to a strong ruler has great advantages when the ruler combines strength with ability, unselfish devotion to the public good and knowledge of what that good calls for. Such a combination is, however, rare and the selection of the right ruler is very difficult. To leave the selection to force is to put a premium on physical strength, chance and intrigue; to make the selection a matter of birth simply transfers the real power from sovereign to selected minister. Inevitably the choice of real rulers must fall on electors.

Then comes the problem. Who shall elect? The earlier answer was: a select few, such as the wise, the best born, the able. Many people assume that it was corruption that made such aristocracies fail. By no means. The best and most effective aristocracy, like the best monarchy, suffered from lack of knowledge; they did not know or understand the needs of the people, and they could not find out, for in the last analysis only the man himself, however humble, knows his own condition. He may not know how to remedy it, he may not realize just what is the matter, but he knows when something hurts, and he alone knows how that hurt feels. Or if, sunk below feeling or comprehension or complaint, he does not even know that he is hurt, God help his country, for it not only lacks knowledge, but has destroyed some of the sources of knowledge!

So soon as a nation discovers that it holds in the heads and hearts of its individual citizens the vast mine of knowl-

edge out of which it may build a just government, then
more and more it calls those citizens to select their rulers
and judge the justice of their acts.

Even here, however, the temptation is to ask only for
the wisdom of citizens of a certain grade, or those of
recognized worth. Continually some classes are tacitly or
expressly excluded. Thus women have been regularly
excluded from modern democracy, because of custom,
because of the persistent theory of female subjection, and
because it was argued that their husbands or other male
folk would look to their interests. Now manifestly most
husbands, fathers and brothers will so far as they know
how, or so far as they realize women's needs look after
them. But remember that the foundation of the argument
is that in the last analysis only the sufferer knows his
sufferings, and that no state can be strong which excludes
from its expressed wisdom, the knowledge possessed by
mothers, wives and daughters. Certainly we have but to
view the unsatisfactory relations of the sexes the world
over and the problem of children, to realize how desperately we need this excluded wisdom.

The same argument applies to other excluded groups:
if a race like the Negro race is excluded from the ballot,
then so far as that race is a part of the economic and
social organization of the land, the feeling and the experience of that race is absolutely necessary to the realization
of the broadest justice for all citizens. Or if the "submerged
tenth" be excluded, then again there is lost experience of
untold value, and the submerged must be raised rapidly
to a plane where they can speak for themselves.

In the same way and for the same reason children must
be educated, insanity prevented and only those put under
guardianship of others who can in no way be trained to
speak for themselves.

The real argument for democracy is then that in the
people we have the real source of that endless life and
unbounded wisdom which the real ruler of men must
have. A given people today may not be intelligent, but
through a democratic government that recognizes not
only the worth of the individual to himself but the worth
of his feelings and experiences to all, they can educate

not only the individual unit, but generation after generation until they accumulate vast stores of wisdom. Democracy alone is the method of storing the whole experience
of the race for the benefit of the future, and if democracy
tries to exclude women or Negroes or the poor or any
class because of innate characteristics which do not interfere with intelligence then that democracy cripples itself
and belies its name.

From this point of view we can easily see the weakness
and strength of current criticism of extensions of the ballot.
It is the business of a modern government to see to it,
first, that the number of the ignorant within its bounds is
reduced to the very smallest number. *Secondly*, it is the
duty of every such government to extend as quickly as
possible the number of grown persons of mature age
who can vote. Such possible voters must be regarded not
as sharers of a limited treasure, but as sources of new
national wisdom and strength.

The addition of the new wisdom, the new points of view
and new interests must of course be, from time to time,
bewildering and confusing. Today those who have a voice
in the body politic have expressed their wishes and sufferings. The result has been a more or less effective balancing
of their conflicting interests. The appearance of new interests and complaints means disarrangement and confusion
to the older equilibrium. But this is not in itself evil — it
is the inevitable preliminary step to that larger equilibrium
in which the interests of no human soul will be neglected.
These interests will not, surely, be all fully realized but they
will be recognized and given as full weight as the conflicting interests of others will allow. The problem of government thereafter will be to reduce the necessary conflict of
human interests to the minimum.

From such a point of view one easily sees the strength
of the demand for the ballot on the part of certain disfranchised classes. When women ask for the ballot they
are asking not a privilege but a necessity. You may not
see the necessity; you may easily argue that women do
not need to vote. Indeed the women themselves in considerable number may feel the same. Nevertheless they do
need the ballot. They need it to right the balance of a

world sadly awry because of its brutal neglect of the rights
of women and children. With the best will and knowledge
no man can know women's wants as well as women themselves. To disfranchise them is deliberately to turn from
knowledge and grope in ignorance.

So too with American Negroes: the South continually insists that a benevolent guardianship of whites over blacks
is the ideal thing. They assume that white people not only
know better what Negroes need than Negroes themselves,
but are anxious to supply those needs. As a result, instead
of knowledge they grope in ignorance and helplessness.
They cannot "understand" the Negro, they cannot protect
him from cheating and lynching and in general instead
of loving guardianship, we see anarchy and exploitation.
If the Negro could speak for himself in the South instead
of being spoken for: if he could defend himself instead of
having to depend on the chance sympathy of white citizens, how much healthier growth of democracy the South
would have.

It is not for a moment to be assumed that enfranchising
women would not cost something. It would for many years
confuse our politics. It would change the composition of
family and social life. It would admit to the ballot thousands of inexperienced persons unable to vote intelligently.
Above all it would interfere with some of the present pre-
rogatives of men and probably for some time to come
annoy them considerably.

So, too, Negro enfranchisement meant Reconstruction
with its theft, bribery and incompetency. It would mean
today that black men in the South would have to be
treated with consideration, have their wishes more respect-
ed and their manhood recognized. Every white southerner
who wants peons beneath him, who believes in hereditary
menials and a privileged aristocracy, or who hates certain
races because of their characteristics, would resent this.

Notwithstanding this, if America is ever to become a
government built on the broadest justice to every citizen,
then every citizen must be enfranchised. There may be
temporary exclusions until the ignorant or their children
are taught, or to avoid too sudden an influx of inexpe-

rienced voters. But such exclusions can be but temporary if justice is to prevail.

While many of those seeking enfranchisement recognize the broad demand of justice for all human beings which underlies their argument, they are often tempted by the exigencies of the situation to ignore the application of those underlying principles to any but themselves, or even to deny and attack the justice of equally just demands for the ballot. The advocates of woman suffrage have continually been in great danger of asking the ballot not because they are citizens, but because they occupy a certain social position, are of a certain grade of intelligence, or are "white." Continually it has been said in America, "If paupers and Negroes vote why not college-bred women of wealth and position?" The assumption is that such a woman has superior right to have her interests represented in the nation and that Negroes and paupers have few rights which society leaders are bound to respect. So, too, many colored people, in arguing their own enfranchisement, are willing to be counted against the enfranchisement of women or foreigners or the unfortunate. Such argument or neglect is both false and dangerous, and while its phrasing may be effective at times it represents a climbing of one class on the misery of another.

The insistent call of democracy is ringing in the ears of all people today as never before in spite of the hard experiences of the past. The cure for the ills of democracy is seen to be more democracy. We are rapidly changing from a form of social control dictated by the interests of a few to one dictated by the interests of a large and larger majority. Not only is this true in what is usually called politics but also in industry. In fact our political interests are becoming more and more industrial and our industry is assuming larger and larger political aspects. In the industrial world we are still under the rule of the strong monarch, with at most the mitigation of the power of the selected few. We feel the consequent confusion. We lack knowledge of industrial conditions. We have no standard of industrial justice. Whence shall knowledge and standards come? Through democracy. Through having the

rights and wishes of every worker represented in the power
that controls industry. This will be hard to attain. The
passing of the strong monarch in industry as in politics
will spell anarchy in many places, but social justice will
eventually come. How necessary then to build a state of
the broadest democracy to cope with the industrial problem
within nations and between nations and races.

W. E. B. Du Bois, *Disfranchisement.* Published by New
York Headquarters, National Woman Suffrage Association, New York, 1912.

20

SOCIALISM AND THE
NEGRO PROBLEM

*In 1904 Dr. Du Bois noted that the Negro problem
was related to the "unjust and dangerous economic conditions" in the country, and indicated that while he was
"scarcely a socialist," he wished the socialist movement
well. Three years later, in* The Horizon, *organ of the
Niagara Movement, he called himself "a Socialist-of-the-
Path," believing that most business should be nationalized
by the government. He agreed that "the socialistic trend"
was the "one great hope of the Negro race," but he still
maintained reservations about the socialists because they
had not succeeded in freeing themselves of racial discrimination.*

*Despite these doubts, Du Bois joined the Socialist Party
in 1911. His stay, however, was brief. In the summer of
1912, he informed the party he was resigning because
he had decided to support Woodrow Wilson, the Democratic candidate for president. Actually, his short experience in the Socialist Party had reinforced his earlier
concern about the racial attitudes of the socialists, and
in a speech to a meeting of Harlem socialists, he developed
this theme fully. The address was published in* The New
Review, *a left-wing socialist monthly, under the title, "Socialism and the Negro Problem."*

One might divide those interested in socialism in two
distinct camps: on the one hand those farsighted thinkers
who are seeking to determine from the facts of modern industrial organization just what the outcome is going to be;

on the other hand, those who suffer from the present industrial situation and who are anxious that, whatever the broad outcome may be, at any rate the present suffering which they know so well shall be stopped. It is this second class of social thinkers who are interested particularly in the Negro problem. They are saying that the plight of ten million human beings in the United States, predominantly of the working class, is so evil that it calls for much attention in any program of future social reform. This paper, however, is addressed not to this class, but rather to the class of theoretical socialists; and its thesis is: in the Negro problem as it presents itself in the United States, theoretical socialism of the twentieth century meets a critical dilemma.

There is no doubt as to the alternatives presented. On the one hand, there are ninety million white people who in their extraordinary development present a peculiar field for the application of socialistic principles; but on the whole, these people are demanding today that just as under capitalistic organization the Negro has been the excluded (i.e., exploited) class, so, too, any socialistic program shall also exclude the ten million. Many socialists have acquiesced in this program. No recent convention of socialism has dared to face fairly the Negro problem and make a straightforward declaration that they regard Negroes as men in the same sense that other persons are. The utmost that the party has been able to do is not to rescind the declaration of an earlier convention.[1] The general attitude of thinking members of the party has been this: we must not turn aside from the great objects of socialism to take up this issue of the American Negro; let the question wait; when the objects of socialism are achieved, this problem will be settled along with other problems.

That there is a logical flaw here, no one can deny. Can the problem of any group of ten million be properly considered as "aside" from any program of socialism? Can the objects of socialism be achieved so long as the Negro is neglected? Can any great human problem "wait"? If socialism is going to settle the American problem of race prejudice without direct attack along these lines by socialists, why is it necessary for socialists to fight along other lines? Indeed, there is a kind of fatalistic attitude on the part of certain transcendental socialists, which often assumes that the whole battle of socialism is coming by a kind of evolution in which active individual effort on their part is hardly necessary.

As a matter of fact, the socialists face in the problem of the American Negro this question: can a minority of any group or country be left out of the socialistic problem? It is, of course, agreed that a majority cannot be left out. Socialists usually put great stress on the fact that the laboring class form a majority of all nations and nevertheless are unjustly treated in the distribution of wealth. Suppose, however, that this unjust distribution affected only a minority, and that only a tenth of the American nation were working under unjust economic conditions: could a socialistic program be carried out which acquiesced in this condition? Many American socialists seem silently to assume that this would be possible. To put it concretely, they are going to carry on industry so far as this mass is concerned; they are going to get rid of the private control of capital and they are going to divide up the social income among these ninety million in accordance with some rule of reason, rather than in the present haphazard way: but at the same time, they are going to permit the continued exploitation of these ten million workers. So far as these ten million workers are concerned, there is to be no active effort to secure for them a voice in the social democracy, or an adequate share in the social income. The idea is that ultimately when the ninety millions come to their own, they will voluntarily share with the ten million serfs.

Does the history of the world justify us in expecting any such outcome? Frankly, I do not believe it does. The program is that of industrial aristocracy which the world has always tried; the only difference being that such socialists are trying to include in the inner circle a much larger number than have ever been included before. Socialistic as this program may be called, it is not real social democracy. The essence of social democracy is that there shall be no excluded or exploited classes in the socialistic state;

that there shall be no man or woman so poor, ignorant or black as not to count one. Is this simply a far-off ideal, or is it a possible program? I have come to believe that the test of any great movement toward social reform is the excluded class. . . .

More than that, assuming that if you did exclude Negroes temporarily from the growing socialistic state, the ensuing uplift of humanity would in the end repair the temporary damage, the present queston is, *can* you exclude the Negro and push socialism forward? Every tenth man in the United States is of acknowledged Negro descent; if you take those in gainful occupations, one out of every seven Americans is colored; and if you take laborers and workingmen in the ordinary acceptation of the term, one out of every five is colored. The problem is then to lift four-fifths of a group on the backs of the other fifth. Even if the submerged fifth were "dull driven cattle," this program of socialistic opportunism would not be easy. But when the program is proposed in face of a group growing in intelligence and social power and a group made suspicious and bitter by analogous action on the part of trade unionists, what is anti-Negro socialism doing but handing its enemies the powerful weapon of four and one-half million men who will find it not simply to their interest, but a sacred duty to underbid the labor market, vote against labor legislation, and fight to keep their fellow laborers down. Is it not significant that Negro soldiers in the army are healthier and desert less than whites?

Nor is this all: what becomes of socialism when it engages in such a fight for human downfall? Whither are gone its lofty aspirations and high resolve—its songs and comradeship?

The Negro problem then is the great test of the American socialist. Shall American socialism strive to train for its socialistic state ten million serfs who will serve or be exploited by that state, or shall it strive to incorporate them immediately into that body politic? Theoretically, of course, all socialists, with few exceptions, would wish the latter program. But it happens that in the United States there is a strong local opinion in the South which violently opposes any program of any kind of reform that recognizes the Negro as a man. So strong is this body of opinion that you have in the South a most extraordinary development. The whole radical movement there represented by men like Blease and Vardaman and Tillman and Jeff Davis and attracting such demagogues as Hoke Smith, includes in its program of radical reform a most bitter and reactionary hatred of the Negro. The average modern socialist can scarcely grasp the extent of this hatred; even murder and torture of human beings holds a prominent place in its philosophy; the defilement of colored women is its joke, and justice toward colored men will not be listened to. The only basis on which one can even approach these people with a plea for the barest tolerance of colored folk is that the murder and mistreatment of colored men may possibly hurt white men. Consequently the Socialist Party finds itself in this predicament: if it acquiesces in race hatred, it has a chance to turn the tremendous power of southern white radicalism toward its own party; if it does not do this, it becomes a "party of the Negro," with its growth South and North decidedly checked. There are signs that the socialist leaders are going to accept the chance of getting hold of the radical South whatever its cost. This paper is written to ask such leaders: after you have gotten the radical South and paid the price which they demand, will the result be socialism?

The New Review, January 1, 1913, pp. 138-41.

21

THE AFRICAN ROOTS OF WAR

Soon after the first World War broke out in August 1914, Dr. Du Bois was speaking to audiences all over the country on the causes of the great conflict. While most commentators emphasized the purely European aspects of the issues leading to the war, Du Bois stressed the African roots of European imperialism as the major factor responsible for the holocaust. The main theme of his speeches was published in an article in the Atlantic Monthly *of May 1915. As James Weldon Johnson pointed out, Dr. Du Bois "showed that when we cut down through the layers of international rivalries and jealousies we found that the roots of the great war were in Africa." Du Bois also saw clearly the role of imperialism in creating a "labor aristocracy" in the home country.*

"*Semper novi quid ex Africa,*"[1] cried the Roman proconsul; and he voiced the verdict of forty centuries. Yet there are those who would write world history and leave out this most marvelous of continents. Particularly today most men assume that Africa lies far afield from the centers of our burning social problems, and especially from our present problem of World War.

Yet in a very real sense Africa is a prime cause of this terrible overturning of civilization which we have lived to see; and these words seek to show how in the Dark Continent are hidden the roots, not simply of war today but of the menace of wars tomorrow.

Always Africa is giving us something new or some metempsychosis of a world-old thing. On its black bosom

arose one of the earliest, if not the earliest, of self-protecting civilizations, and grew so mightily that it still furnishes
superlatives to thinking and speaking men. Out of its
darker and more remote forest fastnesses, came, if we
may credit many recent scientists, the first welding of
iron, and we know that agriculture and trade flourished
there when Europe was a wilderness.

Nearly every human empire that has arisen in the
world, material and spiritual, has found some of its greatest crises on this continent of Africa, from Greece to Great
Britain. As Mommsen says, "It was through Africa that
Christianity became the religion of the world." In Africa
the last flood of Germanic invasions spent itself within
hearing of the last gasp of Byzantium, and it was again
through Africa that Islam came to play its great role of
conqueror and civilizer.

With the Renaissance and the widened world of modern
thought, Africa came no less suddenly with her new old
gift. Shakespeare's Ancient Pistol cries,

> A foutre for the world, and worldings base!
> I speak of Africa, and golden joys.

He echoes a legend of gold from the days of Punt and
Ophir to those of Ghana, the Gold Coast, and the Rand.
This thought had sent the world's greed scurrying down
the hot, mysterious coasts of Africa to the Good Hope
of gain, until for the first time a real world commerce
was born, albeit it started as a commerce mainly in the
bodies and souls of men.

So much for the past; and now, today: the Berlin Conference to apportion the rising riches of Africa among the
white peoples met on the fifteenth day of November, 1884.
Eleven days earlier, three Germans left Zanzibar (whither
they had gone secretly disguised as mechanics), and before
the Berlin Conference had finished its deliberations they
had annexed to Germany an area over half as large
again as the whole German Empire in Europe. Only in
its dramatic suddenness was this undisguised robbery
of the land of seven million natives different from the
methods by which Great Britain and France got four
million square miles each, Portugal three quarters of a

million, and Italy and Spain smaller but substantial areas.

The methods by which this continent has been stolen have been contemptible and dishonest beyond expression. Lying treaties, rivers of rum, murder, assassination, mutilation, rape and torture have marked the progress of Englishman, German, Frenchman, and Belgian on the Dark Continent. The only way in which the world has been able to endure the horrible tale is by deliberately stopping its ears and changing the subject of conversation while the devilry went on.

It all began, singularly enough, like the present war, with Belgium. Many of us remember Stanley's great solution of the puzzle of Central Africa when he traced the mighty Congo sixteen hundred miles from Nyangwe to the sea. Suddenly the world knew that here lay the key to the riches of Central Africa. It stirred uneasily, but Leopold of Belgium was first on his feet, and the result was the Congo Free State—God save the mark! But the Congo Free State, with all its magniloquent heralding of peace, Christianity, and commerce, degenerating into murder, mutilation and downright robbery, differed only in degree and concentration from the tale of all Africa in this rape of a continent already furiously mangled by the slave trade. That sinister traffic, on which the British Empire and the American Republic were largely built, cost black Africa no less than 100,000,000 souls,[2] the wreckage of its political and social life, and left the continent in precisely that state of helplessness which invites aggression and exploitation. "Color" became in the world's thought synonymous with inferiority, "Negro" lost its capitalization, and Africa was another name for bestiality and barbarism.

Thus the world began to invest in color prejudice. The "color line" began to pay dividends. For indeed, while the exploration of the valley of the Congo was the occasion of the scramble for Africa, the cause lay deeper. The Franco-Prussian War turned the eyes of those who sought power and dominion away from Europe. Already England was in Africa, cleaning away the debris of the slave trade and half-consciously groping toward the new imperialism. France, humiliated and impoverished, looked toward a new northern African empire sweeping from the Atlantic to the Red Sea. More slowly Germany began to see the dawning of a new day, and, shut out from America by the Monroe Doctrine, looked to Asia and Africa for colonies. Portugal sought anew to make good her claim to her ancient African realm; and thus a continent where Europe claimed but a tenth of the land in 1875 was in twenty-five more years practically absorbed.

Why was this? What was the new call for dominion? It must have been strong, for consider a moment the desperate flames of war that have shot up in Africa in the last quarter of a century: France and England at Fashoda, Italy at Adua, Italy and Turkey in Tripoli, England and Portugal at Delagoa Bay, England, Germany and the Dutch in South Africa, France and Spain in Morocco, Germany and France in Agadir, and the world at Algeciras.

The answer to this riddle we shall find in the economic changes in Europe. Remember what the nineteenth and twentieth centuries have meant to organized industry in European civilization. Slowly the divine right of the few to determine economic income and distribute the goods and services of the world has been questioned and curtailed. We called the process revolution in the eighteenth century, advancing democracy in the nineteenth, and socialization of wealth in the twentieth. But whatever we call it, the movement is the same: the dipping of more and grimier hands into the wealth-bag of the nation, until today only the ultrastubborn fail to see that democracy in determining income is the next inevitable step to democracy in political power.

With the waning of the possibility of the big fortune, gathered by starvation wage and boundless exploitation of one's weaker and poorer fellows at home, arose more magnificently the dream of exploitation abroad. Always, of course, the individual merchant had at his own risk and in his own way tapped the riches of foreign lands. Later, special trading monopolies had entered the field and founded empires overseas. Soon, however, the mass of merchants at home demanded a share in this golden stream; and finally, in the twentieth century, the laborer at home is demanding and beginning to receive a part of his share.

The theory of this new democratic despotism has not been clearly formulated. Most philosophers see the ship of state launched on the broad, irresistible tide of democracy, with only delaying eddies here and there; others, looking closer, are more disturbed. Are we, they ask, reverting to aristocracy and despotism — the rule of might? They cry out and then rub their eyes, for surely they cannot fail to see strengthening democracy all about them?

It is this paradox which has confounded philanthropists, curiously betrayed the socialists, and reconciled the imperialists and captains of industry to any amount of "democracy." It is this paradox which allows in America the most rapid advance of democracy to go hand in hand in its very centers with increased aristocracy and hatred toward darker races, and which excuses and defends an inhumanity that does not shrink from the public burning of human beings.

Yet the paradox is easily explained: the white workingman has been asked to share the spoil of exploiting "chinks and niggers." It is no longer simply the merchant prince, or the aristocratic monopoly, or even the employing class, that is exploiting the world: it is the nation, a new democratic nation composed of united capital and labor. The laborers are not yet getting, to be sure, as large a share as they want or will get, and there are still at the bottom large and restless excluded classes. But the laborer's equity is recognized, and his just share is a matter of time, intelligence, and skillful negotiation.

Such nations it is that rule the modern world. Their national bond is no mere sentimental patriotism, loyalty, or ancestor-worship. It is increased wealth, power, and luxury for all classes on a scale the world never saw before. Never before was the average citizen of England, France, and Germany so rich, with such splendid prospects of greater riches.

Whence comes this new wealth and on what does its accumulation depend? It comes primarily from the darker nations of the world — Asia and Africa, South and Central America, the West Indies and the islands of the South Seas. There are still, we may well believe, many parts of white countries like Russia and North America, not to mention Europe itself, where the older exploitation still holds. But the knell has sounded faint and far, even there. In the lands of darker folk, however, no knell has sounded. Chinese, East Indians, Negroes, and South American Indians are by common consent for governance by white folk and economic subjection to them. To the furtherance of this highly profitable economic dictum has been brought every available resource of science and religion. Thus arises the astonishing doctrine of the natural inferiority of most men to the few, and the interpretation of "Christian brotherhood" as meaning anything that one of the "brothers" may at any time want it to mean.

Like all world schemes, however, this one is not quite complete. First of all, yellow Japan has apparently escaped the cordon of this color bar. This is disconcerting and dangerous to white hegemony. If, of course, Japan would join heart and soul with the whites against the rest of the yellows, browns, and blacks, well and good. There are even good-natured attempts to prove the Japanese "Aryan," provided they act "white." But blood is thick, and there are signs that Japan does not dream of a world governed mainly by white men. This is the "Yellow Peril," and it may be necessary, as the German Emperor and many white Americans think, to start a world crusade against this presumptuous nation which demands "white" treatment.

Then, too, the Chinese have recently shown unexpected signs of independence and autonomy, which may possibly make it necessary to take them into account a few decades hence. As a result, the problem in Asia has resolved itself into a race for "spheres" of economic "influence," each provided with a more or less "open door" for business opportunity. This reduces the danger of open clash between European nations, and gives the yellow folk such chance for desperate unarmed resistance as was shown by China's repulse of the Six Nations of Bankers. There is still hope among some whites that conservative North China and the radical South may in time come to blows and allow actual white dominion.

One thing, however, is certain: Africa is prostrate. There at least are few signs of self-consciousness that need at present be heeded. To be sure, Abyssinia must be wheedled, and in America and the West Indies Negroes have attempted futile steps toward freedom; but such steps have been pretty effectually stopped (save through the breech of "miscegenation"), although the ten million Negroes in the United States need, to many men's minds, careful watching and ruthless repression.

Thus the white European mind has worked, and worked the more feverishly because Africa is the Land of the Twentieth Century. The world knows something of the gold and diamonds of South Africa, the cocoa of Angola and Nigeria, the rubber and ivory of the Congo, and the palm oil of the West Coast. But does the ordinary citizen realize the extraordinary economic advances of Africa and, too, of black Africa, in recent years? E. D. Morel, who knows his Africa better than most white men, has shown us how the export of palm oil from West Africa has grown from 283 tons in 1800, to 80,000 tons in 1913, which together with by-products is worth today $60,000,000 annually. He shows how native Gold Coast labor, unsupervised, has come to head the cocoa-producing countries of the world with an export of 89,000,000 pounds (weight *not* money) annually. He shows how the cotton crop of Uganda has risen from 3,000 bales in 1909 to 50,000 bales in 1914; and he says that France and Belgium are no more remarkable in the cultivation of their land than the Negro province of Kano. The trade of Abyssinia amounts to only $10,000,000 a year, but it is its infinite possibility of growth that is making the nations crowd to Addis Ababa.

All these things are but beginnings; "but tropical Africa and its peoples are being brought more irrevocably each year into the vortex of the economic influences that sway the western world." There can be no doubt of the economic possibilities of Africa in the near future. There are not only the well-known and traditional products, but boundless chances in a hundred different directions, and above all, there is a throng of human beings who, could they once be reduced to the docility and steadiness of Chinese coolies or of seventeenth and eighteenth-century European laborers, would furnish to their masters, a spoil exceeding the gold-haunted dreams of the most modern of imperialists.

This, then, is the real secret of that desperate struggle for Africa which began in 1877 and is now culminating. Economic dominion outside Africa has, of course, played its part, and we were on the verge of the partition of Asia when Asiatic shrewdness warded it off. America was saved from direct political dominion by the Monroe Doctrine. Thus, more and more, the imperialists have concentrated on Africa.

The greater the concentration the more deadly the rivalry. From Fashoda to Agadir, repeatedly the spark has been applied to the European magazine and a general conflagration narrowly averted. We speak of the Balkans as the storm center of Europe and the cause of war, but this is mere habit. The Balkans are convenient for occasions, but the ownership of materials and men in the darker world is the real prize that is setting the nations of Europe at each other's throats today.

The present world war is, then, the result of jealousies engendered by the recent rise of armed national associations of labor and capital whose aim is the exploitation of the wealth of the world mainly outside the European circle of nations. These associations, grown jealous and suspicious at the division of the spoils of trade-empire, are fighting to enlarge their respective shares; they look for expansion, not in Europe but in Asia, and particularly in Africa. "We want no inch of French territory," said Germany to England, but Germany was "unable to give" similar assurances as to France in Africa.

The difficulties of this imperial movement are internal as well as external. Successful aggression in economic expansion calls for a close union between capital and labor at home. Now the rising demands of the white laborer, not simply for wages but for conditions of work and a voice in the conduct of industry, make industrial peace difficult. The workingmen have been appeased by all sorts of essays in state socialism, on the one hand, and on the other hand by public threats of competition by colored labor. By threatening to send English capital to China and Mexico, by threatening to hire Negro laborers in America, as well as by old-age pensions and accident insurance, we gain industrial peace at home at the mightier cost of war abroad.

In addition to these national war-engendering jealousies there is a more subtle movement arising from the attempt to unite labor and capital in worldwide freebooting. Democracy in economic organization, while an acknowledged ideal, is today working itself out by admitting to a share in the spoils of capital only the aristocracy of labor—the more intelligent and shrewder and cannier workingmen. The ignorant, unskilled, and restless still form a large, threatening, and, to a growing extent, revolutionary group in advanced countries.

The resultant jealousies and bitter hatreds tend continually to fester along the color line. We must fight the Chinese, the laborer argues, or the Chinese will take our bread and butter. We must keep Negroes in their places, or Negroes will take our jobs. All over the world there leaps to articulate speech and ready action that singular assumption that if white men do not throttle colored men, then China, India, and Africa will do to Europe what Europe has done and seeks to do to them.

On the other hand, in the minds of yellow, brown, and black men the brutal truth is clearing: a white man is privileged to go to any land where advantage beckons and behave as he pleases; the black or colored man is being more and more confined to those parts of the world where life for climatic, historical, economic, and political reasons is most difficult to live and most easily dominated by Europe for Europe's gain.

What, then, are we to do, who desire peace and the civilization of all men? Hitherto the peace movement has confined itself chiefly to figures about the cost of war and platitudes on humanity. What do nations care about the cost of war, if by spending a few hundred millions in steel and gunpowder they can gain a thousand million in diamonds and cocoa? How can love of humanity appeal as a motive to nations whose love of luxury is built on the inhuman exploitation of human beings, and who, especially in recent years, have been taught to regard these human beings as inhuman? I appealed to the last meeting of peace societies in St. Louis, saying, "Should you not discuss racial prejudice as a prime cause of war?" The secretary was sorry but was unwilling to introduce controversial matters!

We, then, who want peace, must remove the real causes of war. We have extended gradually our conception of democracy beyond our social class to all social classes in our nation; we have gone further and extended our democratic ideals not simply to all classes of our own nation, but to those of other nations of our blood and lineage—to what we call "European" civilization. If we want real peace and lasting culture, however, we must go further. We must extend the democratic ideal to the yellow, brown, and black peoples.

To say this, is to evoke on the faces of modern men a look of blank hopelessness. Impossible! we are told, and for so many reasons—scientific, social, and what not—that argument is useless. But let us not conclude too quickly. Suppose we have to choose between this unspeakably inhuman outrage on decency and intelligence and religion which we call the World War and the attempt to treat black men as human, sentient, responsible beings? We have sold them as cattle. We are working them as beasts of burden. We shall not drive war from this world until we treat them as free and equal citizens in a world democracy of all races and nations. Impossible? Democracy is a method of doing the impossible. It is the only method yet discovered of making the education and development of all men a matter of all men's desperate desire. It is putting firearms in the hands of a child with the object of compelling the child's neighbors to teach him, not only the real and legitimate uses of a dangerous tool but the uses of himself in all things. Are there other and less costly ways of accomplishing this? There may be in some better world. But for a world just emerging from the rough

chains of an almost universal poverty, and faced by the
temptation of luxury and indulgence through the enslaving of defenseless men, there is but one adequate method
of salvation—the giving. of democratic weapons of self-
defense to the defenseless.

Nor need we quibble over those ideas—wealth, education, and political power—soil which we have so forested
with claim and counterclaim that we see nothing for the
woods.

What the primitive peoples of Africa and the world need
and must have if war is to be abolished is perfectly clear:

First: land. Today Africa is being enslaved by the theft
of her land and natural resources. A century ago black
men owned all but a morsel of South Africa. The Dutch
and England came, and today 1,250,000 whites own
264,000,000 acres, leaving only 21,000,000 acres for
4,500,000 natives. Finally, to make assurance doubly
sure, the Union of South Africa has refused natives even
the right to *buy* land. This is a deliberate attempt to force
the Negroes to work on farms and in mines and kitchens
for low wages. All over Africa has gone this shameless
monopolizing of land and natural resources to force poverty on the masses and reduce them to the "dumb-driven-
cattle" stage of labor activity.

Secondly: we must train native races in modern civilization. This can be done. Modern methods of educating
children, honestly and effectively applied, would make
modern, civilized nations out of the vast majority of human beings on earth today. This we have seldom tried.
For the most part Europe is straining every nerve to make
over yellow, brown, and black men into docile beasts of
burden, and only an irrepressible few are allowed to escape and seek (usually abroad) the education of modern
men.

Lastly, the principle of home rule must extend to groups,
nations, and races. The ruling of one people for another
people's whim or gain must stop. This kind of despotism
has been in later days more and more skillfully disguised.
But the brute fact remains: the white man is ruling black
Africa for the white man's gain, and just as far as possible he is doing the same to colored races elsewhere. Can

such a situation bring peace? Will any amount of European concord or disarmament settle this injustice?

Political power today is but the weapon to force economic power. Tomorrow, it may give us spiritual vision and artistic sensibility. Today, it gives us or tries to give us bread and butter, and those classes or nations or races who are without it starve, and starvation is the weapon of the white world to reduce them to slavery.

We are calling for European concord today; but at the utmost European concord will mean satisfaction with, or acquiescence in, a given division of the spoils of world dominion. After all, European disarmament cannot go below the necessity of defending the aggressions of the whites against the blacks and browns and yellows. From this will arise three perpetual dangers of war. First, renewed jealousy at any division of colonies or spheres of influence agreed upon, if at any future time the present division comes to seem unfair. Who cared for Africa in the early nineteenth century? Let England have the scraps left from the golden feast of the slave trade. But in the twentieth century? The end was war. These scraps looked too tempting to Germany.

Secondly: war will come from the revolutionary revolt of the lowest workers. The greater the international jealousies, the greater the corresponding costs of armament and the more difficult to fulfill the promises of industrial democracy in advanced countries. Finally, the colored peoples will not always submit passively to foreign domination. To some this is a lightly tossed truism. When a people deserve liberty they fight for it and get it, say such philosophers; thus making war a regular, necessary step to liberty. Colored people are familiar with this complacent judgment. They endure the contemptuous treatment meted out by whites to those not "strong" enough to be free. These nations and races, composing as they do a vast majority of humanity, are going to endure this treatment just as long as they must and not a moment longer. Then they are going to fight and the War of the Color Line will outdo in savage inhumanity any war this world has yet seen. For colored folk have much to remember and they will not forget.

But is this inevitable? Must we sit helpless before this awful prospect? While we are planning, as a result of the present holocaust, the disarmament of Europe and a European international world police, must the rest of the world be left naked to the inevitable horror of war, especially when we know that it is directly in this outer circle of races, and not in the inner European household, that the real causes of present European fighting are to be found?

Our duty is clear. Racial slander must go. Racial prejudice will follow. Steadfast faith in humanity must come. The domination of one people by another without the other's consent, be the subject people black or white, must stop. The doctrine of forcible economic expansion over subject peoples must go. Religious hypocrisy must stop. "Bloodthirsty" Mwanga of Uganda killed an English bishop because they feared that his coming meant English domination. It did mean English domination, and the world and the bishop knew it, and yet the world was "horrified"! Such missionary hypocrisy must go. With clean hands and honest hearts we must front high heaven and beg peace in our time.

In this great work who can help us? In the Orient, the awakened Japanese and the awakening leaders of New China; in India and Egypt, the young men trained in Europe and European ideals, who now form the stuff that revolution is born of. But in Africa? Who better than the twenty-five million grandchildren of the European slave trade, spread through the Americas and now writhing desperately for freedom and a place in the world? And of these millions first of all the ten million black folk of the United States, now a problem, then a world salvation.

Twenty centuries before Christ a great cloud swept over sea and settled on Africa, darkening and well-nigh blotting out the culture of the land of Egypt. For half a thousand years it rested there until a black woman, Queen Nefertari, "the most venerated figure in Egyptian history," rose to the throne of the Pharaohs and redeemed the world and her people. Twenty centuries after Christ, black Africa, prostrate, raped, and shamed, lies at the feet of the conquering Philistines of Europe. Beyond the awful sea a black woman is weeping and waiting with her sons on her breast. What shall the end be? The world-old and fearful things, war and wealth, murder and luxury? Or shall it be a new thing — a new peace and new democracy of all races: a great humanity of equal men? *"Semper novi quid ex Africa!"*

Atlantic Monthly, vol. CXV, May 1915, pp. 707-14.

22

THE PROBLEM OF PROBLEMS

Although Dr. Du Bois supported the decision of the United States to enter the World War in 1917, and, as editor of The Crisis, *called upon Negroes to back the nation's war effort, he questioned the ability of the United States to fight a war to save the world for democracy with a clear conscience as long as she maintained racist policies at home. He made his position clear in an address to the Ninth Annual Convention of the Intercollegiate Socialist Society, December 27, 1917. As usual, he minced no words in denouncing racism.*

As the speech makes clear, five years after he had resigned from the Socialist Party, Du Bois still maintained his interest in socialism, and was still critical of the Socialist Party's failure to deal firmly with racism and to abandon its traditional policy that there was nothing special about the Negro question, that it was simply a part of the general problem of the working class.

There are in the United States today nearly twice as many persons of Negro descent as there are Belgians in Belgium; there are three times as many as there are Irish in Ireland or Scotch in Scotland; as compared with twelve million American Negroes, Serbia and Greece together have only six million inhabitants and Bulgaria less than five million. Indeed, the whole population of the Balkan States is only about one-third larger than the Negro population of the United States. The land which American Negroes own in fee simple is as large as the whole island of Ireland and equals in area the land which

the Germans hold in Belgium and France; and the land
which they cultivate as owners and tenants is as large
as half the United Kingdom.

Absolutely, then, this group is of importance in the
world. But the problem which I am to discuss is that
which arises from the fact that this group has been from
the beginning excluded from American democracy and
that this exclusion has had a singular and often well-nigh
fatal effect upon the nation whenever the nation has sought
to follow great ideals or work out any line of unselfish
endeavor. This is easily proven, not simply in the present
crisis but in every spiritual crisis which the territory in the
United States occupied by the nation has passed. Mental
contradiction and moral disintegration have been the price
which the United States has paid again and again for
refusing to face the problem of its Negro population.

Think, for instance, of the earliest of our great social
problems. Late in the fifteenth century the eyes of the
world were opened to see the earth doubled in extent,
to realize vast new territories and unknown possibilities
and not impossible fairy tales beyond the seas. Conceive
the vision, the spiritual uplift that must have followed
such a revelation. With this spiritual exultation, however,
went the keen, cold, calculating realization that sufficient
forces of brute labor could extract untold and immediate
wealth from the known parts of this land. There you
have the first spiritual conflict in which the Negro became
a tremendous part. It was settled by a compromise which
no thoughtful man believed, but which all, thoughtful
and thoughtless, were willing to accept. Import workers
to work in the mines and on the plantations and thus the
heathen would be converted to the kingdom of God! Would
not so meritorious a work excuse the horrors of the slave
trade?

It was characteristic of this conclusion that few dared
go behind it; few dared to call for facts and really argue
and discuss the question. Discussion was interfered with
by dominant public opinion, and America became a land
of slavery.

Then, slowly, in the unwinding of years came a new
spiritual conflict. More and more clearly a splendid ideal

flamed in the minds of Americans. This was to be a land
of refuge and a land of freedom. The disinherited of the
earth were to have here a chance for development such
as the world had never seen before. All men were to be
equal, with an equal chance for life, liberty, and the pursuit of happiness. The land was to exist for itself and not
for Europe, and the forces for the great fight for freedom
gathered themselves. It was exceedingly unpleasant just
here to remember that America, after all, was a land of
slavery, to have the enemy turn frankly to the black
slaves, like Dunmore in Virginia, and cry: "You are free.
Fight for your own liberty against these slave-holding
hypocrites!"[1] Something had to be done and the result,
again, was compromise. Black soldiers shall be free immediately, said the revolutionary fathers, and slavery as
an institution will disappear from the land. But human
changes take time and call for sacrifices. The cost of
uprooting slavery must be spread over many years. Let
the slave trade gradually be abolished; let emancipation
spread state by state and plantation by plantation. Meantime, we will undertake to find a new home in Africa or
elsewhere for the freed Negroes, and thus our dilemma
will be settled. So, our fathers of revolutionary days fought
for freedom and maintained slavery.

Meantime, the world began to change and the new era
of economic expansion swept over it. The nation felt the
impulse, and in the fateful years when the factory system
was being introduced and machinery supplanting crude
labor, they were asked to lay the foundation of the first
American economic kingdom—the kingdom of cotton—
which antedated later kingdoms of iron, of cereals, of
meat, and of lumber. Few in the nation or in the world
understood exactly what was happening. The great ground
swell of the universe revealed itself not as one mighty
movement but rather as a new chance to make money,
particularly in cotton-raising, in tobacco, sugar and wheat.
Gradually a demand gathered itself, a demand for more
land and more labor. The nation took advantage of the
Haitian Revolution and got the empire of the Mississippi
Valley for nothing, seized North Mexico, and annexed
the Northwest. We became a tremendous country, spread-

ing from ocean to ocean and dreaming of a realm from
the pole to the equator.

Right in the midst of this came the problem of American
Negroes. We felt ourselves so large that we tried to sweep
it aside, but persistently it returned. Thoughtful Americans
knew perfectly well that states' rights advocates bent the
Constitution to the breaking point in order to have slave-
ridden Louisiana; that we seized Mexico and Florida in
order to have a larger area for slavery, and for the same
reason we were intriguing in the West Indies; that the real
thing that was expanding was not America but slavery,
and that new laws and new customs were checking emancipation and making the Negro a caste to supplant the old
caste of manual laborers. Rapidly the leaders of the Cotton
Kingdom took the extreme attitude that the new caste of
black labor was an inevitable thing and that so long as
it was confined to inferior people it was the ideal organization of labor and of economic empire.

Thereupon came the great attempt at national compromise. Granted, said the nation, that this is the ideal form
of labor for certain industries; it must be confined within
the climatic belt where those industries are dominant, so
that the black laboring class shall not come in competition
with the rising white laborers who propose to emancipate
themselves from the caste idea and become a real part
of modern democracy. The leaders of the Cotton Kingdom
misread the times and refused to accept the compromise.
They said that their system of caste labor depended upon
expansion for its very existence and that slaves must be
slaves on Bunker Hill as well as in New Orleans; that they
would not and, indeed, could not remain part of the country which did not allow this. On the other hand, the com-
promisers pleaded with them. They did not for a moment
undertake to deny the caste idea for black men. The very
man who is called the Emancipator declared again and
again that his object was the integrity of the Union and
not the emancipation of the slaves; that if he could keep
the Union from being disrupted, he would not only allow
slavery to exist but would loyally protect it.[2]

It took but a few years of murder, anarchy and rapine
to prove to everybody that if the question of black caste

labor were settled there would be no need for disrupting
the Union and no demand for it. It was, therefore, legally
abolished, the Union preserved, and the attention of the
country turned to further economic development. But the
country was, after all, the same country. It loved Negroes
no better after emancipation than it did before and it had
no more respect for them. It was just as willing in 1870
that Negroes should be slaves as in 1860, so long as they
did not endanger the white man's income.

Inevitably the problem continued to face the nation. If
free white labor was not to be menaced by the slave wages
of Negroes then either Negro labor must be confined to
the South or to a certain grade of work or the Negro's
economic and spiritual emancipation must follow his physical freedom. Again came compromise: slavery persisted,
only we called it the plantation system and supported it
by vagrancy laws, the convict-lease system and lynching.
Labor unions carefully guarded against Negro competition in the decently-paid trades, while on the other hand
the price of common labor in the North was kept but a
notch above southern wages by world migration.

This was our economic and moral dilemma when this
World War burst. There can, as it seems to me, be no
real doubt in anyone's mind but that, horrible as war is,
there lies before the world today a stake which may easily
justify it. If at the cost of this World War, the death of
millions and the sorrow and degradation of many millions
more, if at that horrible cost we can put down anarchy
among the nations, reduce them to some system of law
and order, curb the bullying of the highwayman by armed
international police and make the freedom of nations a
freedom under law, as we have done partially with the
individual, then the fight is worth every drop of blood
that it costs. Every thinking man, too, must realize that
if the world battle is a battle for such a stake, for this
nation to keep out of it is either cowardice or insanity.
But when the nation enters, can it enter and fight for such
a stake? Are its hands reasonably clean and its soul sincere? I maintain that the one tremendous handicap which
makes it almost impossible for this nation to fight with
clear conscience or with untrammeled limbs is today, as

yesterday, her attitude toward twelve million American citizens of Negro descent. I can, perhaps, best illustrate my meaning by reminding you briefly of the problems which you are discussing in this conference.

You are discussing, for instance, labor. Now the central problem of American labor is the chronic oversupply of common labor. The oversupply has in the past come from migration, first from Ireland, then from Germany, finally from Italy and Austria, and above all from the millions of Negroes in the South recently emancipated from slavery and systematically kept in ignorance. As soon as this war starts a revolution takes place. Those who were formerly killed in industry in America are now being killed in war in Europe. Common labor becomes scarce and wages rise. The Negro, attracted by higher wages in the North and repelled by the menace of lynching and caste in the South, moves to fill the new labor demand thus created. The common laborer in the North is caught between the tyranny of exclusive trade unions and the underbidding of blacks. The result is murder and riot and unrest. Those who for a generation have been calling the black man a lazy, ignorant burden and incubus on the South have suddenly developed a determination not to allow the rest of the country to share that burden or pay Negroes higher wages. White northern laborers find killing Negroes a safe, lucrative employment which commends them to the American Federation of Labor. No discussion of labor problems arising out of the war can take place, then, without first facing this situation of the Negro laborer.

You are taking up the problem of the freedom of speech. Many of you are vastly upset by the increasing difficulty which you have in discussing this war in America; but I should be much more impressed by your indignation if I did not realize that the greatest lack in freedom of discussion of present American problems comes not in problems which you are not allowed to discuss but rather in those which you are free to discuss but afraid of. I know and you know that the conspiracy of silence that surrounds the Negro problem in the United States arises because you do not dare, you are without the moral courage to discuss it frankly, and when I say *you* I refer not simply to the conservative reactionary elements of the nation but rather to the very elements represented in a conference like this, supposed to be forward-looking and radical. You may, of course, now and then and with some impatience turn from the things which you really want to discuss and listen skeptically and with little interest to a speaker who tries within twenty minutes to untangle a snarl of twenty decades. But you are perfectly willing to leave it at that, to go away without action, to let the mists of half-discussion and half-understanding lie continually upon this human problem. Ten indeterminate half-truths will sum up your whole knowledge of the Negro problem and the knowledge which you are unwilling to have disturbed. For instance: (1) the Negro is lazy; (2) the Negro is unhealthy and is dying out; (3) the Negro is inferior in mind and in body; (4) the Negro misused the ballot and the ballot was rightfully taken from him; (5) the Negro is lynched for rape; (6) the Negro is abnormally criminal; (7) the Negro's one ambition is to marry your sister; (8) efforts to educate Negroes beyond a certain point are a failure; (9) the South is the best friend of the Negro; (10) the Negro problem is insoluble.

There is not a single one of these propositions that is not a half-truth or a whole lie. As a whole they run counter to easily ascertainable facts, to open scientific proof, and to common sense, yet they are allowed to stand. They can be repeated at any time or place without contradiction. Any person anywhere in America, no matter what his standing or reputation, can rise and with proper gestures and embellishments repeat these ten sentences and sit down in nine cases out of ten uncontradicted and unquestioned.

A nation which thus refuses to discuss intelligently or to investigate the problem which historically and at the present is the greatest of its social problems may whine about and pretend that it wishes freedom of speech but it deceives itself.

You are discussing the conscription of wealth for the national weal, and yet this great, rich country has allowed generation after generation of American Negroes to grow up in ignorance and poverty and crime, because they will not spend as many dollars upon a decent public school

system or a system of social uplift for Negroes as they are
perfectly willing to spend upon a single battleship. Under
such circumstances it will be hard to make conscientious
people believe that you believe in the conscription of wealth
for the common weal.

You are talking about the public control of food and
the necessity in great national crisis for the national government to come in and curb and guide the antisocial
action of states and individuals, and in the face of this
you refuse to ask that same national government to come
in and conserve the lives which food feeds. You allow
lynching and murder to become a national pastime. Nine
out of ten of you have practically without protest sat by
your parlor fires while 2,867 colored men have been
lynched and burned and tortured in the last thirty years,
and not a single one of the murderers brought to justice,
not to mention the tens of thousands of Negroes who have
been killed by mobs and murderers in that time.

You wish universal service in war and in peace, but you
are willing that Negroes who are unprotected either in
war or peace should give their services and be compelled
to give them under circumstances of public insult such as
no other part of the nation is asked to endure.

The state socialism which you discuss is in America the
socialism of a state where a tenth of the population is
disfranchised, (not to mention the half who are women),
and where the power which at present controls is the
power which gets its political rights from a franchise based
on the disfranchisement of nine million Americans of
Negro descent; and you raise scarcely a single word of
protest against it.

I was disgusted with pacifists long before their present
prominence. Today they think war a horrible thing, but
yesterday, when war was confined to the Belgian Congo,
to the headwaters of the Amazon, to South Africa and
parts of India and the South Seas it was not war, it was
simply a method of carrying civilization on to the natives,
and there were no national conventions on the subject.
In the peace proposals that are now being made continually, the future of the disfranchised Indians of the Eastern
and Western Hemispheres, and the disfranchisement of

the Negroes in the United States has not only no important part but practically no thought. What you are asking for is a peace among white folk with the inevitable result that they will have more leisure and inclination to continue their despoiling of yellow, red, brown and black folk.

Revolution is discussed, but it is the successful revolution of white folk and not the unsuccessful revolution of black soldiers in Texas. You do not stop to consider whether the Russian peasant had any more to endure than the black soldiers of the 24th Infantry,[3] but you do consider and consider with the utmost care that the black soldiers' cause was lost before they took arms and that for that reason it can be easily forgotten.

Thus, in every question which you discuss and in many other great social questions which you might discuss, frankness and honesty on your part is almost impossible because of the fact that the nation is guilty of continual injustice toward one-tenth of its own citizenship, and that the injustice is deliberate as long as they refuse to investigate it or discuss it, and because if today you saw the righteous and honest solution you would be frankly unwilling to receive it, unwilling to carry it out, since you would not want to live in a world where Negroes were treated as men. Under such circumstances you must remember that the integrity of your own souls and minds is at stake. You cannot thus play with a human problem and not spoil your own capacity for reason. You must face the fact that these human beings cannot always remain in their present relation to world movements. I once suggested in *The Crisis* magazine a method of solving this problem which was received with a certain gasp of horror. Yet I venture to suggest it again. I said that every white family in the United States might choose a person of Negro descent, invite him to their home, entertain him and then through some quick and painless method kill him. In that way, in a single day, we would be rid of twelve million people who are today giving us so much concern, or rather so little concern. Remember, that as ghastly as a proposal of this sort appears that it is a good deal better than forcing these Negroes into slums and ghettos and letting them die slowly by a high death rate. It is a good deal better than forcing them to the lowest wages and letting them die of inanition. It is even better than presenting them with a program of life and education which includes universal and continual insult with absolutely no hope of normal citizenship in modern civilization, and, finally, it is the only one decent alternative to treating them as men.

The Intercollegiate Socialist, December-January, 1917-18, pp. 5-9.

23

THE GREAT MIGRATION NORTH

During the years from 1910 to 1914, an average of over 900,000 Europeans migrated to this country each year. In the following five years, the average fell to about 100,000 per year, due to World War I. In spite of this drop in immigration, the number of workers in manufacturing rose, as did the output of the manufacturing sector. One of the main sources of additional workers for northern industries was southern Negroes. Many firms sent labor recruiters to southern areas and paid the transportation costs of Negroes who would move to such cities as New York, Philadelphia, or Chicago. From 1910 to 1920 over half a million Negroes left the South for northern cities.

Dr. Du Bois spoke frequently on the causes and significance of the great migration North, and in 1918, he incorporated the main points of his speeches in an article entitled, "The Economics of the Negro Problem," published in the American Labor Year Book, *edited by Alexander Trachtenberg and issued by the socialist Rand School of Social Science. It is from this article that the following portion dealing with the migration North is extracted.*

Since 1910, the most significant economic development among Negroes has been a large migration from the South. This has been estimated to have involved at least 250,000 and is still going on.

As to the reasons of the migration, undoubtedly the immediate cause was economic, and the movement began because of floods in middle Alabama and Mississippi and because the latest devastation of the boll weevil came in these same districts.

A second economic cause was the cutting off of immigration from Europe to the North and consequently widespread demand for common labor. The U. S. Department of Labor writes: "A representative of this department has made an investigation in regard thereto, but a report has not been printed for general distribution. It may be stated, however, that most of the help imported from the South has been employed by railroad companies, packinghouses, foundries, factories, automobile plants in northern states as far west as Nebraska. At the present time, the U. S. Employment Service is not cooperating in the direction of Negro help to the North."

The third reason has been outbreaks of mob violence in northern and southwestern Georgia and in western South Carolina.

These have been the three immediate causes, but back of them is, undoubtedly, the general dissatisfaction with the conditions in the South.

A colored man of Sumter, S. C., says: "The immediate occasion of the migration is, of course, the opportunity in the North, now at last open to us, for industrial betterment. The real causes are the conditions which we have had to bear because there was no escape."

These conditions he sums up as the destruction of the Negro's political rights, the curtailment of his civil rights, the lack of the protection of life, liberty and property, low wages, the Jim Crow car, residential and labor segregation laws and poor educational facilities.

The full economic result of this migration and its extent in the future cannot be forecast at the present writing, but the chances are that the demand for labor caused by the European war will result in a large rearrangement of Negro laborers and accelerate all tendencies in the distribution of that labor along lines already noted.

Figures like these are beginning to place the so-called Negro problem beyond the realm of mere opinion and prejudice. Here we see a social evolution working itself out before our eyes. The mass of the freedmen are changing rapidly the economic basis of their social development. They have not given up their close connection with the soil, but they are changing its character tremendously, so that today a fourth of them are peasant proprietors. They are forcing themselves into the trades despite the long opposition of white labor unions. As small businessmen, purveying principally to their own group, they are gaining a foothold in trade. As more or less skilled employees, they form a considerable part of our transportation system and they are rapidly developing a professional class which serves its own group and also serves the nation at large.

Many indications of the effect of this new development are seen in the peculiar incidence of racial prejudice. We hear today less argument about Negro education and more about sumptuary laws to control Negro expenditure, freedom of movement and initiative and residence. Politically handicapped as the colored man is, he is learning to wield economic power, which shows that his political rights cannot long be held back. And finally, in the division of his occupations, there is evidence of forethought and calculation within the group which foreshadows greater cooperation for the future.

Since the above was written, there has been a series of important economic happenings involving the American Negro which ought to be noted.

Severe floods and the cotton boll weevil reduced Negro tenants in many parts of the lower South to great distress during the winter following the declaration of war. They sold their cotton at a low figure or had none to sell. When the price of cotton rose, the plantation owners reaped the benefit and immediately began plans for the next season, calculating on labor at an unusually low price.

Meantime, a great foreign immigration of common laborers was cut off by the war, and there arose in the North an unusual demand for common labor. The Negroes began to migrate. In eighteen months 250,000 left the South and moved into the North. They were chiefly attracted by wages which were from 50 to 200 percent above what they had been used to receiving. And they saw also a chance to escape the lynching and discrimination of the South.

Every effort was made by the South to retain them. They were arrested wholesale, labor agents were taxed $500 to $1,000 or more for licenses, and the daily press of the South began to take on a more conciliatory tone. A slow rise in wages has begun. The migration of Negroes, however, continues, since the demand continues. It is probable that not for a generation after the close of the war will there be any great immigration to the United States from Europe. In that case, the American Negro will have a chance to establish himself in large numbers in the North. We may look for migration of two or even three million.

To offset this, the labor unions have used every effort. The argument was that these blacks kept down the rate of wages. Undoubtedly they did keep wages from rising as high as they otherwise would have, but if Negroes had been received into the unions and trained into the philosophy of the labor cause (which for obvious reasons most of them did not know), they would have made as staunch union men as any. They are not working for low wages because they prefer to, but because they have to. Nine-tenths of the unions, however, are closed absolutely against them, either by constitutional provision or by action of the local unions. It is probable, therefore, that the friction will go on in the North. East St. Louis[1] has already been echoed at Chester, Pa.,[2] and in other industrial centers.

Thus, in his effort to escape industrial slavery, murder, riot and unbelievable cruelty have met the Negro — and this not at the hands of the employers but at the hands of his fellow laborers who have in reality common cause with him.

Alexander Trachtenberg, editor, *The American Labor Year Book, 1917-18*, New York, 1918, pp. 180-82.

24

THE FUTURE OF AFRICA
A PLATFORM

On January 6, 1919, the NAACP sponsored a mass meeting in New York's Carnegie Hall to voice the organization's program for the postwar world being shaped at the Congress of Versailles. Dr. Du Bois had left for Europe on a mission from the NAACP to investigate the treatment of Negro soldiers abroad. He was also asked by a group of black Americans to do what he could to see to it that the interests of Africa were represented during the peace efforts. In his absence, his platform for the future of Africa was read to the Carnegie Hall meeting.

Preceding the reading of Dr. Du Bois's platform, James Weldon Johnson, the distinguished black poet and at that time field secretary of the NAACP, informed the audience that as soon as the Armistice was signed, the Association received many letters from organizations and individuals all over the country, asking that some step be taken to influence world opinion regarding the disposition of the former German colonies in Africa. While these letters were coming in, he pointed out, Dr. Du Bois was already outlining and developing a program. Johnson then read to the audience points eight to eleven from Du Bois's memorandum.

Johnson conceded that the question had arisen as to why the program for the future of Africa did not include the demand for self-determination, and he replied that it was "because of the very practical reason that the question of the former German colonies will come up before the Peace Conference in only three forms: their return to

Germany, their division among the Allies, or their inter-
nationalization."
Here is Dr. Du Bois's platform for the future of Africa.

1. The barter of colonies without regard to the wishes
or welfare of the inhabitants or the welfare of the world
in general is a custom to which this war should put an
end, since it is a fruitful cause of dissension among
nations, a danger to the status of civilized labor, a temptation to unbridled exploitation, and an excuse for un-
speakable atrocities committed against natives.
2. It is clear that at least one of Germany's specific
objects in the present war was the extension of her African
colonies at the expense of France and Portugal.
3. As a result of the war, the German colonies in Africa
have been seized by the Allies, and the question of their
disposition must come before the Peace Conference. Responsible English statesmen have announced that return
of these colonies to Germany is unthinkable.
4. However, to take German Africa from one imperial
master, even though a bad one, and hand it over to
another, even though a better one, would inevitably arouse
a suspicion of selfish aims on the part of the Allies and
would leave after the war the grave questions of future
colonial possessions and government.
5. While the principle of self-determination, which has
been recognized as fundamental by the Allies, cannot be
wholly applied to semicivilized peoples, yet, as the English
prime minister has acknowledged, it can be partially applied.
6. The public opinion which, in the case of the former
German colonies, should have the decisive voice is composed of:
   a. The chiefs and intelligent Negroes among the twelve
and one-half million natives of German Africa, especially
those trained in the government and mission schools.
   b. The twelve million civilized Negroes of the United
States.
   c. Educated persons of Negro descent in South America and the West Indies.

d. The independent Negro governments of Abyssinia, Liberia, and Haiti.

e. The educated classes among the Negroes of French West Africa and Equatorial Africa and in British Uganda, Nigeria, Basutoland, Nyasaland, Swaziland, Sierra Leone, Gold Coast, Gambia and Bechuanaland, and the four and one-half millions of colored people in the Union of South Africa.

These classes comprise today the thinking classes of the future Negro world, and their wish should have weight in the future disposition of the German colonies.

7. The first step toward ascertaining the desires, aspirations and grievances of these people should be the calling together of a *Pan-African Congress*, to meet in Paris some time during the sessions of the Peace Conference.

8. If the world after the war decided to reconstruct Africa in accordance with the wishes of the Negro race and the best interests of civilization, the process might be carried out as follows: the former German colonies, with one million square miles and twelve and one-half millions of inhabitants, could be internationalized. To this could be added by negotiation the 800,000 square miles and nine million inhabitants of Portuguese Africa. It is not impossible that Belgium could be persuaded to add to such a state the 900,000 square miles and nine million natives of the Congo, making an international Africa with over two and one-half million square miles of land and over twenty million people.

9. This reorganized Africa could be under the guidance of organized civilization. The Governing International Commission should represent, not simply governments, but modern culture — science, commerce, social reform and religious philanthropy.

10. With these two principles, the practical policies to be followed out in the government of the new states should involve a thorough and complete system of modern education built upon the present government, religion and customary law of the natives. There should be no violent tampering with the curiously efficient African institutions of local self-government through the family and the tribe;

there should be no attempt at sudden "conversion" by religious propaganda. Obviously deleterious customs and unsanitary usages must gradually be abolished and careful religious teaching given, but the general government set up from without must follow the example of the best colonial administrators and build on recognized established foundations rather than from entirely new and theoretical plans.

11. The chief effort to modernize Africa should be through schools. Within ten years, twenty million black children ought to be in school. Within a generation, young Africa should know the essential outlines of modern culture, and groups of bright African students should be going to the world's great universities. From the beginning, the actual general government should use both colored and white officials, and natives should be gradually worked in. Taxation and industry could follow the newer ideals of industrial democracy, avoiding private land monopoly poverty, promoting cooperation in production and the socialization of income.

12. Is such a state possible? Those who believe in men; who know what black men have done in human history; who have taken pains to follow even superficially the story of the rise of the Negro in Africa, the West Indies, and the Americas of our day, know that the widespread modern contempt of Negroes rests upon no scientific foundation worth a moment's attention. It is nothing more than a vicious habit of mind. It could as easily be overthrown as our belief in war, as our international hatreds, as our old conception of the status of women, as our fear of educating the masses, and as our belief in the necessity of poverty. We can, if we will, inaugurate on the Dark Continent a last great crusade for humanity. With Africa redeemed, Asia would be safe and Europe indeed triumphant.

Africa in the World Democracy, New York, 1919, pp. 28-30. Published by the National Association for the Advancement of Colored People.

NOTES

Editor's Introduction

1. Claude McKay used almost the identical language in his bitter sonnet, "If We Must Die," penned after the Washington race riot in 1919.

1. A Pageant in Seven Decades, 1878-1938

1. Thaddeus Stevens (1792-1868) was the leader of the Radical Republicans in the House of Representatives and a champion of full equality for Negroes, even favoring distribution of the land of the former slaveowners among the freedmen. He was chairman of the committee that prepared impeachment charges against President Andrew Johnson which failed by one vote of carrying in the Senate. Stevens insisted that he be buried in a cemetery in Lancaster, Pennsylvania open to Negroes as well as whites.

2. "Boss" Tweed ruled a political organization in New York City from 1860 to 1871 which gained control of Tammany Hall and through it dominated the government of the city. After exposure of widespread frauds, the ring was overthrown in 1871; Tweed was arrested and died in prison.

3. The New York *Age* was a Negro weekly edited and published by T. Thomas Fortune.

4. Jefferson Davis (1808-1889) was the President of the Confederate States of America.

5. The McKinley Tariff was passed in 1890. It increased tariff rates on iron, steel, glass, tinplate, woolens, cottens, linens, and clothing.

6. Paul Laurence Dunbar (1872-1906), the son of slaves, worked as an elevator boy in Dayton, Ohio, and gained nationwide recognition as a poet, especially for his books of poems, *Major and Minors* and *Lyrics of Lowly Life,* published in 1895 and 1896 respectively.

7. "The Study of Negro Problems" was published in the *Annals of the Academy of Political and Social Science,* vol. XI, 1898, pp. 1-23.

8. Among the volumes published in the series were: *The Negro in Business* (1899), *The College-Bred Negro* (1900), *The Negro Artisan* (1902), *The Negro Church* (1903), and *The Negro American Family* (1908).

9. Joel Chandler Harris (1848-1908) was famous for his Uncle Remus stories, especially *Uncle Remus and Brer Rabbit,* published in 1906.

10. William Monroe Trotter, son of James Trotter, a distinguished Negro leader in Boston, received his B. A. degree *magna cum laude* from Harvard in 1895, and was elected to Phi Beta Kappa, the first Negro at Harvard so honored. He had a lucrative real-estate business in Boston, but gave it up to publish the Boston *Guardian* with George Forbes, and became the most bitter and vigorous critic of Booker T. Washington. "I plunged in," he wrote, "to contend for full equality in all things, governmental, political, civil and judicial, so far as race, creed or color was concerned." As editor of the Boston *Guardian,* of which he was a co-founder, Trotter blasted away at the policies of Booker T. Washington in such harsh language that even Du Bois often winced. However, Du Bois worked closely with Trotter in founding the Niagara Movement. They separated when Trotter refused to follow Du Bois into the NAACP because of his suspicion of any organization in which whites played a dominant role.

11. "A Litany of Atlanta," Du Bois's best-known poem, was published in the *Independent* of October 11, 1906, and has been widely anthologized.

12. "Close Ranks" was published in *The Crisis,* July 1918, p. 111.

13. James Weldon Johnson (1871-1938), distinguished Negro poet and author of *The Autobiography of an Ex-Colored Man,* was the secretary of the NAACP and led the fight for the enactment of the Dyer antilynching bill.

14. When a mob in Detroit gathered in 1925 around the home of Negro physician, Dr. O. H. Sweet, to prevent him from living in a white neighborhood, a white man was killed by gunfire coming from the house. Dr. Sweet, his brother, and his friends in the house were brought to trial. The NAACP came to their defense, employing Clarence Darrow and Arthur Garfield Hayes as defense attorneys. All were finally acquitted.

15. The Sacco-Vanzetti case refers to the arrest, trial, and ultimate execution of two Italian anarchists accused of holding up and murdering a shoe factory paymaster at South Braintree, Massachusetts. The arrests of 1920 led to a trial and appeals extending over a period of

seven years which were conducted in an atmosphere of clear prejudice against the defendants. The case provoked worldwide protests which reached their height in 1927 when the two men were executed. It is generally acknowledged today that they were innocent.

16. In his *Autobiography,* written shortly before his death, Dr. Du Bois described his visits to the Soviet Union during the 1920s and noted: ". . . Russia was and still is to my mind the most hopeful land in the modern world" (p. 290).

17. Only one volume of the *Encyclopedia of the Negro* called "Preparatory Volume" was published by the Phelps-Stokes Fund in 1945.

18. My domain, my domain
   Splendid, far and wide!
   The epoch is my domain —
   My acre is time!

2. The Conservation of Races

1. Toussaint L'Ouverture (1743-1803), the great Haitian liberator, was a slave who rose to become master of the western third of the French island of Saint Domingue which later became Haiti. Although Toussaint was tricked into visiting France for negotiations where he died in prison, he had successfully organized the slaves into a powerful force which established in 1804 the first black republic in the history of the world and the second republic in the Americas.

2. These are the famous words in the first issue of *The Liberator* (January 1, 1831) issued by William Lloyd Garrison (1803-1879), the great abolitionist.

4. The Study of the Negro Problems

1. A bibliography of the American Negro is a much needed undertaking. The existing literature may be summarized briefly as follows: in the line of historical research there are such general studies of the Negro as William's *History of the Negro Race in America,* Wilson's, Goodell's, Blake's, Copley's, Greeley's and Cobb's studies of slavery, and the treatment of the subject in the general histories of Bancroft, Von Holst and others. We have, too, brief special histories of the institution of slavery in Massachusetts, Connecticut, New York, New Jersey, Pennsylvania, the District of Columbia, Maryland, and North Carolina. The slave trade has been studied by Clarkson, Buxton, Benezet, Carey and others; Miss McDougall has written a monograph on fugitive slaves; the Slave Codes have been digested by Hurd, Stroud, Wheeler, Goodell, and Cobb; the economic aspects of the slave system were brilliantly outlined by Cairnes, and a great amount of material is available, showing the development of antislavery opinion.

Of statistical and sociological material the United States government has collected much in its census and bureau reports; and congressional investigations, and state governments and societies have added something to this. Moreover, we have the statistical studies of DeBow, Helper, Gannett and Hoffman, the observations of Olmsted and Kemble, and the studies and interpretations by Chambers, Otken, Bruce, Cable, Fortune, Brackett, Ingle and Tourgée; foreign students, from de Tocqueville and Martineau to Halle and Bryce, have studied the subject; something has been done in collecting folklore and music, and in studying dialect, and some anthropological material has been collected. Beside this, there is a mass of periodical literature, of all degrees of value, teeming with opinions, observations, personal experiences and discussions.

[Note by Dr. Du Bois]

2. The reference is to W. E. B. Du Bois's *The Philadelphia Negro: A Social Study. Together with a special report on domestic service,* by Isabel Eaton, published by the University of Pennsylvania in 1899 as volume XLV in its Series on Political Economy and Public Law.

6. On Booker T. Washington

1. Booker T. Washington was frequently called upon as a public speaker, but it was his speech at the Cotton States and International Exposition at Atlanta, Georgia, September 18,1895, which gained the Tuskegee educator acclaim and recognition as the leading Negro in the country, succeeding Frederick Douglass who had just died. He spoke at a time when Negroes in the South were being denied the ballot in deliberate defiance of the Fourteenth and Fifteenth Amendments and were being forced to live under a system of strict racial segregation. Washington proposed a compromise by which the Negro would not ask for social or political equality in return for a pledge that he would be provided with industrial training and the opportunity to take a place in the economic development of the New South. He stressed that the Negro must win dignity and respect by self-help and emphasized Negro responsibilities rather than rights.

7. The Training of Negroes for Social Power

1. The Freedmen's Savings and Trust Company, commonly known as the Freedmen's Bank, was created by the federal government in 1865 to assist the emancipated freedmen in their new adjustment from slavery and to aid them "in securing a stronger economic position in the social order." Under the impression that the bank was a government institution, the freedmen responded enthusiastically. Before the end of 1865, ten branches had been set up. By 1872 there were thirty-four branches in existence, thirty-two of them in the southern states. By 1874 the deposits in all branches totaled $3,299,201. But careless bookkeeping and incompetence hurt the bank from the beginning, and loans,

secured through fraud and political influence, to speculators and financiers, many without assets, drained the resources of the institution. With the Panic of 1873, the bank was left holding worthless notes. Despite the efforts of Frederick Douglass, who assumed the presidency of the bank in 1874 and loaned the institution $10,000 of his own money, the establishment was forced to close its doors. It was a long time after the bank was closed before the depositors received any of their money, and even then they were paid less than fifty cents on the dollar.

In *The Souls of Black Folk,* Du Bois noted that the disappearance of "all the hard-earned dollars of the freedmen" was "the least of the loss" caused by the failure of the bank; ". . . all the faith in saving went too, and much of the faith in men; and that was a loss that a nation which today sneers at Negro shiftlessness has never yet made good."

9. The Niagara Movement

1. The Afro-American Council was an outgrowth of the Afro-American League of the United States founded in 1890 by T. Thomas Fortune. By 1898 the League was all but dead, but it continued as the Afro-American Council which met annually for about ten years thereafter but accomplished little.

2. The National Negro Business League was founded by Booker T. Washington, but as Louis R. Harlan points out, "the idea . . . was born in the brain of W. E. B. Du Bois."

10. The Economic Future of the Negro

1. The following statistics of the percentages of the Negro population that were urban from 1890 to 1910 bear out Dr. Du Bois's point:

	Total USA	South	North and West
1890	19.8	15.3	61.5
1900	22.7	17.2	70.4
1910	27.4	21.2	77.5

U. S. Bureau of Census, *Negro Population: 1790-1915,* pp. 33,90.

2. For a discussion of the methods used by the unions to exclude black workers, see Philip S. Foner, *History of the Labor Movement in the United States,* vol. III, New York, 1964, pp. 233-44.

3. See, in this connection, Herbert Gutman, "The Negro and the United Mine Workers," in Julius Jacobson, editor, *The Negro and the American Labor Movement,* New York, 1968, pp. 49-127.

4. Under the crop-lien system, the Negro sharecropper's share of the crop was mortgaged in advance to the planter-storekeeper and he obtained no part of it until his debts cleared. Since the debts often

amounted to more than the value of his share of the crop, the Negro sharecropper lived in a perpetual system of dependence upon the planter-storekeeper, rarely saw any cash, and sank into a permanent status of debt slavery.

5. In 1904 the Supreme Court upheld laws enacted at the close of the nineteenth century eliminating peonage, but neither the laws nor court decisions accomplished much in eliminating peonage.

11. We Claim Our Rights

1. Colonel Robert Gould Shaw commanded the 54th Massachusetts Infantry, a black regiment, and was killed in the storming of Fort Wagner, South Carolina, in 1863.

2. The reference is to the Russian Revolution of 1905 which though unsuccessful served as the "dress rehearsal" for the 1917 Revolution.

12. The Value of Agitation

1. Thomas Clarkson (1760-1846), pioneer British abolitionist, was active for over sixty years with William Wilberforce in the battle against slavery and the slave trade. Clarkson's interest in abolition was aroused during his student days at St. John's College, Cambridge. His Latin essay, "Is it right to make men slaves against their will?" brought him into contact with Granville Sharp and Wilberforce and into the ranks of the movement for the universal abolition of the slave trade and the universal freeing of slaves.

2. Mrs. Charlotte P. Gilman (1860-1955), an influential woman suffragist and reformer, was the author of *Women and Economics* (1898), *Concerning Children* (1900), and *The Man-Made World* (1910).

13. Is Race Separation Practicable?

1. Stone's paper opened with a description of the meeting held by the colored citizens of Boston, December 17, 1855, to honor William C. Nell for his untiring activity in aiding to achieve the removal of the color line from the public schools of Boston. He pointed out that speakers like Wendell Phillips and William Lloyd Garrison rejoiced at the gathering over the fact that "the prejudice against color was dying out," and that this was the keynote of all the addresses delivered — "the faith that the final surrender of this long-stormed citadel marked the passing of the prejudice of race." Stone then observed that fifty-two years later, November 1907, a meeting was held by the colored citizens of Boston in Faneuil Hall "to protest against the steady and wide increase of race prejudice in America."

2. The reference is to William Monroe Trotter.

3. Franz Boas (1858-1942) was the first professor of anthropology at Columbia University (where he began his duties in 1899). A pioneer in statistical analysis of physical measurements of man, he was vigorously opposed to theories of racial supremacy. His famous work, *The Mind of Primitive Man*, was published in 1911.

4. In the treaty ending the Spanish-American War, Spain granted the United States the Philippines for a payment of $20 million. In the debate on ratification of the treaty in the Senate, the annexation of the Philippines became the main issue. Opposition to annexation was led by the American Anti-Imperialist League, of which Dr. Du Bois was a member, but the treaty was ratified by one vote. The Filipinos, however, insisted on independence, and it took a cruel war of several years' duration before the United States conquered the Philippines and forced the Filipinos to accept annexation.

5. The reference is to the Kishineff massacres of Jews in Russia which was protested by the government of the United States and which brought the reply from Russia that the treatment of Negroes in the United States should cause the government in Washington to look to its own atrocities.

14. Politics and Industry

1. The Atlanta Riot occurred in September 1906. On September 22, climaxing a local political campaign, with Negro disfranchisement as an issue and featured by the whipping up by the press of anti-Negro sentiment, attacks on Negroes began. When on September 24 Negroes organized to defend themselves, the police joined the white mobs. At least ten Negroes (including two women) and two whites were killed, sixty Negroes and ten whites seriously injured, and scores of Negro homes were looted and burned. Du Bois was in Alabama when the riot broke out, and he hastened home to his family at Atlanta. En route, he wrote his magnificent "Litany of Atlanta."

2. The strike of white firemen against the employment of Negro firemen on the Georgia Railroad began in May 1909. It was the beginning of a successful drive to eliminate all the black firemen from the southern railroads.

15. The Evolution of the Race Problem

1. Benjamin R. Tillman of South Carolina and J. K. Vardaman of Mississippi were both outstanding white racists and open advocates of Negro disfranchisement. They regularly vilified the Negro people in speeches in the U. S. Senate.

16. Race Prejudice

1. The reference is to the Open-Door Policy originally enunciated by Secretary of State John Hay in 1899. It was applied to the conditions in China in the period when England, France, Russia, and Japan had marked out for themselves spheres of influence and extraterritorial rights in that country. The policy declared the desire of the United States that equal commercial, tariff, and railroad rights be granted to all nations.

17. Socialism and the Negro Problem

1. The reference is to the resolution adopted at the founding convention of the Socialist Party in 1901 which declared the party's sympathy for the Negro and urged him to join the socialist movement and vote his way to emancipation. The resolution was never rescinded, but, on the other hand, nothing further was added to implement it.

21. The African Roots of War

1. "Always something new from Africa."

2. There is wide disagreement as to the exact number of people lost to Africa during the three centuries of the international slave trade. Most recently, Professor Philip Curtin has estimated in his book, *The Atlantic Slave Trade: A Census* that not more than nine million Africans were landed in the New World during the slave trade. But he does note that the total figure lost to Africa was much higher. "For every slave landed alive," he writes, "other people died in warfare, along the bush paths leading to the coast, awaiting shipment, or in the crowded and unsanitary conditions of the middle passage."

22. The Problem of Problems

1. On November 7, 1775, Lord Dunmore, the governor of Virginia, issued a proclamation which declared all Negroes free who were willing to join the British against the American colonists. Dunmore's proclamation led to many slaves running over to the British and to the recruitment of Negroes into the Continental Army.

2. In his letter to Horace Greeley, August 22, 1862, Abraham Lincoln wrote: "My paramount object in this struggle is to save the Union. . . . If I could save the Union without freeing any slave I would do it; and if I could save it by freeing all the slaves I would do it; and if I could save it by freeing some and leaving others alone I would also do that. What I do about slavery, and the colored

race, I do because I believe it helps to save the Union. . . ." For a keen analysis of Lincoln's attitude toward slavery and the Negro during the Civil War, see Du Bois's *Black Reconstruction in America,* New York, 1935, pp. 81-87.

3. In September 1917, the black soldiers of the 24th Infantry became involved in a battle with white citizens of Houston, Texas. This was caused by constant insults hurled at the black soldiers by the white citizens. The Negro soldiers were disarmed, but when the goading and insults continued, they seized arms and killed seventeen whites. After a hurried trial, thirteen Negro soldiers were hanged for murder and mutiny, forty-one were imprisoned for life, and forty others held pending further investigation. The treatment of the members of the 24th Infantry aroused a great anger among black Americans.

23. The Great Migration North

1. In East St. Louis, Illinois, in 1917, at least forty Negroes lost their lives in a riot that grew out of the employment of Negroes in a factory holding government contracts. Negroes were stabbed, clubbed, and hanged. On July 28, 1917, Dr. Du Bois headed the great "Silent Protest Parade" on Fifth Avenue in New York staged by the NAACP in protest of the East St. Louis riots and other violence to Negroes. Some of the banners carried in the parade read: "Mr. President, why not make America safe for democracy?" and "Pray for the Lady Macbeths of East St. Louis."

2. On July 26, 1917, a race riot broke out in Chester, Pennsylvania, and continued on the twenty-seventh. It began when a mob of whites attacked two Negroes, one of whom shot someone in the mob in self-defense. On the twenty-seventh the mob overcame the local and state police and, before it could be suppressed by the arrival of additional guards, had killed three Negroes.

INDEX

Abbott, Lyman, 40, 44
Abyssinia, 36, 60, 250
Addams, Jane, 55
Adler, Felix, 41
Africa, 6-7, 13, 14, 59, 60, 114, 125-27, 173, 184, 206, 207, 208, 227, 244-57, 272-75
Afro-American Council, 145, 280
Agitation, 174-77
Aldridge, Ira, 222
"A Litany of Atlanta," 49, 277
Amenia Conference, 56, 67
American Academy of Political and Social Science, 102
American Economic Association, 150
American Federation of Labor, 263
American Historical Association, 70
American Indians, 204
American Negro Academy, 73, 82-85
American Revolution, 260
American Sociological Society, 179
Anti-Lynching Crusaders, 63
Appeal to England and Europe, 1910, 53-54
Atlanta Conferences, 38, 40, 48
Atlanta Exposition Speech, 223
Atlanta riot of 1906, 49, 191, 282
Atlanta studies, 39, 48-49
Atlanta University, 6, 7, 21, 36, 38-41, 42, 49, 50, 57-59, 70-71, 102, 140, 182
Autobiography of W. E. B. Du Bois, 21

Baker, Newton, 62
Baldwin, William H., Jr., 41
Balkan War, 50, 56
Banneker, Benjamin, 222
Baptiste, Dr. Jean, 218
Barber, J. Max, 144
Bellegarde, Dantes, 64
Bethune, Mary McCleod, 64
Bismarck, Otto von, 28
Black Academy of Arts and Letters, 10
Black Folk, Then and Now, 7
Black Reconstruction in America, 7, 15-16, 70
Blaine, James G., 23
Boas, Franz, 69, 282
Bond, Dr. Horace Mann, 5-6
Boston *Guardian*, 44, 45
"Boston Riot," 46
Broun, Heywood, 64
Brown, Henry B., 127
Brown, John, 4, 47, 170, 172, 173, 202, 203
Brownie's Book, 59
Bryan, William Jennings, 36, 50
Bull Moose Campaign, 50, 54-55
Bumstead, Horace, 36, 38, 45, 57-58
Burghardt, Tom, 26
Burroughs, Charles, 36
Burroughs, John, 67
Buttrick, Wallace, 41

Calhoun School, 49, 163-64
Carnegie, Andrew, 44, 48
Chesnutt, Charles W., 22
Chicago, 158-59

China, 35, 56, 184, 204, 206, 207, 214, 249-50, 251
CIA, 19
Civil War, 107
Cleveland, Grover, 23
"Close Ranks," 62
Cobb, Irwin, 57
Coffin, Rev. William Sloane, 16
Coleridge-Taylor, Samuel, 40
Columbia University, 122, 182, 187
Committee of Twelve, 44
Communism, 18, 66, 68
Communist Party of the United States, 8
Congo Free State, 127, 246, 265
Congress of British West Africa, 64
Convict-lease system, 262
Cook, Will, 222
Cornell University, 187
Cotton Kingdom, 261
Council of African Affairs, 7
"Credo," 142-43
Crop-lien system, 136, 168, 280
Crummell, Reverend Alexander, 73
Czar Nicholas II, 35

Darkwater, 7, 21, 59
Darrow, Clarence, 277
Darwin, Charles, 75, 89, 202, 203, 205
Davis, Jefferson, 1-2, 30, 205, 243, 276
De Land, Margaret, 7
Diagne, Blaise, 59, 60
Dillingham, Pitt, 164
Douglass, Frederick, 8, 126, 173, 222, 279, 280
Dreyfus Case, 35
Dunbar, Paul Laurence, 36, 222, 276
Dyer Lynch Bill, 63
Du Bois, Shirley (Graham), 11
Du Bois, W. E. B., as speaker, 8-9; at Atlanta University, 38-41; at University of Berlin, 32-34; at Wilberforce University, 35-36; calls for race organizations, 81-82; calls for study of the Negro, 48-49, 83, 182, 208-10; college career, 27-30; criticizes Socialist

Party, 239-43; death, 3-4, 17; debt white America owes to, 18-19; early life, 22-26; editor of *The Crisis,* 51-53, 59, 68; empathy with oppressed, 19; joins Communist Party of the United States, 8, 18; leaves NAACP, 68-69; lifelong aim, 6; makes study of Lowndes County (Ala.), 48-49; makes study of Negro in Philadelphia, 37; migrates to Ghana, 17; and NAACP, 51-53; on how to achieve peace, 253-54; organizes Niagara Movement, 47-48; and Pan-Africanism, 7, 40, 59-60, 61, 64, 124-27; and Progressive Party, 54-55; relations with Marcus Garvey, 61-62; relations with NAACP, 66-69; relations with Booker T. Washington, 41-46, 53-54, 128-129, 223-24; supports U.S. in World War I, 62, 218; U.S. government tries to imprison, 7; views on economic organization for Negroes, 67-68
Dunmore, Lord John M., 260, 283
Dusk of Dawn, 7, 21, 124

East St. Louis Riot, 56, 271
Education, 168-69, 172, 201-02, 208-09, 220
Elaine riots, 63
Eliot, Charles William, 28, 30
Emancipation Proclamation, 200, 226
Encyclopedia of the Negro, 69, 278
England, 50, 54, 58, 61, 185, 206, 247, 251, 254, 255
Evans, Glendowen, 57

Fascism, 66
Fauset, Jessie, 59
Fifteenth Amendment, 23, 199, 200, 279
Fisk Herald, 28
Fisk University, 27-28, 63, 90, 136
Forbes, George, 44, 46

Force Bill, 83
Fortune, T. Thomas, 2, 276, 280
France, 50, 58, 185, 247, 251
Freedmen's Bank, 136, 279

Gale, Zona, 64
Garrison, William Lloyd, 126, 173, 203, 278, 281
Garvey, Marcus, 61-62
Germany, 32-34, 58, 206, 247, 251, 255, 272-75
Grandfather Clause, 63
Great Barrington, 22-27

Haiti, 260, 274, 278
Hall, G. Stanley, 48
Hampden, Walter, 64
Hampton Institute, 41, 42, 63
Harris, Joel Chandler, 39, 277
Hart, Albert Bushnell, 29, 57, 70
Harvard University, 13, 28-30, 122
Hayes, Arthur Garfield, 277
Hayes, Rutherford B., 23, 31-32
Haynes, Lemuel, 222
Hewlett, Maurice, 54
Hope, John, 39, 57, 70
Hose, Sam, 39
Houston, Negro soldiers rebellion in, 56, 266, 284
Howard University, 56, 63

Immigration, 168
Imperialism, 17, 50, 65, 206, 213-14, 244-57
India, 256
Industrial education, 130, 191

James, William, 25, 29, 69
Japan, 35, 79, 184, 206, 213, 249
Jim Crow, 214, 216, 269
John Brown, 7, 50-51
Johnson, Andrew, 22
Johnson, James Weldon, 63, 244, 272, 277
Johnson, Rosamond, 222
Johnston, Sir Harry, 54, 69, 218

Kelly, Florence, 60
King, Martin Luther, Jr., 12-20

Labor and imperialism, 248
Laski, Harold, 61
League of Nations, 58, 60, 61
Lemon, John, 164
Lewis, William H., 46
Leys, Norman, 60
Liberia, 7, 60, 274
Lincoln, Abraham, 18, 100, 261, 283
Livingstone, David, 89
Louisiana Purchase, 261
Lowndes County (Ala.), 48-49, 162-64, 166
Lynching, 4, 35, 39, 56, 63, 262, 265
Lynch law, 74

MacDonald, Ramsay, 61
McKinley, William, 36
McKinley tariff, 30, 276
Marx, Karl, 18, 64
Mexican War, 261
Mexico, 252
Milholland, John, 53, 54
Miller, Henry, 9-10
Miller, Kelly, 43, 222
Monroe Doctrine, 247, 251
Moore, Fred Atkins, 10
Morel, E. D., 40, 250
Morgan, Clement, 30
Moskowitz, Henry, 55

National Negro Committee, 187
National Woman Suffrage Association, 230
Negroes, and Americanism, 79-81; as "scabs," 192; businesses among, 152-53; cannot buy land in South, 160-61; crime among, 137, 147; disfranchisement of, 189-95, 211-12, 265; economic activities of, 94-96; economic future of, 150-169; economic status of in South, 191; education of, 130-41, 156-57, 168-69, 201-02, 220; genius of, 79; half-truths about, 264; history of, 104-06; in North, 158; in Philadelphia, 37, 122; in South, 159; insurance companies among, 159-60; lynchings of, 4, 35, 39, 56, 63

265; migration of to North, 56, 263, 268-71; ministers among, 97-98; need for study of, 6, 37, 48-49, 83, 102-04, 110-23, 181-82, 208-10; and organized labor, 64, 165, 166-67, 190-92, 193-94, 262-63, 267, 280; socialist and, 56, 239-43, 283; status of in U. S., 108-09, 128-29, 169, 219-20; treatment of in France, 59-60, 63; urban and rural, 153-54, 280; will not submit to discrimination, 185

Negro Business League, 145, 280
Negro colleges, 96-100, 139-41
Negro problem, 104-10, 132-33, 219-25
Negro Renaissance, 59
Negro students, 63, 86, 135-36
Negro suffrage, 188-95, 197-200, 211-12, 232-33
Nell, William C., 180, 281
Neruda, Pablo, 18
New England Suffrage League, 145
New York, 158
Niagara Movement, 4, 46-48, 70, 144-48, 170-78
Norton, Charles Eliot, 40

O'Casey, Sean, 18
Ogden, Robert, 41
Olivier, Sir Sidney, 60, 61
O'Neill, Eugene, 64
Open Door, 215, 249, 283
Organized labor and the Negro, 68, 156, 165, 166-68, 190-92, 262-63, 271

Page, Walter Hines, 40
Palmer, George, 29
Pan-African Congresses, 7, 14, 59-61, 64, 124, 274
Pan-Negroism, 79
Peabody, George Foster, 41, 46
Peace Information Center, 7, 16
Peonage, 136, 168, 281
Perry, Bliss, 40
Petrie, Flinders, 69
Phelps-Stokes Fund, 69, 278
Philadelphia, 37, 158

Philippine Islands, 184, 282
Phillips, Wendell, 26, 126, 173, 281
Phylon, 7, 14
Progressive Party, 54-55

Race friction, 179-86
Race prejudice, 155-56, 167, 213-17
Race problem, 179-86, 196-210
Races, classification of, 74-78
Reconstruction after the Civil War, 15-16
Red Cross, 63
Riots against Negroes, 63, 271, 284
Roosevelt, Theodore, 50, 55, 57
Rosenwald Fund, 70
Royce, Josiah, 29
Russia, 35, 58, 66, 173, 185, 249, 266, 282
Russian Revolution, 50, 173, 281

Sacco-Vanzetti case, 63, 277
Santayana, George, 29
Sayre, Dr. Etta, 54
Schiff, Jacob, 42, 45-46
Schurz, Carl, 48
Shaler, Nathaniel, 29
Share-cropping, 152
Slater Fund, 31, 32
Slavery, 104-06, 139, 151, 197
Slave trade, 14, 112-13, 246
Smith, Hoke, 243
Socialist Party, 8, 56, 239-43, 258-67, 283
Sociology, 102
South Africa, 206, 254
Spingarn, Joel E., 55, 56, 67
Spock, Benjamin, 16
Springfield Republican, 24
Stanley, Henry M., 246
Stevens, Thaddeus, 22, 276
Stone, Alfred Holt, 179, 281
Sumner, Charles, 23, 173
Sweet, Dr. O. H., 63, 277
Sylvain, George, 64
Sylvester-Williams, Henry, 124, 127

Taft, William Howard, 50, 55

Talbert, Mary, 63
"Talented Tenth," 86
Tanner, H. O., 222
The Crisis, 4-5, 8, 49-55, 59, 61, 63, 68-69, 258, 266, 277
The Gift of Black Folk, 59
The Horizon, 49-50, 239
The Moon, 49
The Negro, 51
The Negro in the South, 50
The Philadelphia Negro, 7, 14, 279
"The Star of Ethiopia," 59, 226
The Suppression of the Slave Trade to the United States of America, 7
The Voice of the Negro, 144
The World and Africa, 7
Thorn, Charlotte, 164
Tillman, Ben, 205, 243, 282
Traubel, Horace, 40
Trotter, William Monroe, 44, 46, 181, 276, 281
Turner, Nat, 173
Tuskegee Institute, 41, 42, 44, 45-46

United Mine Workers, 155, 280
Universal Races Congress of 1911, 9, 50, 54, 218-25
University of Berlin, 13, 32-34

University of Pennsylvania, 36-37, 122

Vardaman, J. K., 205, 243, 282
Vietnam, 19
Villard, Oswald Garrison, 56
Virchow, Rudolf, 33

Walters, Bishop Alexander, 40, 55-56, 127
Washington, Booker T., 41-46, 50, 53, 56, 128-29, 174, 187, 222, 223, 279, 280
Webb, Mrs. Sidney, 61
Weber, Max, 40
Wells, H. G., 61
Wendell, Barrett, 29
Wheatley, Phillis, 222-23
Whitman, Walt, 40
Wilberforce University, 35-36, 63
Willcox, Walter F., 48
Williams, Talcott, 40, 48
Wilson, Woodrow, 50, 55-56, 239
Woman suffrage, 230-38
Woods, Granville, 222
World War I, 50, 56, 62-63, 64, 244-57, 262, 268

"Yellow Peril," 249
Young, Charles, 36, 56

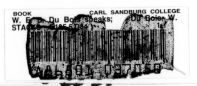